THE BIG ATLAS OF THE
EARTH & SEA

By Susanna van Rose and Anita Ganeri
Illustrated by Richard Bonson and Luciano Corbella

COVENT
GARDEN
BOOKS

A DK PUBLISHING BOOK
www.dk.com

Produced for Dorling Kindersley by
PAGEOne, United Kingdom

Art Editors Martyn Foote, Rachael Foster
Project Editors John C. Miles, Laura Buller
US Editor B. Alison Weir
Production Shelagh Gibson
Managing Editor Susan Peach
Managing Art Editor Jacquie Gulliver
Consultant Keith Lye, Brian Bett

First American Edition, 1999
2 4 6 8 10 9 7 5 3 1

Published in the United States by
DK Publishing, Inc.
95 Madison Avenue,
New York, NY 10016

Copyright © 1999
Dorling Kindersley Limited, London

ISBN 0-7894-4385-3

A catalog record is available from the Library of Congress.

Reproduced in Essex by Dot Gradations
Printed in Spain by Artes Graficas Toledo
D.L. TO: 1121 - 1999

CONTENTS

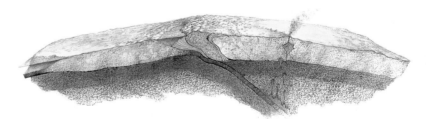

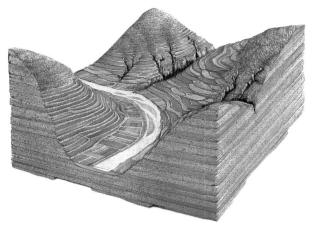

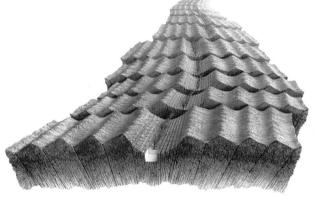

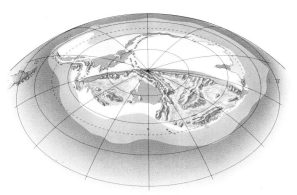

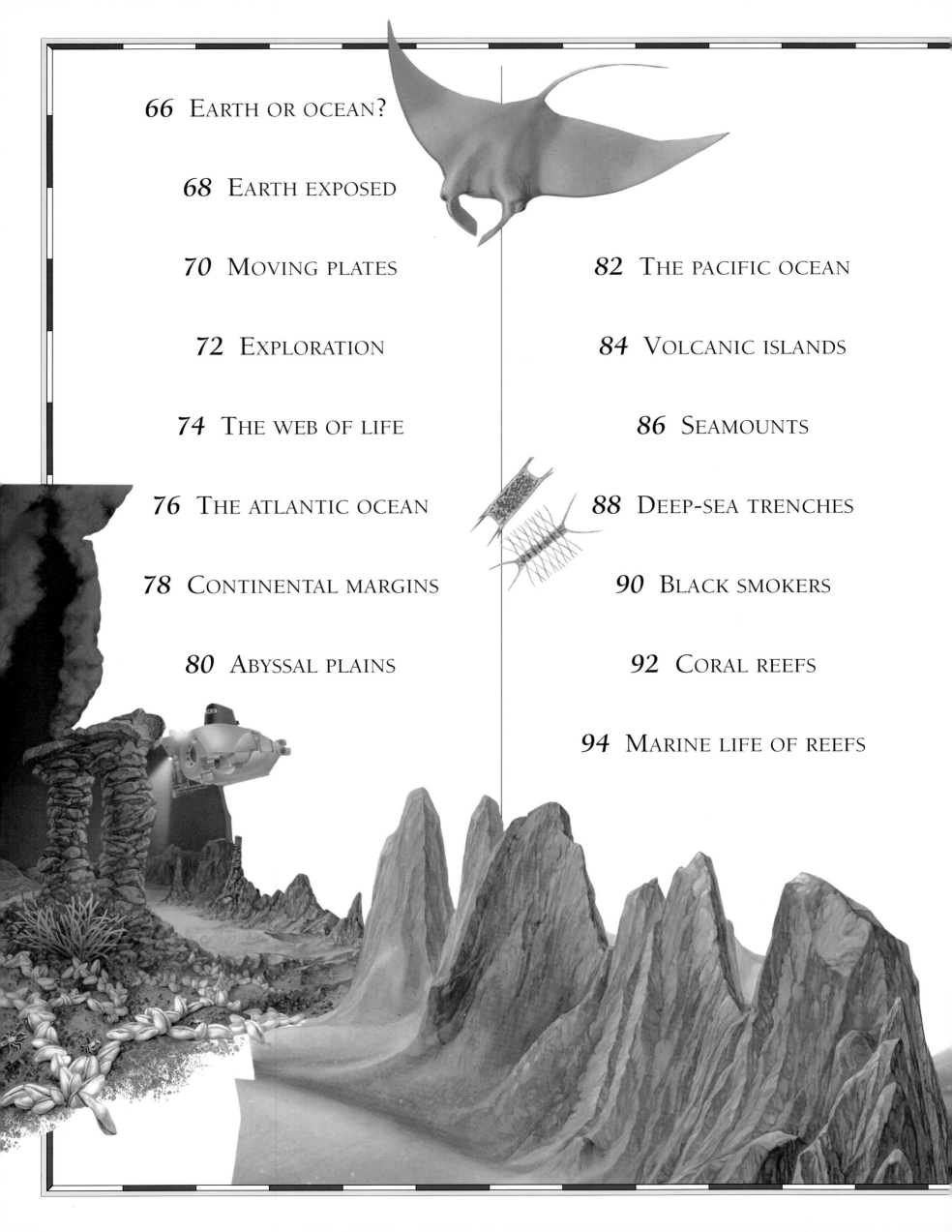

You are a child of the universe,
No less than the trees and stars;
You have a right to be here,
And whether or not it is clear to you,
No doubt the universe is unfolding as it should.
—Max Ehrmann

PUTTING THE EARTH IN A BOOK

HOW CAN THE ENTIRE EARTH – from high mountains to deep valleys, from vast oceans to flat deserts – be squeezed between the pages of a book? In order to explain how the Earth looks, this book uses several different ways to show the round Earth on flat paper. The rocky outer surface that humans and animals live on is just a small part of the whole Earth. To understand the forces that have shaped and changed its surface, the illustrations in this book sometimes cut through Earth's layers right down into its fiery center. In addition, maps, photographs, and diagrams help to show the huge variety of Earth's landscapes, and explain how they were created. Together, the elements in this book show how the Earth really works.

The Americas   *Africa and Europe*   *East Asia and Oceania*   *The Pacific Rim*

Four faces of the Earth

Because Earth is round, it is not possible to see all sides at once. Above are four faces, or views, of the globe, each focusing on a different area. One of these four faces appears on most pages of the book, to give a general idea of the location of the main illustration for that page.

A page explained

The double page below shows how information is presented in this book. An introduction gives an outline of the most important facts and ideas. Most pages feature an illustration of a particular place on Earth, chosen to represent a particular geographical feature. Details are explained by smaller illustrations.

Box marks the area shown in the main illustration

Box marks the area shown on the map

Understanding the maps

Each globe view of the Earth includes a box marking the area shown on a more detailed, flat map. A section of the Earth's surface is cut from this map, then lifted out and laid down with the sky uppermost. This section is featured in the main illustration. Areas not shown are marked with a dashed line.

Marked area in the middle is left out of the illustration

Illustration features these two areas from the map

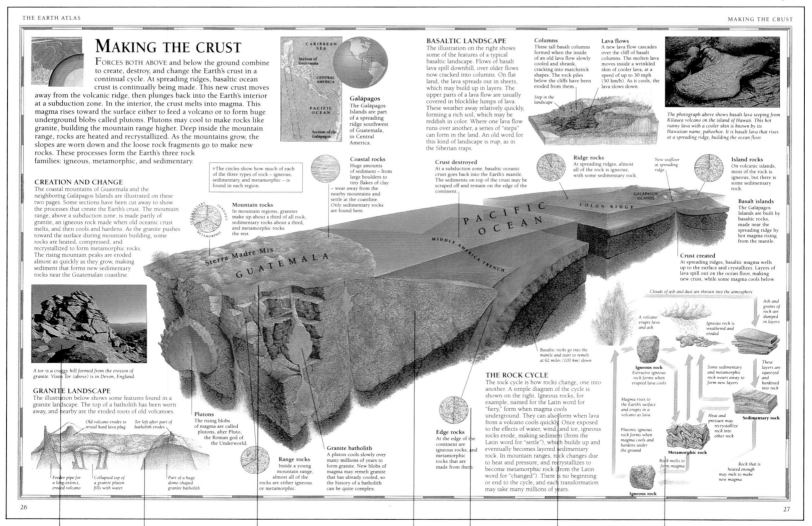

(Main illustrated double-page spread, pages 26–27: "MAKING THE CRUST")

Photographs
These show what landscapes look like when they are made of the rocks, or formed by the geological processes, described on the double-page spread.

Place names help to locate the illustrations

Small illustrations show details of landscapes related to the main illustration

Main illustrations
Different colors are used to show the different kinds of rock that are found in the places featured in the main illustrations.

This detail shows the rock types found in this part of the Earth

Captions
These work closely with the illustrations to present facts and information.

Charts and diagrams
Ideas that relate to the main illustration are often explained by charts and diagrams. Some step-by-step diagrams show how a landscape was formed.

Cutting up mountains

Some of the main illustrations feature huge chunks of the Earth. This one, representing the Himalayas and Tibet, shows a section of the Earth which is really hundreds of miles (kilometers) long. The Himalaya mountains, the highest mountains on Earth, look tiny on the page.

The section of the Earth featured in the illustration is boxed on the globe view

The section is cut out, lifted, and then laid flat

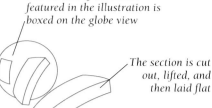

Once the illustration is laid flat, it is easier to understand

Ancient maps (right) were based as much on imagination as on fact. Today, mapmakers can check the accuracy of their measurements by comparing their maps with satellite photographs (above).

Mapping the Earth

Although the nearly round Earth is most accurately represented as a globe, flat maps provide an almost complete picture of a large area. The maps in this book are used to show specific areas featured in the illustrations. Others show the major mountain ranges, deserts, and frozen regions on Earth.

A closer look

A piece of the main illustration is often pulled out and made bigger, so that details are easier to see. This cross section, for example, shows what the rocks inside the mountains look like.

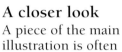

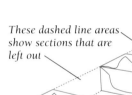

This block has been cut out of the main artwork and made larger

Below the surface

The pulled-out blocks of the illustration show us not only the land surface, but also what is going on in the layers underneath. Sometimes this is important in helping to understand the surface landscape and rocks.

These dashed line areas show sections that are left out

This is the most distant section

This is a section taken from the middle of the glacier

This is the end, or snout section of the glacier

Cutouts

This illustration of the Athabasca Glacier in Canada shows inside and underneath the glacier – views it is not usually possible to see. The inside of the glacier is shown in cross sections of, or cuts through, the illustration, which are pulled apart to give a better view. In one section of the illustration the whole glacier is removed, along with all the boulders and rock fragments trapped in the ice, to show the rocky surface below.

Times change

Landscape is always changing, but usually very slowly. This book explains the forces that are continually changing the Earth's surface. Sometimes change happens rapidly – the volcanic eruption at Mount St. Helens, Washington, blew the side of the mountain away in only hours (right). Other changes have happened slowly, over tens of thousands of years, or even over a time span long before humans had evolved. Illustrations such as the sequence below are used to show these changes.

This is Mount St. Helens before its eruption.

This is a landscape as it might have looked 100 million years ago. Dinosaurs roamed over swamps, and left their footprints in the wet sand.

This is the same place 40 million years later. The dinosaurs are now extinct, their footprints long since buried. The land has sunk and is under a shallow, young sea.

Today the sea is gone, and dry land is left behind. The muddy ooze that was on the seabed has hardened into chalk, which is being eroded into steep cliffs.

After the eruption, there is a large hole where the mountain summit once was.

EARTH IS UNIQUE

AMONG THE PLANETS of the solar system, Earth is unique in many ways. It is enveloped in a cloud of gas called the atmosphere. One gas in particular, oxygen, makes a very special contribution: supporting life. Oxygen makes up a critical one-fifth of the Earth's total atmosphere; if there were slightly more oxygen in the atmosphere, plants would spontaneously catch fire. Water covers most of the Earth's surface, keeping temperatures moderate and releasing essential water vapor into the atmosphere. Inside the Earth, restless currents of molten rock create a magnetic field which shields the Earth from space radiation. Other internal movements cause the surface to slowly churn over, so that the crust constantly renews or reshapes itself.

THE INNER EARTH

Nothing seems as substantial as the rocky surface we live on, but in relation to the vast inner layers of the Earth it is no more than an eggshell. The surface rocks are made mostly of the chemical elements oxygen and silicon, along with some metals. Beneath this is a thick layer of heavier rock called the mantle, which encloses the inner and outer cores. The solid metal inner core is the densest part of the Earth. The liquid outer core is continually moving, causing a constantly changing magnetic field to envelop the planet.

Earth imagined

Ancient people had no way of knowing about the inner Earth. The painting below illustrates the world system of the Babylonians. The Earth is a round, hollow mountain resting on water. The sky, with fixed stars, meteors, and planets, forms a hollow chamber. The sun rises each day through a door in the east, and sets through a door in the west. Even today, no one has ever seen or taken a sample of the Earth's mantle and core. Most of what we know is based on indirect measurement.

Green planet
From space, the plants on Earth's land surface make the continents look green. Plants take in carbon dioxide gas from the atmosphere, and use it to grow new leaves and branches. In the process they give out oxygen, used by animals and people.

Land planet
Earth's land areas cover only a small part of its surface, where the continents rise above sea level.

Air planet
The mixture of gases and water vapor wrapped around the Earth is its atmosphere. Its swirling white clouds are continually on the move, warmed or cooled by the land and sea below, or whipped around by the Earth's rotation.

Water planet
Three-quarters of the Earth's surface is covered by water, most of it within its vast oceans.

Crust
The solid, rocky surface that we live on is called the crust. It is thickest under the continents, and thinnest below the oceans.

Lithosphere and asthenosphere
The outermost 62 miles (100 km) of the mantle is firmly attached to the Earth's outer crust. Together, these make up the lithosphere (from the Greek word for "rock sphere"). Below the lithosphere is a layer of hotter, softer rock another 62 miles (100 km) thick. This is called the asthenosphere, from the Greek word for "weak sphere."

Mantle
Making up about nine-tenths of the total bulk of the Earth, the mantle is a thick shell of hot, rocky silicate (silicon and oxygen) minerals. Although the mantle is solid, it does slowly circulate over millions of years.

Outer core
Surrounding the solid inner core is the liquid outer core. Its molten iron and nickel metals are at the slightly cooler temperature of 10,000°F (5,500°C), and are under less pressure than the inner core. The movement of the hot liquid here generates the Earth's magnetic field. Changes in the strength and the polarity of the magnetic field are linked to changes in the circulation.

Inner core
At the heart of the planet is its inner core, made of the same metals that make up the outer core. The temperature is so high here – up to 10,800°F (6,000°C) – that these metals should be molten liquid. But the immense pressure is enough to compress them into solids.

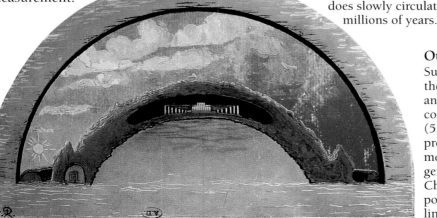

Summer solstice

On June 21, the tilt of the Earth's axis means the strongest and most direct light from the sun is in the northern hemisphere. The longest day of the year occurs at this time; the Arctic Circle has 24 hours of daylight.

Northern hemisphere summer

Note: This diagram is not to scale.

Northern hemisphere spring

Spring equinox

At the spring equinox on March 21, the Sun is directly overhead at the Equator. Days and nights have equal length all over the Earth. Equinox means "equal nights."

Northern hemisphere winter

Autumnal equinox

As in the spring equinox, the sun is directly overhead at the equator during the autumnal equinox. Day and night are once again the same length of time in both hemispheres.

Northern hemisphere autumn

Winter solstice

On December 21, the tilt of the Earth means the sun's direct light and heat strike south of the Equator. This is the longest day of the year in the southern hemisphere. The northern hemisphere has its shortest day and longest night.

THE EARTH'S ORBIT

Like the other planets, Earth travels around the sun; it takes a year to make one complete round-trip. The pathway is called its orbit. Earth's orbit is not quite circular, but is slightly oval in shape. As it makes its orbit, Earth is also spinning around an imaginary line running between the north and south poles, called its axis. Each complete spin takes about 24 hours. When light from the sun illuminates half the globe, this region has day while the dark half has night. Our seasons (above) are also a result of the Earth's orbit and rotation.

A beautiful result of the Earth's magnetism is an aurora – a shimmering display of light seen in the night sky in and near Arctic and Antarctic regions. The Earth's magnetic poles attract charged particles in the atmosphere which radiate colored light.

The Earth's plates

The Earth's lithosphere is broken into fewer than a dozen large and many smaller plates. These move slowly and steadily. Everything carried on them moves, too – from huge continents to entire oceans.

Hydrosphere

The watery layer of the Earth, the hydrosphere, includes its oceans, lakes, rivers, underground water, and snow and ice. The hydrosphere covers the oceanic crust almost totally, to an average depth of 3 miles (5 km). The water laps onto and submerges the edges of the continents.

Atmosphere

The total thickness of the atmosphere is at least 620 miles (1,000 km), with almost all of the gas molecules hugging tight to the Earth. The atmosphere is densest in the lowest 6 miles (10 km), the troposphere. Above this is the stratosphere, where the atmosphere is thinner because it contains fewer molecules.

A gas within the atmosphere called ozone shields the Earth from some of the sun's rays

Upper part of the mantle and the crust forms the lithosphere

Thick continental crust

Thin oceanic crust

Hydrosphere

Troposphere

Stratosphere

Mesosphere

Thermosphere

Exosphere and magnetosphere

THE OUTER EARTH

The solid rocky surface of the Earth is a place of continual change. Here the Earth's rocks meet – and interact – with the watery layer of the hydrosphere and the gassy layer of the atmosphere. The rocks react both chemically and physically with these turbulent layers. Moving air and water, and temperature changes, break down the rocks physically. Oxygen from the atmosphere reacts with silicates in the rocks to change them chemically, making new rocky minerals. The Earth's outer layers are so closely interlinked that a change in one layer is likely to affect the others.

BOMBARDMENT FROM SPACE

THE EARLY HISTORY OF THE EARTH is shrouded in mystery. Most clues about the young planet have long been worn away. But the events of this turbulent first billion years – nearly a quarter of the Earth's history – set the scene for the planet of today. During that time, the Earth evolved out of a cloud of dust to a cooling, encrusted planet wrapped in an envelope of gases. Its first rocky skin was ripped apart by the impact of huge meteorites. This bombardment of the Earth and other planets went on while the crust grew thick enough to withstand the impact, and cool enough for rainwater to collect in pools – the earliest oceans.

Chemical clouds
Billowing clouds of steam and smelly chemical gases poured from the Earth. Gravity held most of these near the surface, but some of the lighter gases escaped.

Crust cooling over hot interior

Cooler crust
The thin surface crust over the Earth gradually grew thicker. From time to time, slabs of cooled crust probably plunged back into the molten mantle below and were melted again. Wherever the crust was cooling and crystallizing, thick clouds of gases bubbled out, building the Earth's first atmosphere.

Meteorites pound the Earth
One after another, meteorites pounded the molten surface of the Earth. A thin, brittle skin barely covered the Earth; it was not yet tough enough to resist the impact of the falling meteorites.

Piercing the skin
As a meteorite landed, hot liquid rock splashed out around the hole in the surface. The meteorite itself plunged into the hot interior. Torrents of lava probably surged up to the hole punched in the surface, spilling out around it in thick sheets.

Large meteorite about to land on the Earth

Flows of lava spreading from the impact crater

Meteorites
These arrivals from space are pieces of an exploded planet, one of the Earth's long-ago neighbors. Some, like this meteorite, are rich in iron, and probably came from the core of the exploded planet.

Craters
Meteorites make an impact crater when they land. The impact may be so intense that the meteorite shatters or even evaporates altogether. Meteor Crater in Arizona is 3,936 ft (1,200 m) across and 557 ft (170 m) deep.

Lava fountains

Lazy molten lava bubbles underneath a huge volcano. When it erupts, gas escapes from the hot lava, and its intense bubbling forces the lava to spill out in fountains.

Dust from volcanic eruptions can cause lightning because it is electrically charged by friction

The first rainfall

The steam escaping from the cooling crust may condense to form rain clouds. If the clouds become big or cool enough, rain falls.

The surface is still so hot that rain instantly turns to steam

HOT FIERY PLANET

The Earth was probably a hot, fiery planet around 4.5 billion years ago, covered with a thin, rocky skin. The skin cracked and remelted over and over, solid crusts sinking back into the hot interior to melt again, while new crust grew and cooled. Like the other planets in the solar system, the Earth was continually bombarded by meteorites – loose rock fragments plummeting onto its thin skin. These may have come from the explosion of an older planet that had a rocky surface and an iron-rich core. The asteroids orbiting Earth today may be the remains of this exploded planet.

THE THICKENING CRUST

As the molten Earth began to grow a thicker, more solid crust, the cooling lava at the surface bubbled and gave off vast clouds of gases. These became the Earth's first atmosphere, a smelly mixture very different from the atmosphere today. It included steam, carbon dioxide, and nitrogen – but no oxygen. Some of its gases, such as the lightweight hydrogen and helium, easily escaped Earth's gravity. Others, such as hydrogen chloride, became combined with rocks during weathering.

THE FIRST OCEANS

Volcanoes punctuated the Earth's still hot, steamy surface. The gases that poured out of the volcanoes with each eruption were added to the thick, choking chemicals of the atmosphere. Some volcanic mountains may have grown high enough to cause the water in the atmosphere to cool and condense (turn back into liquid). The tiny drops of water gathered to form clouds, so that it could rain. At first, the solid surface of the Earth may have been so hot that the rain evaporated as soon as it fell. Eventually, some parts of the surface became cool enough for the rain to collect there in hot pools.

Lava layers

Massive volcanoes pour out seething hot lava, which spreads out in runny sheets to cover the surface. Layer by layer, the lava builds the volcanoes higher, and thickens the cooling crust.

Hot water collects in steaming pools on top of the hardening layers of lava

Sizzling surface

At first, rain that falls to the Earth sizzles like water on a hot griddle. But after many rainstorms, the surface of the Earth is cool enough for pools of steaming water to collect.

Sizzling water boils as it skids over the hot rocky surface.

Bubbling pool

A bubbling hot pool of sulfurous water has some mud at the bottom, from the first weathering of rocks.

Ropelike coils are found today in a type of lava called "pahoehoe"

The steam rises and may condense again to make clouds

Cooling coils

As the skin of the lava cools, it is twisted and pulled by the movements of the still-molten lava into ropelike coils.

Rock reactions

Rocks reacted chemically with the gases in the primitive atmosphere – the first signs of chemical weathering, the breaking down of the Earth's rocky materials. For example, sulfur gases and hydrogen chloride react with minerals in the rocks to transform them into clay minerals, forming the first muds on Earth.

11

DAWN OF EARTH HISTORY

THE ARCHEOZOIC HISTORY of the Earth, from the Greek word for "beginning," represents its first 2 billion years. After its rocky crust formed and the surface cooled enough for steaming pools of rainwater to collect, the Earth entered a new stage of development. During this dawn of Earth history, the continents came into being. They were made of granite-like rocks that thickened the crust and eventually built the first mountains. The oceans were not just low places filled with water; instead, they had a rocky crust quite different from that of the continents. How this separation into two types of crust happened, we do not know. Oxygen was added to the atmosphere from tiny sea plants. Although much of the oxygen was at first consumed by chemical reactions, in time, enough built up to support primitive life forms. Then, 600 million years ago, there was an explosion of life forms with skeletons. At last, the stage was set for the Earth we know today.

Hot lava
Komatiite lava erupted at temperatures as high as 3,100° F (1,700° C) – twice as hot as many lavas today.

Fast flowing
Some of the fastest-flowing lavas today move at about 30 mph (50 km/h), but runny komatiite moved much more quickly.

THE ARCHEOZOIC EARTH
It is not easy to reconstruct the Archeozoic Earth, because the rocks of that age have changed so much since they formed. Around 3.5 billion years ago the continents began to form as light, molten rock similar to granite rose under giant volcanoes. The volcanoes have long ago been eroded away, but their granite "roots" formed the first continents. An unusual lava unlike those known today formed the first ocean crust. This kind of lava, called komatiite, seems to have been very runny and very hot – so hot that it melted the rocks it flowed over.

Komatiite crystals
Komatiite was very much hotter than modern lavas. It cooled to form huge crystals, which looked like coarse blades of grass.

Cool crust
This lava has cooled to form a rough-textured crust of rock.

Traces in the rocks
Today, the only traces of the first ocean floor are tiny rock scraps containing komatiite. It seems that whatever mechanism made this strange lava stopped happening 2.5 billion years ago. The modern ocean crust is made from a very different hardened lava known as basalt.

Slow the flow
As a lava flow cools, it becomes stickier and more solid, and it slows down.

A river of lava
When komatiite lava erupted, it melted the rocks over which it flowed. As a result, it cut its path or channel lower and lower, just like a river.

Crusty black cooled lava

Layers of old cooled lava

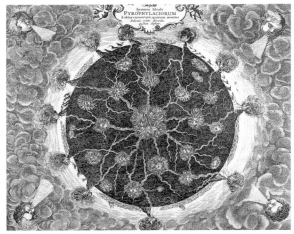

This 17th-century engraving by Anthanasius Kircher illustrates his theory that the Earth's interior was still molten, and that perpetual fire fed volcanoes. His theory was not accurate for the Earth of today, but could have described its first billion years.

Cutting through the rocks
A komatiite lava flow that flowed for a week could cut a channel 65 ft (20 m) deep, just by melting the rocks underneath.

Quick-moving lava shooting through the crusty channel

Long-distance lava
The lava is able to flow through its eroded channel for long distances from its original eruption.

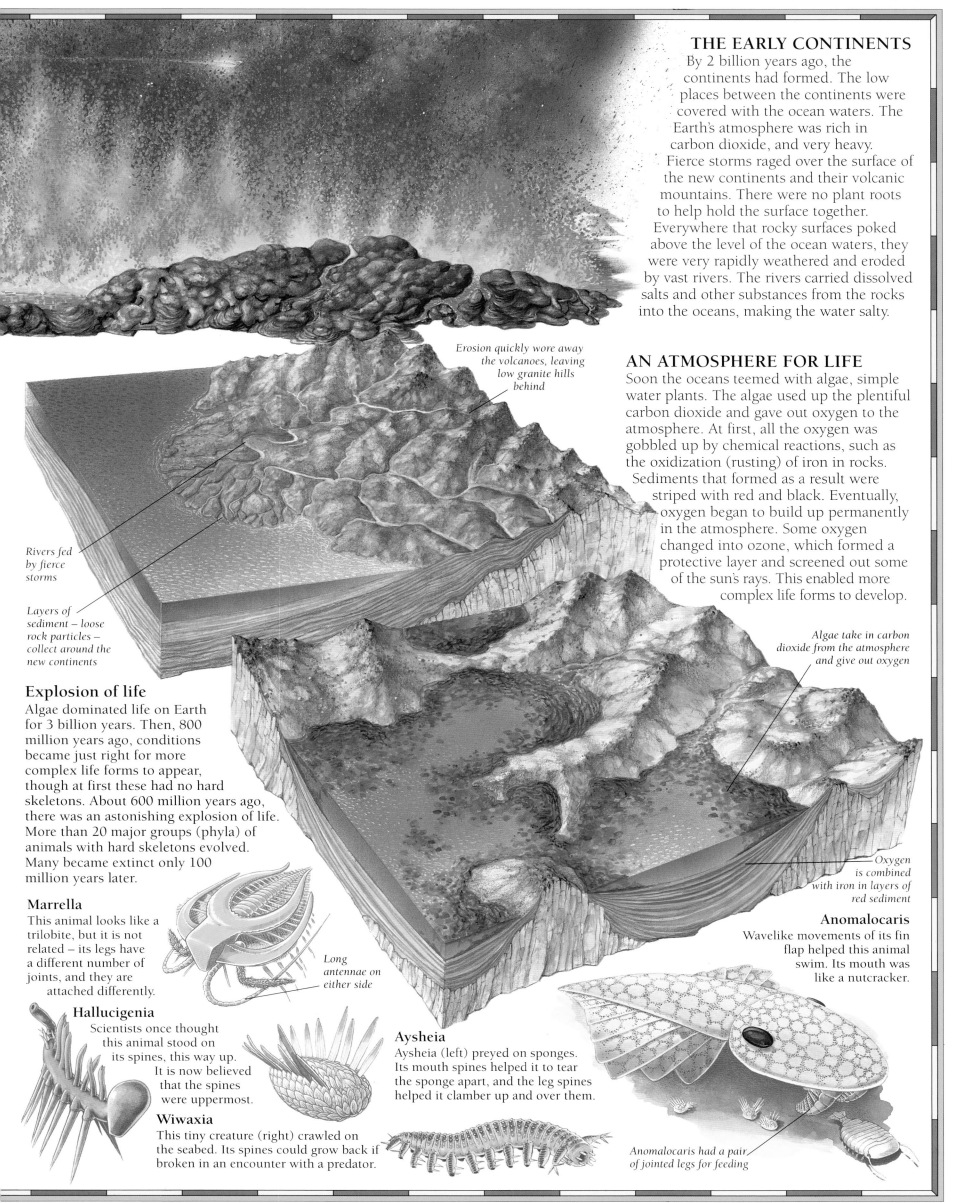

THE EARLY CONTINENTS

By 2 billion years ago, the continents had formed. The low places between the continents were covered with the ocean waters. The Earth's atmosphere was rich in carbon dioxide, and very heavy. Fierce storms raged over the surface of the new continents and their volcanic mountains. There were no plant roots to help hold the surface together. Everywhere that rocky surfaces poked above the level of the ocean waters, they were very rapidly weathered and eroded by vast rivers. The rivers carried dissolved salts and other substances from the rocks into the oceans, making the water salty.

AN ATMOSPHERE FOR LIFE

Soon the oceans teemed with algae, simple water plants. The algae used up the plentiful carbon dioxide and gave out oxygen to the atmosphere. At first, all the oxygen was gobbled up by chemical reactions, such as the oxidization (rusting) of iron in rocks. Sediments that formed as a result were striped with red and black. Eventually, oxygen began to build up permanently in the atmosphere. Some oxygen changed into ozone, which formed a protective layer and screened out some of the sun's rays. This enabled more complex life forms to develop.

Erosion quickly wore away the volcanoes, leaving low granite hills behind

Rivers fed by fierce storms

Layers of sediment – loose rock particles – collect around the new continents

Algae take in carbon dioxide from the atmosphere and give out oxygen

Oxygen is combined with iron in layers of red sediment

Explosion of life

Algae dominated life on Earth for 3 billion years. Then, 800 million years ago, conditions became just right for more complex life forms to appear, though at first these had no hard skeletons. About 600 million years ago, there was an astonishing explosion of life. More than 20 major groups (phyla) of animals with hard skeletons evolved. Many became extinct only 100 million years later.

Marrella

This animal looks like a trilobite, but it is not related – its legs have a different number of joints, and they are attached differently.

Long antennae on either side

Hallucigenia

Scientists once thought this animal stood on its spines, this way up. It is now believed that the spines were uppermost.

Wiwaxia

This tiny creature (right) crawled on the seabed. Its spines could grow back if broken in an encounter with a predator.

Aysheia

Aysheia (left) preyed on sponges. Its mouth spines helped it to tear the sponge apart, and the leg spines helped it clamber up and over them.

Anomalocaris

Wavelike movements of its fin flap helped this animal swim. Its mouth was like a nutcracker.

Anomalocaris had a pair of jointed legs for feeding

LINES OF FIRE

MOST VOLCANOES lie along lines of fire that encircle the planet. These are places where the turbulence of the Earth's fiercely hot interior is revealed along giant cracks at the surface. Many earthquakes also happen near these cracks. This uneven distribution on the Earth was noticed early in the nineteenth century, though at that time there was no way of explaining why it should be. An especially large number of volcanoes and earthquakes happen around the shores of the Pacific Ocean, shown here. This explosive area is sometimes called the Pacific Ring of Fire. Its amazing landscapes are a result of its fiery past.

The Valley of Ten Thousand Smokes
A huge ashy eruption blanketed this valley in Alaska in 1912. The first explorers to venture into the valley saw countless bubbling volcanic "smokes" rising from the ash. The ash itself is up to 164 ft (50 m) deep in places.

Key to map
Three types of margins, or boundaries between plates, are shown on this map: constructive margins are fiery red, destructive margins are brown, and conservative margins are purple. They will be explained on the next two pages.

Valley of Ten Thousand Smokes, Alaska

NORTH AMERICAN PLATE

ALEUTIAN TRENCH

KURIL TRENCH

JAPAN TRENCH

JUAN DE FUCA PLATE

EURASIAN PLATE

PHILIPPINE PLATE

MARIANA TRENCH

BISMARCK PLATE

JAVA TRENCH

PACIFIC PLATE

CARIBBEAN PLATE

COCOS PLATE

Galápagos Islands

PERU-CHILE TRENCH

NAZCA PLATE

INDO-AUSTRALIAN PLATE

SOUTHEAST INDIAN RIDGE

ANTARCTIC PLATE

Whakarewarewa, New Zealand

TONGA TRENCH

EAST PACIFIC RISE

CHILE RISE

PACIFIC-ANTARCTIC RIDGE

There may be minutes, hours, or days between geysers

Whakarewarewa
Geysers are a kind of hot spring that gushes out as a fountain of hot water every now and then. This geyser and these bubbling mud pools are in New Zealand's Whakarewarewa, south of Rotorua.

Volcanic gases bubble out through soft mud

Galápagos calderas
Huge craters, called calderas, pockmark the summits of the Galápagos Islands.

Calderas form when a volcano erupts so much lava that it collapses

Surtsey born from the sea

In 1963 a bubbling volcano broke through the waves south of Iceland. The new island, named Surtsey after an ancient Icelandic fire god, grew larger as more and more lava poured out over the first loose ash layers. Surtsey is now home to a variety of plants, insects, and birds.

Surtsey sits astride the Mid-Atlantic Ridge, where two of the Earth's plates are slowly pulling apart. New magma from inside the Earth cools to heal the crack, making new ocean crust.

A YEAR IN THE LIFE OF A PLANET

About 30 volcanoes are erupting in any one year. Of these, some continue to erupt for several years, or even decades, while others may erupt only once during that time. One or two have been active for thousands of years. Thousands of earthquakes happen each year, but most are far too small to be noticed. A few dozen cause shaking which can be felt, and fewer than ten are really large. There is no sign that today earthquakes and volcanic eruptions are happening either more or less often.

Fingal's Cave

The basalt columns that built the island of Staffa off western Scotland are formed from lava which cracked into regular shapes as it cooled slowly, 60 million years ago.

Le Puy in France

This church in southern France is built atop a volcanic rock 250 ft (76 m) high. The rock hardened inside the volcano two million years ago. It was exposed when softer, ashy rocks were eroded away from around it.

Urgup Cones, Turkey

These pillars in Turkey are sculpted out of volcanic ash, from eruptions of long ago. Volcanic gases, like the "smokes" in Alaska, welded the ash in places. Wind and rain have shaped it into pillars.

Karum salt pillars

Rain weathers salt out from volcanic rocks, washing it into the Assale Lake in Ethiopia. The water is so salty that the surface crystallizes over, with salt pillars growing 10 ft (3 m) overnight.

Map labels

REYKJANES RIDGE

EURASIAN PLATE

• Surtsey, Iceland

• Fingal's Cave, Scotland

• Le Puy, France

Urgup Cones, Turkey
ANATOLIAN PLATE

IRANIAN PLATE

ARABIAN PLATE

Karum Pillars, Ethiopia •

AFRICAN PLATE

Réunion •

SOUTH AMERICAN PLATE

MID-ATLANTIC RIDGE

RIDGE

ATLANTIC-INDIAN RIDGE

SCOTIA PLATE

ANTARCTIC PLATE

Réunion

One of the Earth's largest volcanoes is Réunion island, which rises from the deep ocean floor to its summit craters 10,068 ft (3,069 m) above sea level.

SIGNS OF THE TIMES

Old, eroded volcanic features in the landscape are an indication that millions or even tens of millions of years ago, there were volcanoes at this place. Not all of these features lie along the lines of fire we know today. This means the old lines were in different places, and shows that the Earth's plates move as time passes. This movement is evidence of change in the churning motions of the Earth's turbulent interior.

THE MOVING CRUST

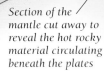

NOT ONLY IS OUR PLANET spinning through space, but also the Earth's surface is heaving about, though very slowly. Each year, the continents move nearly half an inch (a centimeter) or so – some getting closer together, others moving apart. This sounds like a small amount, but over a million years it adds up to about 6 miles (10 km). The movement happens because the inside of the planet is hot and turbulent. Its motion disturbs the cool rocky surface and causes the huge plates of the crust move around. New ocean floor is made at spreading ridges; over tens or hundreds of millions of years it moves toward a subduction zone, where it is destroyed. This slow movement of the Earth's plates has been going on for billions of years.

In 1919, German scientist Alfred Wegener (above) proposed the idea that the continents move. His theory is known as continental drift.

THE PLATE DEBATE

Wegener himself wasn't sure how continents moved, imagining them to somehow plow their way through the rocky ocean floor. Wegener's theory has been transformed by the understanding that each plate of the Earth's crust (shown lifted off the mantle in the artwork below) carries both continents and oceans, which move together.

Destructive margin in Indonesia

Thin oceanic plate *Thick continental plate*

Subduction zone

Destructive margins
Old ocean crust is destroyed where it dives (or subducts) beneath a continent and melts into the mantle. This kind of margin is also called a subduction zone.

PLATE BOUNDARIES

A plate edge meets another at three possible kinds of margins. If a plate carrying an ocean meets a continental plate, the ocean crust plunges down, or subducts, under the continent and disappears. When solid rocky crust of one plate crunches sideways against another equally solid plate, the rocks fracture and earthquakes occur. Where two plates move apart, there is a widening crack in the Earth's outer skin, which fills with hot magma rising from the mantle.

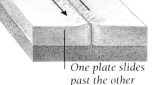

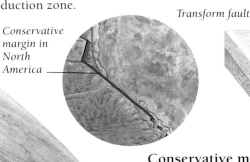

Conservative margin in North America

Transform fault

One plate slides past the other

Conservative margins
Where two plates slide past each other, the rocks grind and crunch and make earthquakes. No new crust is made and no old crust is destroyed. The line along which the plates slide is a transform fault.

Constructive margin in the Atlantic Ocean

Magma oozing up from the mantle

Constructive margins
New ocean crust is made where plates are spreading apart. The gap between the plates fills with magma. These margins are also known as spreading ridges.

Section of the mantle cut away to reveal the hot rocky material circulating beneath the plates

Earth's turbulent mantle
The mantle is more or less solid, but over long periods of time – millions, or tens of millions of years – it flows like a thick, sticky plastic. Some parts of the mantle are cooler and more solid than others. Other regions, under constructive margins and volcanoes, are hotter and contain some liquid, which will rise to become magma.

DRIFTING CONTINENTS

Continual shifting and drifting of the plates which cover the Earth's surface is what changes the shapes of the continents and oceans. Three stages in one continent's drift toward another are shown here. Old ocean crust is swallowed and destroyed at a subduction zone. At the same time, a new ocean grows at the far margin of the plate. Eventually the entire ocean crust disappears back into the mantle, bringing the two continents together. Continental crust cannot subduct – it is too light in weight to go down into the mantle. Instead it grafts onto the other continent.

Ocean crust meets this continent and subducts

Plates pushed apart to make room for the new crust

Spreading ridge

First push
A spreading ridge pushes one continent towards another. The ocean crust between them has nowhere to go, and begins to subduct at the edge of the far away continent.

Spreading ridges are almost all under ocean water, except in Iceland (above), where magma is coming to the surface so fast that the ridge has built up a huge land mass made of oceanic crust.

The ocean floor spreads as magma rises, trying to plug the gap between plates, only to be added to the plate edges

Subduction zone

The push continues
As the new ocean grows bigger, the old ocean gets smaller. Some of the old ocean crust is melted at the subduction zone. It rises to feed volcanoes at the surface, and a mountain range starts to grow.

Continental drift means the ocean floor is always renewed – today, there is no ocean crust left on Earth older than 200 million years.

200 Million Years Ago

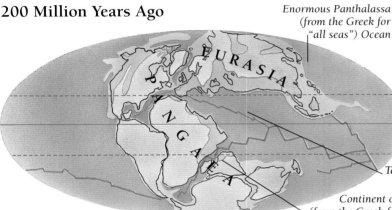

Enormous Panthalassa (from the Greek for "all seas") Ocean

Tethys Ocean

Continent of Pangaea (from the Greek for "all lands")

The continents meet
The mountains buckle up and fold as the continents come closer. Finally, there is no more old ocean crust left to subduct. The continents meet, and one grafts onto another, making a bigger continent.

200 million years ago
An ocean separated Europe and Asia (Eurasia) from the southern supercontinent, Pangaea. There was no Atlantic Ocean, and India was attached to Antarctica.

100 Million Years Ago

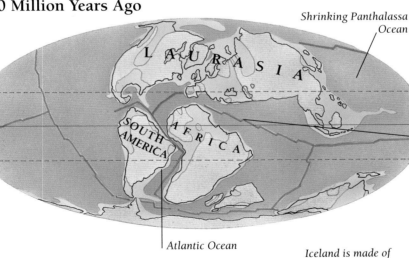

Shrinking Panthalassa Ocean

Tethys Ocean

Atlantic Ocean

100 million years ago
Africa and South America had already begun to separate from each other as they broke away from Antarctica. As new ocean floor was built by a spreading ridge between North America and Europe (Laurasia) and Africa, the young Atlantic Ocean was born.

Present day
Antarctica is now separated from all the other continents; it is totally surrounded by new ocean floor which has been made by a spreading ridge encircling it. India has rammed into Asia, and the ancient Tethys Ocean has all but disappeared.

THE WORLD LONG AGO
The shapes and locations of the continents and oceans were very different in times gone by. It is easy to put together the history of the last two hundred million years, by imagining that today's ocean crust is no longer there. In this way we know that two hundred million years ago there was a giant continent, called Pangaea. This supercontinent came about through the collision and grafting together of yet older continents. It is not so easy to reconstruct what happened before Pangaea. There was an even earlier supercontinent, also pieced together from even older continents which themselves had been formed by previous continental splitting.

Present Day

Iceland is made of oceanic crust

NORTH AMERICA
EUROPE
ASIA
ATLANTIC
PACIFIC OCEAN
AFRICA
OCEAN
SOUTH AMERICA
INDIAN OCEAN
ANTARCTICA

Remains of Tethys Ocean

Himalayas formed where India rammed into Asia

Spreading ridge around Antarctica

EXPLOSIVE VOLCANOES

EARLY IN 1980, THE SIDE of Mount St. Helens started to bulge. As pressure built up inside the volcano, the bulge got bigger and bigger. On May 18, the entire volcano exploded. Explosive volcanoes like Mount St. Helens (shown here) produce thick, sticky lava, and erupt infrequently. Between eruptions, there is time for gas to build up in the magma below the volcano. Eventually the pressure of the gas blows the overlying rocks apart. The gassy lava froths up and explodes, shattering into tiny fragments. Propelled by the force of the explosion and the continuing release of gas, the fragmented lava billows out. It launches down the steep slope of the volcano as a high-speed ash flow, engulfing everything in its path.

FIRE MOUNTAIN

Mount St. Helens is shown on the right, with two sections pulled away to expose its explosive center. The last major eruption had been in the 1800s, so the volcano had been silent for over a hundred years before its devastating eruption in 1980. Mount St. Helens at last lived up to the name given to it by its native peoples – Tahonelatchah, or "fire mountain."

Eruption cloud

A vertical column of ash and steam rose high into the atmosphere, where it formed a mushroom cloud directly over the erupting volcano.

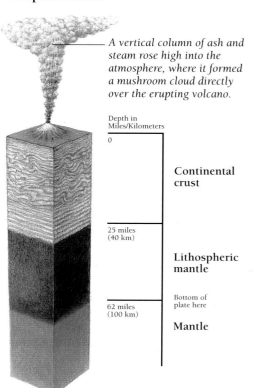

Depth in Miles/Kilometers
0

Continental crust

25 miles (40 km)

Lithospheric mantle

62 miles (100 km)

Bottom of plate here

Mantle

MAGMA

Magma is generated about 62 miles (100 km) under the ground. It rises through the solid rock in red-hot blobs, and collects in a reservoir. During decades or even centuries of slow cooling, the magma crystallizes and gas bubbles rise to the top. When pressure is suddenly released in an eruption, pressure from the gas blows out the crystals and explodes the magma, which chills to lava glass and falls as ash.

A cloud of ash

The dense cloud of ash from a large eruption may rise 19 miles (30 km) or more into the atmosphere. Winds can carry the choking cloud over great distances. Ash from Mount St. Helens spread more than 150 miles (240 km) in just two hours.

Hot ash

The temperature inside the cloud reached 680°F (315°C).

Blast force

The force of the eruption blew out the side of the mountain.

Mud flows

Glaciers on the volcano slopes were suddenly melted in the eruption, making destructive mud flows which spread far down the river valleys.

Section of mountainside removed to show the interior of the volcano

Below the volcano

Lava crystallizes slowly in the magma reservoir below the volcano. The arrival of a new blob of magma from greater depth below may trigger an eruption.

Bubbling under

As the magma rises, the gases contained in it escape and form larger and larger bubbles. These balloon out against the rock, trying to find an escape route.

Washington's Cascade Range

Mount St. Helens is a volcano in the Cascade mountain range, along the northwestern coast of North America.

Bird's-eye view

This color-enhanced photograph of Augustine volcano in Alaska shows the explosive force of an ashy eruption. The plume of ash rises high into the atmosphere, then rains down to cover land and sea. Traces of ash clouds can spread around the Earth, affecting the weather and creating spectacular sunrises and sunsets on the other side of the globe.

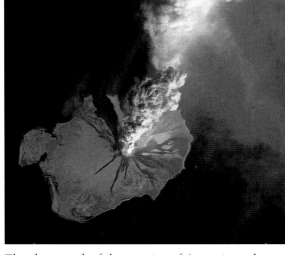

The photograph of the eruption of Augustine volcano was taken from the safety of a Landsat satellite. The ash cloud is about 7 miles (11 km) high.

Avalanche

After a small earthquake shook the volcano, its entire north face trembled slightly, then suddenly broke loose to slide downhill as a massive avalanche.

Rock glows red-hot

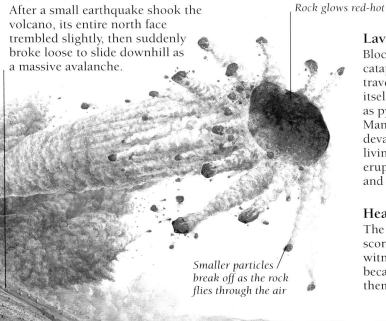

Smaller particles break off as the rock flies through the air

Lava bombs

Blocks of hot rock and new magma were catapulted out of the explosion cloud, traveling even faster than the ash cloud itself. Fragments of new lava are known as pyroclasts, meaning fiery fragments. Many are tiny, but together they make up devastating ash flows, which sear every living thing they meet. Ash flows and the eruption clouds flash with lightning bolts, and may cause torrential rainstorms.

Heat blast

The intense heat from the blast scorched the surrounding forest. Some witnesses said that nearby streams became so hot that fish leaped out of them to escape.

THE AFTERMATH

After Mount St. Helens' great ash flow eruptions in 1980, it began to emit thick, almost solid lava, which squeezes slowly up into the crater. It moves by slipping along many tiny cracks that riddle the sticky lava. As this lava builds up inside the crater, it forms a dome shape. Occasionally the dome becomes so steep that hot, solid lava bursts off as an avalanche from the side of the dome. Mount St. Helens will regrow, but it may take tens of thousands of years to rebuild to its original size.

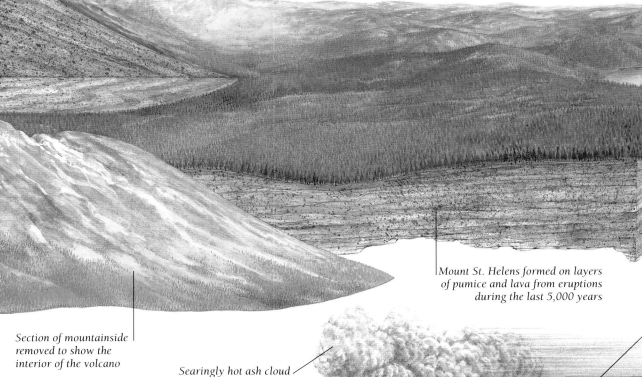

Spirit Lake
Spirit Lake, dammed up by lava from an eruption in prehistoric times, was covered with floating tree trunks and gray ash after the enormous eruption.

Mount St. Helens formed on layers of pumice and lava from eruptions during the last 5,000 years

Traveling in front of the ashy cloud, the hot blast of air blew down the forest

Section of mountainside removed to show the interior of the volcano

Searingly hot ash cloud

As the heat rolls over the landscape, it boils resin from the trees and turns the water in plants and animals instantly into steam

BLASTED TREES

The initial blast of the explosion from Mount St. Helens was so powerful that it ripped mature trees out of the ground, along with their roots and the soil from the volcano slopes. Farther away, it felled hundreds of trees, snapping them off just above ground level, stripping their branches, or splintering their trunks as though they were flimsy sticks.

LAVA ERUPTIONS

IN A VIOLENT ERUPTION, an explosive volcano can devastate the land and throw clouds of searing hot ash into the sky. But other types of volcanoes erupt more quietly and gently, oozing floods of runny, red-hot magma from deep within the Earth's mantle. Because this lava cools to a dark-colored rock called basalt, these volcanoes are known as basalt-lava volcanoes. Basalt-lava volcanoes usually erupt frequently, so they do not build up a huge head of pressure. Instead, the volcano may spit fountains of lava into the air, along with long lava flows that spread out over the surrounding countryside. Over time, these eruptions build huge, broad mountains with very gentle slopes. The islands of Iceland and Hawaii were formed in this way. Volcanic islands grow bigger as lava flows spread into the sea. New islands appear when undersea volcanoes grow large enough to become islands.

This volcano has not erupted for about four million years. The oldest islands are growing smaller as they slowly sink into the sea.

The base of each island is buried in sediment worn from the island itself

Older islands
The islands in the distance are older than Hawaii. They were once above the hot spot, but have been carried away as the Pacific plate moved northwest. Scientists have found evidence for plate movement by taking rock samples from each island. The farther the rocks are found from Hawaii, the older they are.

ISLANDS OF FIRE
The island of Hawaii lies in the middle of a great plate underlying much of the Pacific Ocean. Two of the largest and most active volcanoes on Earth – Mauna Loa and Kilauea – are found here. In this illustration, Mauna Loa is split in half to reveal its red-hot interior. Basalt magma from a hot spot in the mantle wells up beneath the volcano, sometimes erupting near its summit. If the magma finds a crack inside the volcano and spreads out sideways, lava may come out from lower on the volcano slopes.

Hawaiian island chain
The Hawaiian Islands are the tops of huge volcanoes rising from the Pacific Ocean floor. Hawaii is the biggest and youngest of a chain of 130 islands. The eight largest islands are seen above.

Sliding sides
Occasionally the side of a volcano falls away in an underwater rock slide. Blocks of island up to 1,650 ft (500 m) across slide deep into the ocean.

HOT SPOT VOLCANOES
The formation of the Hawaiian Islands was a puzzle to geologists, because unlike most volcanoes, they are in the middle of a plate. By determining the age of the volcanoes, geologists reasoned that the entire chain had formed over a stationary "hot spot" deep in the mantle. A volcano forms over the hot spot, but as the plate carrying it moves, the volcano stops erupting and a new, younger volcano forms. In this way, the hot spot builds a chain of volcanoes that increase in age the farther they are found from the hot spot.

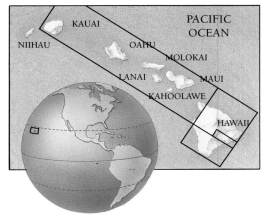

The volcanoes grow older the farther they have been carried from the hot spot

Older volcanoes are no longer active

The plate is now moving northwest at about 4 in (10 cm) a year

Path traveled by moving plate

Each volcano stays over the hot spot for about a million years

The youngest volcano forms right over the hot spot, and erupts frequently

Hot spots in the mantle appear to stay fixed in position for tens of millions of years. Some hot spots are found under continents.

Hidden depths
Only a small part of the volcano is above sea level. Measured from the ocean floor, the volcano is over 29,530 ft (9,000 m) tall – one of the largest volcanoes on Earth.

Pillows on the seabed
When hot lava erupts under cold water, pillow lavas form. These are rounded blobs of lava with a thin skin. Inside the skin, red hot lava continues to flow until eventually the skin splits and another pillow-shaped blob begins to form. This happens over and over until a jumble of pillows piles up on the seabed.

Fire goddess
Pele, the Hawaiian goddess of fire, is said to have traveled down the chain from the oldest island to the youngest, where she lives today. This myth roughly coincides with the way these "hot spot" volcanoes formed.

BASALT MAGMA
Basalt magma comes from the "guts" of the Earth – called the mantle. As a result, it is hotter and runnier than the type of magma that forms from melting crust at a subduction zone. Only the mantle rocks that melt most easily make up basalt magma; the materials that melt at higher temperatures stay behind in the mantle, making it dense and heavy. When basalt magma comes to the surface, it solidifies to basalt rock. If it crystallizes slowly below the surface, the crystals grow large, forming a coarse rock called gabbro.

At Kilauea volcano on Hawaii, basalt lava makes a red-hot fountain while lava flows pour over the dark volcanic landscape. Shreds of lava from the fountain collect in a heap as they cool, building a cindery cone.

Crust layers
The lowest layer of the ocean crust is made of coarse-crystallized gabbro rocks. Above this is a wall-like layer formed by magma that has solidified inside dikes. The volcano has grown on top of these layers.

The uppermost mantle is part of the moving plate

The island has been split in two to show the layers of the volcano.

Volcano layers
Because the lowest layers of the volcano erupted under water, they are made up of piles of rounded pillow lavas. Once the volcano broke the surface, the lava erupted on top of the pillows in long gentle flows stretching to the sea.

Each flood of lava covers the older layers formed by earlier eruptions, continuously building the volcano

Under a volcano
Lava that erupts at Hawaii comes from the mantle, well below the bottom of the Pacific Plate.

Lava dikes
The channels that feed magma to the surface are known as dikes. Dikes cut an angled path through the rock layers that they invade.

Loihi, Mauna Loa, and Kilauea are the only active volcanoes in the Hawaiian chain.

Loihi volcano
South of Hawaii lies an active submarine volcano called Loihi. Its summit is 900 m (2,950 ft) below sea level, but one day it will erupt enough lava to become an island.

Loihi is fed by magma from the same hot spot that built Hawaii

Magma curtain
A curtain of magma seeps upward into a crack in a volcano mountain. The magma might eventually reach the surface and seep out as a lava flow. The magma that is not erupted turns into solid rock, forming a dike.

Depth in Miles / Kilometers	
Oceanic crust	0
	3 miles (5 km)
Lithospheric mantle	
Bottom of plate here	
	60 miles (100 km)
Mantle	
Magma originates here	

SHAKING THE CRUST

WHEN ROCK MASSES under stress suddenly slip apart and break, the crust trembles in an earthquake. It takes a massive amount of force to snap rock apart. Stress can build up for years in the rock before it is swiftly released. The broken rock moves along a crack called a fault. Most faults are underground, but faults break through to the surface and may even show up in the landscape. The Alpine Fault in New Zealand, shown on these pages, has divided the landscape in two, with rising mountains on the east side, and flat plains to the west of the fault line. Like many faults, it is a result of complex plate movements.

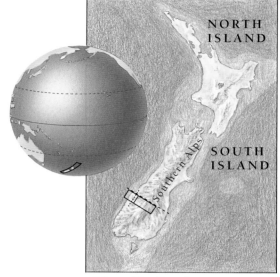

New Zealand
The junction of two plates runs right through the North and South islands of New Zealand, in the Pacific Ocean.

WHY EARTHQUAKES HAPPEN

The three steps below show how stress building in the rocks along a fault line may lead to an earthquake. Two sliding plates lock together, and pressure builds up along the fault line. The stress grows and grows until the strength of the rocks is overcome: the plates suddenly unlock and move, causing an earthquake. The main illustration shows a quake along New Zealand's Alpine Fault.

Volcanic landscapes – from geysers to active volcanoes – are found on North Island.

Stress builds
One plate is moving past another, but the fault line where they meet has gotten stuck. Stress builds up in the rocks of the fault plane, at each side of the fault.

Stress against strength
The stress deforms the rocks, and cracks open in them. Eventually, the stress is greater than the strength of the rocks.

Breaking point
The place where the rock starts to break is called the focus of the earthquake; and the point above, on the Earth's surface, is the epicenter.

Earthquake
When their strength is overcome, the rocks break, and an earthquake occurs.

The earthquake's vibrations travel out from its focus in all directions.

Focus of earthquake

Mt. Tasman

Mt. Cook

Mt. Sefton

Up and down
The New Zealand Alps grow a little higher with each quake, but they are eroded by wind and snow and ice as fast as they are pushed up.

Section of main artwork pulled out and made larger

River courses offset (moved apart) along the fault line

Rocks near the surface at the fault are crushed to a greenish rocky mush which erodes easily

Deeper down, rocks in the fault plane may be melted by heat caused by friction

Fault plane
The fault plane is unlikely to be a straight line; it is probably wavy. The irregularities along its length are part of what makes the fault stick between quakes. The more firmly it sticks, the longer time it will be until the next quake, and the bigger that quake will be.

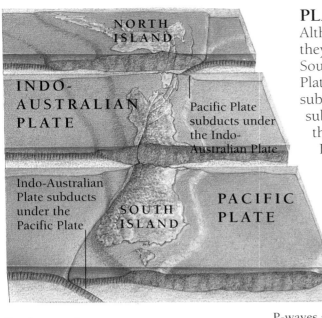

PLATE BOUNDARIES
Although earthquakes can strike anywhere, they are most common near plate edges. South of New Zealand, the Indo-Australian Plate is diving beneath the Pacific Plate in a subduction zone. In North Island, subduction is in the other direction, with the Pacific Plate subducting below the Indo-Australian Plate. This results in a gigantic tear through South Island – the Alpine Fault. In North Island, the subduction causes earthquakes, both in the diving Pacific Plate and the overriding Indo-Australian Plate.

San Francisco, California, sits astride the San Andreas Fault. This photo shows streetcar tracks split apart by shaking during a huge earthquake in 1906.

Rocks on the move
The geology of the rocks found here in the western plains matches up with that of rocks found on the mountain side of the fault. But because of the sideways movement along the fault, these sets of matching rocks are now hundreds of miles (kilometers) apart. They have been separated by countless earthquakes.

Primary waves
P-waves are like sound waves, as they compress and stretch rocks they pass through. Their simple push-and-pull movement lets the waves travel fast.

Secondary waves
S-waves have a more complicated, shearing motion, moving not only up and down, but sideways in all directions at the same time.

EARTHQUAKE WAVES
The vibrations that travel out from the focus are called seismic waves. These waves move fastest through dense rocks, and more slowly through loose sediments and water. Different kinds of waves cause the rocks to vibrate in different ways. The two kinds that travel fastest are P-waves (primary) and S-waves (secondary). After the vibrations pass, there is no sign of change to hard, solid rocks, but soft sediments may be compacted and pressed together.

Shaken to the foundations
Shaking ground can collapse buildings, bridges, and other structures. The damage is often most intense nearest to the epicenter.

Sometimes the most damaging vibrations are intensified by soft rocks, where the vibrations travel more slowly.

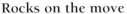

C A N T E R B U R Y   P L A I N S

I S L A N D

Lake Tekapo

TSUNAMIS
Earthquakes that occur near ocean coastlines, or that cause the sea floor to slip, can trigger gigantic waves in the ocean water. They are known by their Japanese name, tsunami. Tsunamis have long wavelengths and can travel vast distances, far from the earthquake that causes them – even across the entire Pacific Ocean. When the waves finally meet the continental shelf, the water heaps up into monster waves – on average 100 ft (30 m) high – which can drown a coastline with devastating effects.

Moving north
West of the mountains is a vast plain that has moved at least 300 miles (500 km) north over the last 20 million years. In fact, every time an earthquake hits, the plains move a few inches (centimeters) northward.

The displaced rocks disturb the water above, generating waves

The train of waves travels through the water away from the epicenter

At the continental shelf, the waves break – that is, the water heaps up into huge waves

Waves sweep the shore about every ten minutes

An underwater earthquake causes seabed rocks to break along the fault plane

MOUNTAIN BUILDING

THE EARTH'S SPECTACULAR mountain ranges have been buckled up from relentless plate movements. Most mountains are over a subduction zone at the edge of a continent, but some are the result of uplift caused by huge rifts in a splitting continent. As soon as mountains are lifted up, erosion starts to wear them away. The higher the mountains become, the more rain and snow fall on them – and the more the mountains are carved down by water and ice. Tall, rugged mountains are an indication that mountain building is still taking place. Once there is no more uplift, erosion takes over, and the mountains are worn lower, until eventually only hills remain. Even these low hills contain clues within their rocks to their past as a lofty mountain range.

The Rocky Mountains grew as subducting ocean crust carried islands to the edge of the coast, and packed them together to add to the mountains.

South America's Andes mountain range is formed by subduction of Pacific Ocean crust.

BALANCING FORCES

Most mountain ranges have been shaped by a balance between tectonic (building) forces, which make the region higher, and weathering and erosion, which wear the rocks away. The shapes of the mountains are a result of this balance. Other mountains are built by volcanic activity. A volcanic mountain may sit on top of a tectonic mountain range, making up the very highest peaks. The map on these pages shows the Earth's main mountain ranges.

The folding that formed Sheep Mountain in Wyoming has been revealed by erosion.

Kilimanjaro, Tanzania
An old volcano built of alternating layers of ash and lava, Kilimanjaro is the highest point in Africa at 19,344 ft (5,896 m).

Mt. Elbrus, Russian Federation
Mt. Elbrus is 18,510 ft (5,642 m) high. It is a volcano but it has not been active for many thousands of years.

Mt. McKinley, Alaska
Mt. McKinley stands glacier-clad 20,322 ft (6,194 m) high in the Denali National Park in Alaska.

Snow line
The snow line falls lower the farther the mountain is from the equator.

Kilimanjaro is on the Equator, but it has a permanent ice cap

Because Mt. Elbrus is farther from the equator, the snow line is lower

At Mt. McKinley, the tree line drops with the snow line

In the polar regions, permanent ice exists at sea level

Altitude

Snow line

Tree line

Kilimanjaro

Mt. Elbrus

Mt. McKinley

0° 10° 20° 30° 40° 50° 60° 70° 80° 90°
Latitude

Tree line
Lower than the snow line is the tree line; above it, trees find it impossible to grow because of the cold.

SNOWY TOPS
Near the equator, where the direct angle of the sun's rays warms the land, the snow line is over 16,000 ft (5,000 m) up. Only at such heights is it cool enough for permanent ice to exist. Away from the equator, where the Sun's heat rays are more and more slanted, they heat the land less, and the snow line is progressively lower. Sections of three mountains, at different distances from the equator, are shown here.

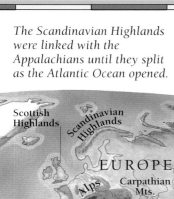

The Scandinavian Highlands were linked with the Appalachians until they split as the Atlantic Ocean opened.

It is so long since the old Ural Mountains were lifted up that erosion has worn them down to only 3,281 ft (1,000 m) high.

The Himalayas are a huge, young mountain range that represents the closing of the old Tethys Ocean.

Scottish Highlands
Scandinavian Highlands
Ural Mts.
EUROPE
ASIA
Verkhoyansk Range
Alps
Carpathian Mts.
Mt. Elbrus
Tien Shan
Kunlun Shan
Himalayas
Atlas Mts.
AFRICA
Ethiopian Highlands
INDIAN OCEAN
East African Rift Valley
Kilimanjaro
OCEAN
AUSTRALIA
Great Dividing Range
Drakensberg Mts.
SOUTHERN OCEAN
ANTARCTICA
Transantarctic Mts.

The mountain ranges in Mongolia were formed 450 to 600 million years ago

Mountains of the East African Rift Valley have been uplifted as Africa prepares to split apart

The Alps, Atlas, and Carpathian mountains formed as Africa moved northward against Europe.

The Transantarctic Mountains developed along a rift within the Antarctic continent.

Since the Great Dividing Range formed 300 million years ago, there has been little tectonic activity in Australia.

This satellite image shows the peaks of the Andes Mountains near Santiago, Chile, under their cover of winter snow.

Key to map

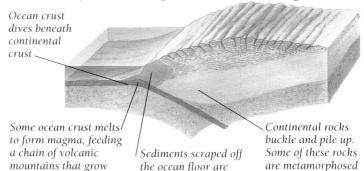

Cenozoic mountains, less than 65 million years old

Mesozoic mountains, between 65 and 250 million years old

Younger Paleozoic mountains, between 250 and 450 million years old

Older Paleozoic mountains, between 450 and 565 million years old

MOUNTAINS FROM SUBDUCTION

Some mountain ranges result from ocean crust being subducted under a continent. They are built partly by rising magma from the melted ocean crust, which may erupt or may cool underground as masses of granite.

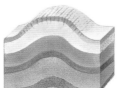

Ocean crust dives beneath continental crust

Some ocean crust melts to form magma, feeding a chain of volcanic mountains that grow with each eruption.

Sediments scraped off the ocean floor are added to the mountains.

Continental rocks buckle and pile up. Some of these rocks are metamorphosed or recrystallized.

Worn-down mountains

America's Appalachian Mountains were built about 250 million years ago, parallel to an even older mountain range. Forces of erosion have attacked the range since its creation, leaving snakelike ridges of hard quartzite rock standing. The softer rocks in between the ridges wear away much more easily, forming valleys. A satellite image of the Appalachians in Pennsylvania (left) shows the distinctive patterns left behind by erosion.

MOUNTAIN STRUCTURES

Making mountains involves both stretching and compression. These illustrations show different types of folding and fracturing that may be seen in mountain ranges.

When rocks are stretched apart, they fracture. This type of fault is called a normal fault.

Rocks also fracture when they are compressed. This type of fault is known as a reverse fault.

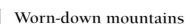

Rocks crack when they are folded. This allows erosion to wear them away faster. So, the tops of upfolds do not become the tops of mountains.

Folded rocks

The layered sediments begin to fold as the rocks of the crust become more and more compressed.

Faulted fold

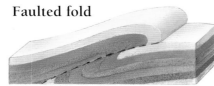

When the folding is so intense that the rocks cannot bend any more, they break, forming a thrust fault.

Folds and faults

In a mountain range, layers of rock are squeezed and folded, then may fracture to form thrust faults. Erosion wears away the tops of the thrust mass of rocks to make the mountain peaks.

CONTINENTS COLLIDE

OVER THE LAST 70 MILLION YEARS, a mighty collision between two continents has created the most spectacular mountain range on Earth – the Himalayas. The continent of India began to move slowly but steadily northward toward Asia, swallowing up an old ocean in its path. Some small continents in the ocean were pushed into Asia first, forming the young Himalayas. As the two continents came closer together, the ocean floor was pushed beneath them, or subducted. When all the ocean had been subducted, India finally met up with the Asian mountains. India has continued to move northward, and Asia has buckled and been pushed up, forming the world's highest mountains and highest plateau.

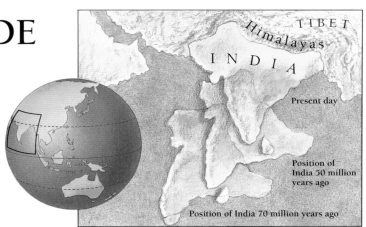

Present day

Position of India 50 million years ago

Position of India 70 million years ago

India's northward charge
Before its collision with Asia, the plate carrying India was moving north at 4 in (10 cm) a year. Once the continents met, this slowed to 2 in (5 cm) a year. The Himalayas are the youngest mountains so far formed in this collision.

INSIDE A MOUNTAIN RANGE
India (on the left) has pushed into Asia much like a battering ram. The collision has hardly changed India, but Asia has buckled up and its crust has become almost twice as thick as it was before. This is partly a result of folding and fracturing of the Asian crust, and partly due to blobs of molten rock rising upward to add to the continental mass. As the mountains rise, they are eroded by wind, ice, and rain, making new sediments.

New oceanic crust is formed on the sea floor south of India

Wedge of sediment
This fan-shaped wedge of sediment was scraped off the subducted plate and accreted, or joined, to Asia. It is known as an accretionary wedge.

Young sediments formed from erosion of Himalayan mountains

Old hard continental crust of India

INDIA

SRI LANKA

INDIAN OCEAN

Ganges River

Himalayas

The stark, glacier-hung peaks of Thamserku soar over the Everest region of Nepal.

The roof of the world
The Himalaya range includes the tallest mountain on Earth – Mount Everest – soaring to a height of 29,028 ft (8,848 m). Many other mountains in the range tower to heights of more than 26,240 ft (8,000 m). The exact height of Everest is difficult to determine. This is because the depth of the snow covering it changes all the time.

• Mt. Everest

HIMALAYAS CROSS-SECTION
The rocks that now make up the high mountain peaks of the Himalayas were formed on the floor of the Tethys Ocean, which once separated India and Asia. When the continents met, the heavy oceanic crust was subducted. But the lighter seafloor sediments were scraped off, one slice after another. Through folding and faulting, they became part of the Himalayan mountain range. Faults push one slice of rock over another. This close-up view of a section of the main illustration shows how the rock sequence created by faulting is repeated over and over again.

Glaciers keep the mountain slopes steep

Fractures caused by crushing of rock layers

The youngest rocks of one slice are beside the oldest rocks of the next slice

Folding in rock layers

INDIA'S LIFE HISTORY

India became separated from the old southern continent of Gondwanaland when a new ocean formed between it and Antarctica, pushing the landmasses apart. North of India there were several small continents which were added on to Asia as the Tethys Ocean floor was subducted. When India met Asia at last, no more subduction could happen, because continental crust is too light to subduct. Instead the edge of the Asian continent collapsed and was crushed to make room for India.

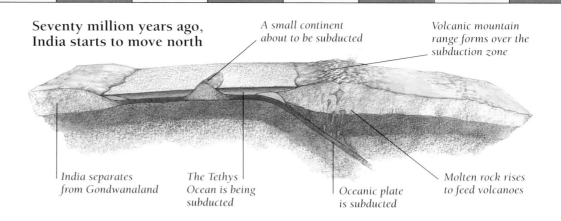

Seventy million years ago, India starts to move north

A small continent about to be subducted

Volcanic mountain range forms over the subduction zone

India separates from Gondwanaland

The Tethys Ocean is being subducted

Oceanic plate is subducted

Molten rock rises to feed volcanoes

Fifty million years ago, India collides with Asia

The last remains of the Tethys Ocean are subducted

The old line (suture) where the small continent added on to Asia

Volcanic activity continues

The southern edge of Asia starts to collapse

Ocean sediments are thrust and stacked on top of each other

Earthquake zone

Deep, violent earthquakes under the west end of the Himalayan mountains show that the subduction process is continuing.

Karakorams

The Karakoram range is home to K2, the second highest peak in the Himalayas at 28,250 ft (8,611 m).

High and dry

Because the massive mountains block the monsoon rains, much of Tibet is a desert.

TIBETAN PLATEAU

Experts think continental may be at its thickest under Tibet. Here, the land surface of the plateau is a lofty 3 miles (5 km) above sea level. The plateau is a stark, treeless land dotted with low mountains. Its plains are thick with sediment worn from nearby mountains. Probably because of fracturing, the mountains seem to be collapsing like wobbly jelly. As a result, the mountains are burying themselves in the sediment they shed.

Tibetan hot springs

There are few active volcanoes over the remains of the subduction zone in Tibet. Tibet does have hot springs, however, which are heated by the cooling igneous rock.

Kailas Range

T I B E T

Tien Shan Mts

Kunlun Shan Mts

Tibetan Plateau

LAKE BAIKAL

The results of the crushing of Asia are visible thousands of miles (kilometers) north, as far away as Lake Baikal, in Siberia. Lake Baikal sits in a huge rift which has been opening for 25 million years. The rift is about 5.5 miles (9 km) deep – almost as deep as the Mariana Trench. Over the years, the rift has filled with sediment, but today Baikal is still the deepest lake on Earth, holding about one-fifth of the planet's fresh water. As India continues to barge northward, Baikal may one day become a new ocean which will split Siberia apart.

Rocks formed by remains of the small continent

Compression of Asia results in a split

Subduction zone

When two plates collide, particularly at the edge of an ocean, the impact can force one plate right underneath the other. This is known as subduction. As the subducted plate dives downward, it starts to melt. Earthquakes and volcanoes are common in subduction zones.

Melted crust

Subducted oceanic crust starts to melt at a depth of about 62 miles (100 km). The fiercely hot molten rock pushes up through any cracks and weak spots in the rocks above. It gathers in huge underground blobs called plutons, which may cool and harden to form igneous rock, such as granite.

Thickened crust under Tibet

Lake Baikal

MAKING THE CRUST

FORCES BOTH ABOVE and below the ground combine to create, destroy, and change the Earth's crust in a continual cycle. At spreading ridges, basaltic ocean crust is continually being made. This new crust moves away from the volcanic ridge, then plunges back into the Earth's interior at a subduction zone. In the interior, the crust melts into magma. This magma rises toward the surface either to feed a volcano or to form huge underground blobs called plutons. Plutons may cool to make rocks like granite, building the mountain range higher. Deep inside the mountain range, rocks are heated and recrystallized. As the mountains grow, the slopes are worn down and the loose rock fragments go to make new rocks. These processes form the Earth's three rock families: igneous, metamorphic, and sedimentary.

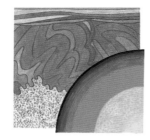

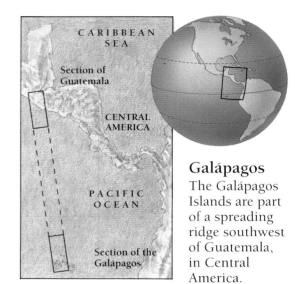

Galápagos
The Galápagos Islands are part of a spreading ridge southwest of Guatemala, in Central America.

CREATION AND CHANGE
The coastal mountains of Guatemala and the neighboring Galápagos Islands are illustrated on these two pages. Some sections have been cut away to show the processes that create the Earth's crust. The mountain range, above a subduction zone, is made partly of granite, an igneous rock made when old oceanic crust melts, and then cools and hardens. As the granite pushes toward the surface during mountain building, some rocks are heated, compressed, and recrystallized to form metamorphic rocks. The rising mountain peaks are eroded almost as quickly as they grow, making sediment that forms new sedimentary rocks near the Guatemalan coastline.

◦ The circles show how much of each of the three types of rock – igneous, sedimentary, and metamorphic – is found in each region.

Coastal rocks
Huge amounts of sediment – from large boulders to tiny flakes of clay – wear away from the nearby mountains and settle at the coastline. Only sedimentary rocks are found here.

Mountain rocks
In mountain regions, granites make up about a third of all rock, sedimentary rocks about a third, and metamorphic rocks the rest.

A tor is a craggy hill formed from the erosion of granite. Vixen Tor (above) is in Devon, England.

GRANITE LANDSCAPE
The illustration below shows some features found in a granite landscape. The top of a batholith has been worn away, and nearby are the eroded roots of old volcanoes.

Old volcano erodes to reveal hard lava plug

Tor left after part of batholith erodes

Feeder pipe for a long-extinct, eroded volcano

Collapsed top of a granite pluton fills with water

Part of a huge dome-shaped granite batholith

Plutons
The rising blobs of magma are called plutons, after Pluto, the Roman god of the Underworld.

Range rocks
Inside a young mountain range, almost all of the rocks are either igneous or metamorphic.

Granite batholith
A pluton cools slowly over many millions of years to form granite. New blobs of magma may remelt granite that has already cooled, so the history of a batholith can be quite complex.

BASALTIC LANDSCAPE

The illustration on the right shows some of the features of a typical basaltic landscape. Flows of basalt lava spill downhill, over older flows now cracked into columns. On flat land, the lava spreads out in sheets, which may build up in layers. The upper parts of a lava flow are usually covered in blocklike lumps of lava. These weather away relatively quickly, forming a rich soil, which may be reddish in color. Where one lava flow runs over another, a series of "steps" can form in the land. An old word for this kind of landscape is *trap*, as in the Siberian traps.

Columns

These tall basalt columns formed when the inside of an old lava flow slowly cooled and shrank, cracking into pencil shapes. The rock piles below the cliffs have been eroded from them.

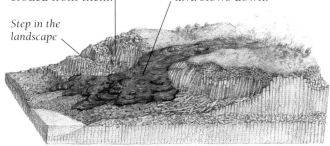

Step in the landscape

Lava flows

A new lava flow cascades over the cliff of basalt columns. The molten lava moves inside a wrinkled skin of cooler lava, at a speed of up to 30 mph (50 km/h). As it cools, the lava slows down.

The photograph above shows basalt lava seeping from Kilauea volcano on the island of Hawaii. This hot runny lava with a cooler skin is known by its Hawaiian name, pahoehoe. It is basalt lava that rises at a spreading ridge, building the ocean floor.

Crust destroyed

At a subduction zone, basaltic oceanic crust goes back into the Earth's mantle. The sediments on top of the crust may be scraped off and remain on the edge of the continent.

Ridge rocks

At spreading ridges, almost all of the rock is igneous, with some sedimentary rock.

New seafloor at spreading ridge

Island rocks

On volcanic islands, most of the rock is igneous, but there is some sedimentary rock.

Basalt islands

The Galápagos Islands are built by basaltic rocks, made near the spreading ridge by hot magma rising from the mantle.

GALÁPAGOS ISLANDS

COLON RIDGE

P A C I F I C
O C E A N

MIDDLE AMERICA TRENCH

Crust created

At spreading ridges, basaltic magma wells up to the surface and crystallizes. Layers of lava spill out on the ocean floor, making new crust, while some magma cools below.

Clouds of ash and dust are thrown into the atmosphere

Ash and grains of rock are dumped in layers

A volcano erupts lava and ash

Igneous rock is weathered and eroded

Basaltic rocks go into the mantle and start to remelt at 62 miles (100 km) down

THE ROCK CYCLE

The rock cycle is how rocks change, one into another. A simple diagram of the cycle is shown on the right. Igneous rocks, for example, named for the Latin word for "fiery," form when magma cools underground. They can also form when lava from a volcano cools quickly. Once exposed to the effects of water, wind, and ice, igneous rocks erode, making sediment (from the Latin word for "settle"), which builds up and eventually becomes layered sedimentary rock. In mountain ranges, rock changes due to heat and pressure, and recrystallizes to become metamorphic rock (from the Latin word for "changed"). There is no beginning or end to the cycle, and each transformation may take many millions of years.

Igneous rock
Extrusive igneous rock forms when erupted lava cools

Magma rises to the Earth's surface and erupts in a volcano as lava

Plutonic igneous rock forms when magma cools and hardens under the ground

Some sedimentary and metamorphic rock wears away to form new layers

These layers are squeezed and hardened into rock

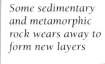

Sedimentary rock

Heat and pressure may recrystallize rock into other rock

Metamorphic rock

Rock melts to form magma

Rock that is heated enough may melt to make new magma

Edge rocks

At the edge of the continent are igneous rocks, and metamorphic rocks that are made from them.

Igneous rock

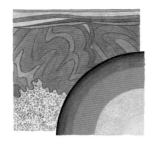

THE CRUST WEARS DOWN

AS NEW CRUST is created, forces act upon it all the time to wear it down again. These forces might be as obvious as a gigantic landslide, or as invisible as a flake of clay carried in a raindrop. Changes in the weather bring continual fluctuations in temperature and dampness. These changes affect surface rocks. The rocks expand and contract, and become waterlogged and dried out. Mineral grains that make up the rocks loosen and separate, creating many tiny rock fragments. The fragments may remain in place or be carried away by rain, by melting snow and ice, by the wind, or by rivers, such as China's mighty Huang He, seen here. Plant roots play their part by wedging rocks apart along cracks, allowing water to penetrate more deeply. Weathering is the breaking apart or chemical "rotting" of the rocks, and erosion is the removal and transport of rock grains.

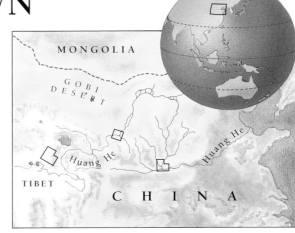

Course of the Huang He
The Huang He (Yellow River) of China travels 3,000 miles (4,830 km) from its source in the mountains of northern Tibet, through a loop near Mongolia, and south to the Yellow Sea.

Meandering to the sea
Nearer to the sea, the river travels over the gentle slopes of the flood plain. By this point the river is loaded with yellow sediments. As it meanders across the land here in great, slow-moving curves, it drops much of its load of silt. The river flows between banks made of silt that has already been deposited. Each year, the river drops more silt, filling up the river channel.

The Huang He is so loaded with yellow silt that it is the same color as the silt of the riverbanks.

Turning yellow
The river water is clear in the rocky mountains. But the soft, fertile yellow silt of the loess region is easily washed away, especially from plowed fields. Here the river picks up the bulk of the yellow sediments that give it its

When it leaves the loess lands, almost a third of the river's total volume is sediment

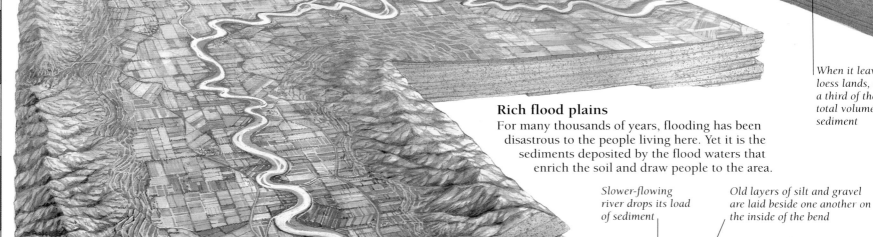

Rich flood plains
For many thousands of years, flooding has been disastrous to the people living here. Yet it is the sediments deposited by the flood waters that enrich the soil and draw people to the area.

Slower-flowing river drops its load of sediment

Old layers of silt and gravel are laid beside one another on the inside of the bend

A CURVING COURSE

As water rounds a curve in the river course, it flows fastest on the outside of the bend. The river is also deepest here. On the inside, the water is shallower and flows more slowly, so silt and pebbles are dropped. Over time, the river bed moves outward, making a gentle bend into a sharp curve. In this way the course of the river moves sideways as it snakes across flat land.

Fast-flowing water on the outside of the bend

Deeper water erodes the sand and gravel banks

CHINA'S HUANG HE

Three sections of the Huang He are shown on these pages. The river carries some sediment from its mountainous source in Tibet. Farther downstream is the loess region, where soft silts are easily weathered and eroded. The river picks up the fine, silty loess grains and carries them away. In the flat plains near the sea, the river flows slowly and can no longer carry the silt, which drops to the riverbed, building it ever higher.

In the mountainous regions, turbulent streams flow over rocky valley floors

Valleys have steep sides

Crumpled peaks
The Kunlun Shan (or mountains) are eroded into rugged peaks. As the rivers cut valleys ever deeper, the peaks become steeper and more unstable.

Ups and downs
The higher the mountains are pushed up by forces within the Earth, the faster erosion wears them down.

The mountain region
In winter, snow and glaciers cover the high mountains. The mountain rocks may be broken apart as water in cracks within them freezes at night and thaws during the day. In summer, the snow melts to feed fast-flowing torrents. These torrents carry the loose rock fragments swiftly downstream.

Carving a valley
These river valleys have steep sides because layers of very hard rock make up the mountains. Where the underlying rock is softer, valleys are less rugged.

HILLSLOPE EROSION
The pull of gravity means the surface on almost every slope is slowly inching downhill. Slope erosion happens most rapidly on steep hillsides that are unstable or barely stable. Gentle slopes and tree-covered slopes are less easily eroded.

Enlarged cross-section of area in the loess

Layers of pebbly silt are soft and easily eroded

Falling rock
At the foot of steep, rocky slopes there is usually a heap of rock fragments that have fallen from the cliff face. This heap, or talus, makes the slope less steep and reduces the rate of erosion.

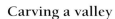

The loess lands
The hill slopes in the middle course of the Huang He are rapidly eroding. These slopes are made of soft loess, young layers of wind-blown silt that were blown from the deserts of central Asia and deposited here during the Pleistocene Ice Age. The river valley is flat in places where the valley is wide and layers of sediment line the riverbed. In others parts, where the river goes through harder rocks, its silty water flows in torrents through steep-walled gorges.

A series of steps called terraces have been cut into the slopes. These allow farmers to grow crops on level ground right up to the hilltops, and helps prevent heavy rains from washing the soil away

Tree grows up toward sunlight despite the sliding soil

Slipping land
Steplike landslips happen along curved cracks in the rock. These too make the slope more gentle, unless the "toe" at the bottom of the slip is eroded by a river in the valley.

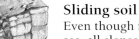

Sliding soil
Even though its movement may be too slow to see, all slopes show some evidence of the continual downhill creep of soil. Each rainstorm and frost moves soil and broken rock fragments in the subsoil slightly farther downhill. Heavy rainfall can wash whole slopes clear of soil and talus, especially where there are few trees to hold the loose slope material in place.

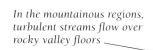

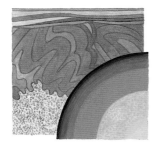

LAYERING THE LAND

THE SEDIMENT that is carried by rivers and glaciers from mountain regions eventually finds a resting place. This might be as boulders and gravel at the foot of a mountain, sand dunes in a desert, silt and salt in a desert lake, or as sand or pebbles on a riverbank or on a coastline. Sediments are laid down in layers, each younger layer on top of older ones. These layers are exposed to view where they have been uplifted and then cut through by eroding rivers. Perhaps the most spectacular example on Earth is the immensely deep Grand Canyon, carved into the layered rocks of the Colorado Plateau by the Colorado River.

This spectacular view of the Grand Canyon was taken from Mather Point on the South Rim. The higher North Rim is just visible in this picture.

North Rim
More than 1,000 ft (300 m) higher than the South Rim, the North Rim is covered with snow until late spring.

Weathered walls
Over millions of years, weathering has chiseled and shaped the curves and gulleys of the canyon walls.

Canyon colors
The layers of different types of rock give the canyon its spectacular colors, from gray limestone, yellow sandstone, to pink granite, and dark schist.

Bright Angel Point

BRIGHT ANGEL CANYON

Manu Temple

Widforss Point

Buddha Temple

KAIBAB PLATEAU

HAUNTED CANYON

Cheops Pyramid

Tivo Point

Isis Temple

HOW COAL FORMS

Coal began to form when vast swampy forests flourished on a river delta. As the trees died, they fell into the swampy bogs. Instead of decaying as they would in air, the dead tree remains were preserved under the water, sticking together to form a dark, fibrous material called peat. This was buried by layers of new sediment – sand, lime, and mud. As more and more sediments were laid down, each peaty layer of forest remains became compressed. After many millions of years, the peat was compressed and heated, forming coal.

Coal deposits, or seams, are removed from the Earth by mining.

Surface works of coal mine

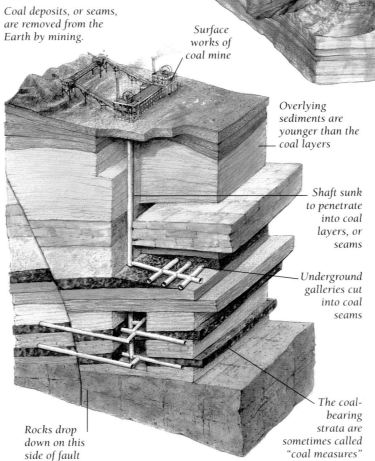

Overlying sediments are younger than the coal layers

Shaft sunk to penetrate into coal layers, or seams

Underground galleries cut into coal seams

Rocks drop down on this side of fault

The coal-bearing strata are sometimes called "coal measures"

HOW OIL FORMS

Some sediments contain large amounts of the remains of tiny sea plants. When these are buried, they are "cooked" by heat and pressure to become oil.

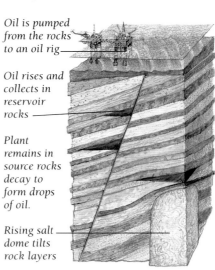

Oil is pumped from the rocks to an oil rig

Oil rises and collects in reservoir rocks

Plant remains in source rocks decay to form drops of oil.

Rising salt dome tilts rock layers

Trees to peat
Soft, nonwoody trees that grow in a tropical swamp may form peat.

Peat to coal
Layer after layer of new sediment compresses the peat to coal.

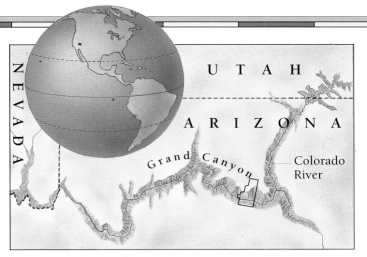

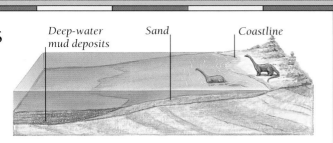

CHANGING SEDIMENTS

As sea level changes with time, so coastlines move. Sea level rises when spreading ridges are more active. The undersea mountains push aside ocean water, so that it floods the continental shelves.

Deep-water mud deposits   Sand   Coastline

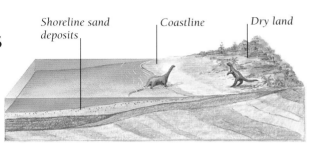

Shoreline sand deposits   Coastline   Dry land

CHANGING SHORELINES

At times when sea level is lower, during an ice age, or when spreading ridges are less active, the continental shelves dry out. Shoreline sediments such as sand are then deposited on top of the older, deeper water sediments.

Arizona's Grand Canyon and Colorado River

The Colorado River has carved the awesome Grand Canyon through Arizona, in the southwestern United States. The canyon is 217 miles (349 km) long, up to 18 miles (30 km) wide, and 1 mile (1.6 km) deep.

Rocks of the rims

The rocks near the canyon rims were formed from sediments laid down 250 million years ago. Each layer reflects the changing history of the area. Some layers were once ancient seabeds, while others were desert sands.

South Rim

Little rain falls on the desert plateau on the South Rim, so there is little water to run down and erode the canyon walls. As a result, the South Rim of the canyon has the steepest slopes, and the river runs right at the foot of the cliff walls.

Fossil finds

Fossils found in the canyon walls record a changing history of life. Older life forms such as trilobites are found near the bottom of the canyon, while reptile fossils are nearer the top.

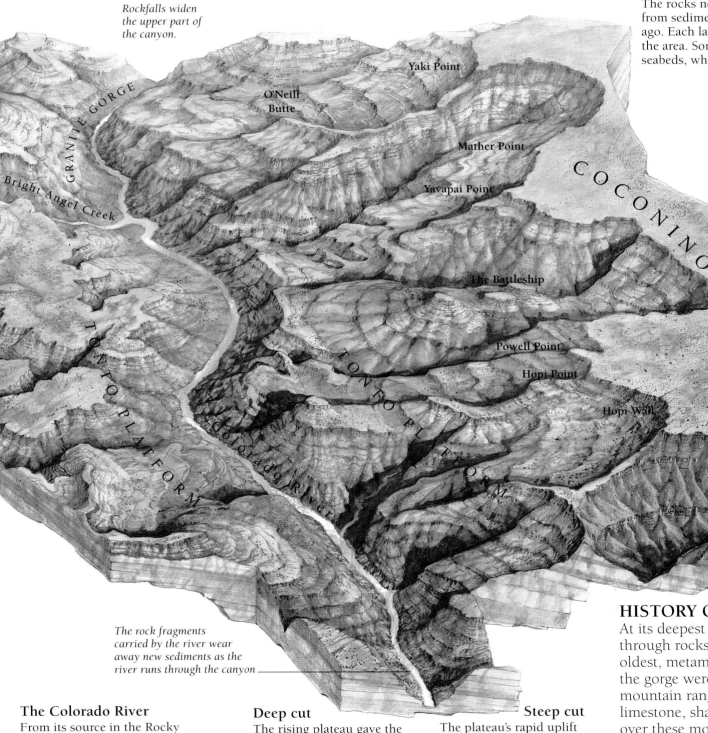

Rockfalls widen the upper part of the canyon.

Yaki Point
O'Neill Butte
Mather Point
Yavapai Point
The Battleship
Powell Point
Hopi Point
Hopi Wall
Great Mohave Wall

GRANITE GORGE
Bright Angel Creek
TONTO PLATFORM
Colorado River
COCONINO PLATEAU

The rock fragments carried by the river wear away new sediments as the river runs through the canyon

HISTORY OF THE CANYON

At its deepest point, the Grand Canyon cuts through rocks 2 billion years old. The oldest, metamorphic rocks at the bottom of the gorge were formed as part of an ancient mountain range. Younger layers of limestone, shale, and sandstone were laid over these mountains, then lifted up into the Colorado Plateau. As the plateau rose and domed up in the middle, the river carved its course deeper, keeping pace with the uplift. The rocks of the canyon rim are about 250 million years old.

The Colorado River

From its source in the Rocky Mountains of Colorado, the river falls sharply through several canyons and into the desert. The Colorado River itself may be as much as 30 million years old, while the high plateau itself is younger.

Deep cut

The rising plateau gave the river a steeper slope on its journey to the sea. This made the river flow faster, so it had more energy to cut away its riverbed and deepen the canyon floor.

Steep cut

The plateau's rapid uplift means the river has carved an even steeper canyon over the last two million years. In its long history, the canyon may never have been so impressive as it is today.

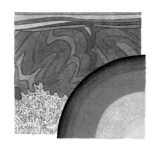

THE CRUST CHANGES

AT THE HEART of the Earth's mountain ranges lie metamorphic rocks. They are different from sedimentary and igneous rocks – they have unique textures and structures, and contain new and different minerals. Metamorphic rocks are igneous or sedimentary rocks that have been changed. The changes are brought about by heat given off at nearby igneous rock intrusions, by the immense pressure from the weight of the overlying mountains, or by chemical reactions. Heat and pressure cause the rocks to recrystallize without melting. Metamorphic rocks in a landscape show there was once a mountain range there, though there may be no high ground any longer.

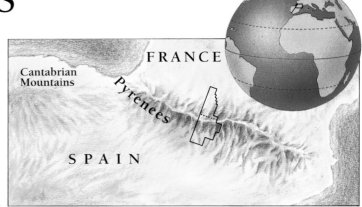

The Pyrenees Mountains
Forming a border between France and Spain 270 miles (435 km) long, the Pyrenees are one of the Earth's young, still growing mountain ranges.

METAMORPHIC MOUNTAINS
The Pyrenees mountain range, seen on these pages, has granite intrusions at its core. The hot molten granite swelled upward, heating the surrounding rocks and pushing them aside. Over many millions of years, the sedimentary rocks and older igneous rocks were metamorphosed within the mountain range. Today, many miles (kilometers) of rock have been eroded off the top of the Pyrenees, to reveal its metamorphic heart.

These layers of sedimentary rock at Pico de Vallibierna have been folded and over-folded until they are lying down, or recumbent. Part of the fold is eroded.

Pico de Vallibierna, Spain
The folded rock pattern shown in the photograph on the left is outlined here.

Folding up rocks
In mountain ranges, sedimentary rock which was first laid down in horizontal layers is folded. The forces that make the mountain range push and fold the layers, sometimes forming intricate patterns later exposed by erosion.

Change in the range
Metamorphism that happens over a wide area, especially in mountain ranges, is known as regional metamorphism.

Lago Helada, Spain
The outline shows a recumbent fold in the strata of Lago Helada, seen on the right. The folding is so intense that some of the layers are now upside down. The top of the fold has been cut away by erosion.

This icy lake in Spain's Ordesa National Park shows a reflection of the folded rocks of Lago Helada above.

Section through granite intrusion

Intrusion
This granite intrusion cooled many miles (kilometers) down in the crust. It is now exposed at the Earth's surface by erosion.

Country rock round intrusion

HISTORY OF THE PYRENEES

A hundred million years ago, the great Tethys Ocean stretched between Europe and Africa. As immense forces in the Earth pushed Africa northward, the ocean was swallowed at a subduction zone. Sediments from the ocean floor were buckled and crushed and intensely over-folded, as great rock masses were pushed one over another to make the Pyrenees. Some rocks deep in the mountain range were heated, just by their deep burial. These rocks became hot enough and were buried for long enough to recrystallize into metamorphic rocks.

200 million years ago
In the Tethys Ocean, sediments were laid down on the ocean bed and along its shorelines.

100 million years ago
Iberia and France crunched together, and a mountain range began to grow.

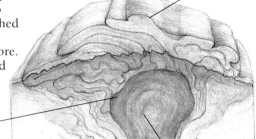

Rocks are folded and pushed one over another

Two million years ago
Older granite pushed up into the folded and crushed rocks, complicating the mountain range even more. All the rocks were heated and metamorphosed.

Rocks nearest the intrusion are heated the most

Old granite intrusion deep within the mountains

IBERIAN DRIFT

As Africa moved northward, Iberia (the landmass of Spain and Portugal) crunched sideways against Europe. Layers of sediment from the old ocean floor were probably scraped up and eventually eroded away, so there is no record left of their existence. Today, the Mediterranean Sea is all that remains of the ancient Tethys Ocean.

Rock which formed many miles (kilometers) deep has been worn from the peaks

Ice carving
The high slopes of the Pyrenees have been carved into rugged peaks by the glaciers that covered them during the Pleistocene Ice Age.

Shared history
The Pyrenees are among the world's youngest mountain chains, the same age as the Alps and Carpathians in Europe and the Himalayas in Asia.

Foothills
The rocks of the foothills show less complicated folding and less intense metamorphism.

Folded and metamorphosed rocks near the granite

The dark rock at the center of Pic la Canau has eroded more easily, making a gully on the slope.

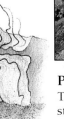

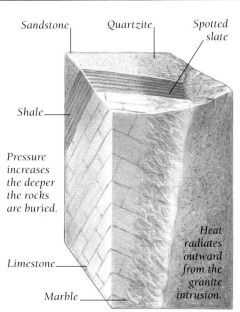

HOW ROCKS CHANGE

As rocks are compressed and heated, their mineral grains gradually rearrange themselves in response to the changing pressure and temperature. Atoms move from places where pressure is greatest to the places where it is less intense. New minerals grow which are stable at high pressures and temperatures. The type of metamorphic rock that forms depends on the composition of the original rock, and how much heat or pressure – or both – brings about the change.

Sandstone
Quartzite
Spotted slate
Shale
Pressure increases the deeper the rocks are buried.
Limestone
Marble
Heat radiates outward from the granite intrusion.

Pic la Canau, France
The outline shows how the rock was stretched and cracked over the top of the fold, allowing erosion to bite in. The top of the fold has all worn away.

AMAZING EARTH

EARTH'S LANDSCAPES show an amazing variety – from deserts and polar ice regions to spectacular waterfalls and graceful volcano cones. Each has its own unique geological history. Some landscapes are the result of recent erosion or tectonic (building) processes, which in the vast time scale of Earth's history means changes over the last few tens of millions of years. Others were sculpted by the same processes, but have changed little for hundreds of millions of years. Several amazing landscapes – from hoodoos to inselbergs – are shown here.

Bryce Canyon, Utah

The hoodoos (from an African word meaning "spirit") of Bryce Canyon are a mass of pinnacles sculpted from layers of soft young rock. The canyon's pink-orange limestone is sediment that collected in a lake only 60 million years ago. The attack of wind, snow, and rain has worn the rocks into colorful hoodoos.

Loose rock collects at the base of the hoodoos.

These red sandstone towers are the North and South Mittens.

Monument Valley, Utah

The large mesas and smaller buttes that tower over Monument Valley are isolated flat-topped mountains, made of horizontal layers of sedimentary rock. Over hundreds of thousands of years they have worn away, leaving behind tall towers of rock.

The falls plunge off a flat plateau.

The Pantanal, Brazil

In the back country of Brazil, seasonal rainfall in the mountains feeds mighty rivers. Where these rivers travel over the level swamplands of the Pantanal, they spread out, flooding the land. When the rains stop, hundreds of shallow pools are left behind.

The swamps cover an area the size of Great Britain.

Angel Falls, Venezuela

The waterfall with the longest drop in the world tumbles 3,212 ft (979 m) off the wet swamplands of a plateau called Auyán Tepuí in Venezuela. It is named after the pilot Jimmy Angel, the first outsider to see the falls in 1935. The water changes into white mist before reaching the bottom.

Canadian tundra

In summer, soggy plains stretch in all directions in the Arctic regions of northern Canada and Siberia. Below the surface the ground is permanently frozen, so the summer meltwater has nowhere to go and collects in swampy pools. At the end of the summer these pools of water freeze again. When water just beneath the surface expands to form ice, it may push the soil up into small domes called pingoes.

Tundra

NORTH AMERICA

Bryce Canyon • • Monument Valley

Tropic of Cancer

ATLANTIC

Equator

PACIFIC OCEAN

Angel Falls •

SOUTH AMERICA

Tropic of Capricorn

The Pantanal •

The icecap contains 90 percent of all the ice on Earth.

Antarctic icecap

A vast sheet of ice makes up the cold deserts of Antarctica. The icecap has formed from frozen snow that has accumulated over tens of thousands of years. Covering nearly the entire continent, the ice is over 14,764 ft (4,500 m) thick in places. Only the tallest summits of the Transantarctic Mountains break through the ice.

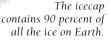

Ahaggar Mountains, Algeria

From the desolate Sahara desert plain rise the majestic Ahaggar Mountains. The tallest of these spiny peaks is about 9,840 ft (3,000 m) high. The mountains are made of igneous rocks – granites and lavas including phonolite. Phonolite, meaning "sound stone," is so called because when it is hit with a hammer, it gives off a musical note.

Fuji is a sacred place of pilgrimage. Thousands of people each year climb the mountain to watch the sun rise.

The phonolite cooled and cracked into long, thin shapes that give the Ahaggars their ribbed surface.

Mount Fuji, Japan

The majestic snow-capped volcano Mount Fuji is 12,388 ft (3,776 m) high. The volcano has been active for thousands of years. When it last erupted in 1707, black ash fell in the streets of Tokyo, 62 miles (100 km) away. Its name comes from "fuchi," which means fire, a word of the Ainu, the original people of the Japanese islands.

EUROPE ASIA

Ahaggar Mts.

AFRICA

• Mt. Fuji

• Guilin

PACIFIC OCEAN

OCEAN

INDIAN OCEAN

• The Olgas

AUSTRALIA

Table Mountain •

SOUTHERN OCEAN

ANTARCTICA

Antarctic icecap

Guilin hills, China

Over hundreds of millions of years, the limestone in the hills of Guilin has been slowly dissolved by rain, creating a landscape called tower karst. The flat lands at the bottoms of the hills, covered by rice paddy fields, are layered with vast amounts of clay washed away with the limestone. Rivers snake their way around these strange, weathered remains.

Table Mountain, South Africa

The sandstone layers of South Africa's Table Mountain were laid down 500 million years ago. Over time, the sand hardened into rock and was uplifted without folding, so its layers are still horizontal. Erosion has worn away everything but the distinctive table rock that remains.

Kata Tjuta, the Aboriginal name for the Olgas, means "many heads."

Table Mountain rises 3,566 ft (1,087 m) above Cape Town.

The Olgas, Australia

Resembling huge red rock haystacks, the Olgas (or Kata Tjuta) are clustered on the sandy Australian plains. The plain is covered with regolith – rock-sand and clay weathered from the underlying solid rocks. Erosion does not remove the regolith, so over time it gets thicker, until it is burying all but the highest points of the underlying solid rock. These island mountains are called inselbergs. Uluru (formerly Ayers Rock) is another example.

PLANET WATER

EARTH IS ENVELOPED in a watery shroud, with almost three-quarters of its surface covered by ocean waters. The largest ocean, the Pacific, is also the oldest, and is about one third of the Earth's entire surface. Around its fringes lie the deepest places on the Earth's surface, the great ocean trenches. Some trenches are much deeper even than the nearby land mountains are high. The ocean floor is studded with volcanoes and flat-topped mountains that may rise much higher than those on land, and is crisscrossed by massive mountain chains. Layers of sediment carpet the entire deep ocean floor. Shallow water surrounds each continent; these continental shelves are the flooded margins of the continents.

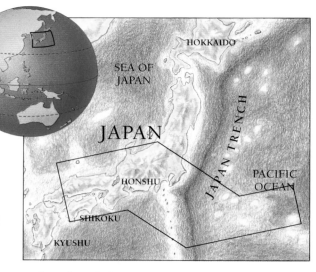

Islands of the rising sun
Japan is a chain of islands east of Asia. Its name means "land of the rising sun" in Japanese. A deep ocean trench lies along its Pacific coast, and a small young ocean separates it from Asia.

Seabed sediment
Thick layers of sediment collect on the shallow seabed. Some is made from the shells of sea creatures, and some is sand and mud from the continent.

Young mountains
High mountains with steep slopes make up much of Japan's landscape. The young mountain rocks erode rapidly, pouring loose sediment into the ocean.

Loose sediment settles in layers on the edge of the slope

At the edge of the continent
The continental slope stretches from the edge of the continental shelf all the way down to the ocean deep. It is covered with layers of mud, sand, and the fine sediments eroded away from the nearby continent.

JAPAN TRENCH
Japan lies on an active continental margin, where the Pacific Ocean plate is being subducted underneath Japan. The deep Japan Trench shown on these pages marks the place where the ocean floor plunges beneath its neighboring plate. As the plate crunches underneath, earthquakes are generated. Sometimes the shaking dislodges loose sediment from the sides of the trench, which then cascades down into deeper water.

Sea canyons
Undersea avalanches of muddy sediment carve out steep-sided canyons into the depths of the trench.

PASSIVE MARGINS
The continental shelves fringing most land areas in the Atlantic Ocean are wide and shallow. They are known as passive margins. As Europe and the Americas split and the ocean between them grew, the continental edge was pushed from the spreading ridge. Much of the continental shelf was flooded at the end of the Ice Age.

An old avalanche of sediment from the coastal water

Ocean trench
A trench is deep and narrow, with steep walls. Some of the sediment that collects here is carried back into the Earth with the subducting plate.

Passive margins have no subduction zone, and few earthquakes

Continental slope ends at a pile of sediment called the continental rise

Continental shelf is part of the neighboring continent

LAND HEMISPHERE

Although Africa, Asia, and Europe dominate this view of the globe, they are surrounded by the waters of the Atlantic, Indian, and Antarctic oceans. The Atlantic is a young ocean, split down the middle by a huge underwater mountain chain. The Atlantic and the Antarctic oceans have been growing larger over the past 200 million years, as the continents have drifted apart. At the same time, an old ocean that once separated the northern and southern continents has shrunk to become the Mediterranean Sea.

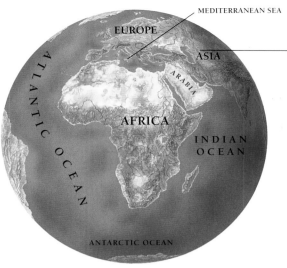

The Aral Sea is a landlocked salty lake, which straddles Uzbekistan and Kazakhstan in western Asia. Diversion of its water for irrigation has made the lake shallower, so the water evaporates faster. These ships are stranded in the shrinking sea.

OCEAN HEMISPHERE

The Pacific Ocean is so vast it extends across a whole hemisphere, stretching nearly halfway around the globe at its widest point. Within the Pacific is the lowest point on Earth – the Mariana Trench. The Pacific is dotted with more than 25,000 islands, which are actually huge mountains rising from the ocean floor. Although subduction has been swallowing the ocean crust along its margins for many tens of millions of years, the spreading ridges to the south and east of the ocean, where new crust is formed, are keeping pace.

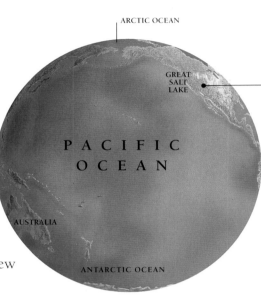

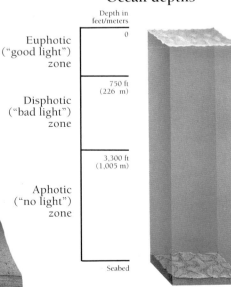

This is a satellite view of the Great Salt Lake and Desert in Utah. No plants can grow in the vast salt flats north of the lake. The lake looks as if it is two colors because it is split by a rocky causeway. A river feeds the left side of the lake, but the fresh water cannot circulate to the saltier right side.

Undersea volcanoes
Volcanoes pepper the ocean floor. Some are active and grow large enough to rise above the water, forming islands.

Guyots
A guyot is a sunken flat-topped mountain. Guyots were once islands, but their tops were worn flat by pounding waves. They sank under the sea as the sea floor subsided.

Age of the seafloor
The ocean floor being subducted under Japan today is about 200 million years old. It was once part of Panthalassa, a massive ocean nearly twice the size of the Pacific that surrounded Pangaea.

Tipping toward the trench
Flat-topped guyots tip over at an angle as they are pulled into the ocean trench by the subducting ocean floor.

Sediment
Layers of sediment made mostly of red-brown clay build up on the ocean floor.

Final resting place
Buried in the deep sea sediment are whale earbones, skeletons of microscopic creatures – even bits of meteorites from space.

Ocean depths

Depth in feet/meters

Euphotic ("good light") zone	0
Disphotic ("bad light") zone	750 ft (226 m)
Aphotic ("no light") zone	3,300 ft (1,005 m)
	Seabed

Sunlight penetrates only the euphotic and disphotic zones. The oxygen-rich water supports a vast range of life. The aphotic zone is inky black with cold waters and immense pressure –few life forms can survive here.

THE OCEAN FLOOR

THE DEEP OCEAN FLOOR is crisscrossed by the longest mountain chains on Earth. These are the spreading ridges, where magma oozes up to form new oceanic crust. The ocean floor today is the youngest part of the Earth's crust. It has all formed at oceanic spreading ridges over the past 200 million years. No older ocean crust is left, because it has all been swallowed back into the mantle at subduction zones near the continental margins. New crust is made at cracks in the spreading ridges. When the crust beneath the cracks stretches, rift valleys form. As the continents on either side of the rift valley move farther apart, there is continually space for more and more new crust. Tall chimney stacks called black smokers billow thick black clouds along cooler parts of the spreading ridge.

RIDGES AND RIFT VALLEYS

A section of the vast underwater mountain chain that snakes through the Atlantic Ocean, the Mid-Atlantic Ridge, is shown here. Its massive peaks rise up to 13,000 ft (4,000 m) above the ocean floor. The rift valley at the center of the ridge is where the ocean floor is spreading. Several black smokers dot the middle of the valley. A section of the rift valley is pulled out and shown larger, to reveal its structure.

Faults

As the growing ocean floor stretches, it cracks along lines (faults) more or less parallel to the rift valley. Steep cliffs along the fault lines gradually grow less steep as blocks of rock break off and fall to the bottom.

Each section of ocean floor breaks along a sloping fault, so its layers become tilted

The rising cloud of water looks black because of the minerals it contains

A black smoker grows when the boiling water shooting from a crack meets the cold water near the ocean floor

The chimneys are brittle and break off from time to time, leaving heaps of broken fragments around the smokers

Pillow lava

Magma oozing up from the mantle becomes basalt lava, a dark-colored rock rich in iron and magnesium. When the hot lava cools in contact with seawater, it makes lumpy round shapes called pillow lava.

Dikes

Under the pillows is a layer of vertical dikes, where magma crystallized as it came up through the rift valley crack.

BLACK SMOKERS

These tall stacks are made of mineral deposits. The black "smoke" they belch out is actually tiny grains of metal sulfides. Originally, the sulfides were in the new rocks of the ocean floor. As ocean water seeps through cracks in the cooling rock, it dissolves the sulfides. Hot magma below the center of the rift makes this water boil. As the water bubbles up through the cracks, it deposits the sulfides and other minerals, building chimneys up to 33 ft (10 m) tall.

Mysteries of the deep

A hundred years ago, the unexplored deep waters of the ocean were a great mystery. The instruments and ways to study the seabed had not been invented. Instead, many people believed folktales of fantastic undersea cities, or fearsome sea monsters prowling the icy depths. In those days, the deep ocean was the setting for science fiction books, such as Jules Verne's *Twenty Thousand Leagues Under the Sea* (left), in the same way as space and other planets are the setting for fantasy novels today.

MID-ATLANTIC RIDGE

Two hundred million years ago, there was no ocean between Europe and Africa, and the Americas. Then a crack developed which grew and widened, and new ocean crust filled in the gaps along the Mid-Atlantic Ridge to form the Atlantic Ocean. By dating ocean-bed rocks, scientists know that the oldest oceanic crust is nearest to the continents, and "strips" of ocean floor are younger the nearer they are to the still-active ridge. The map below shows the age of the crust in each of its sections.

The longest mountains on Earth

The Mid-Atlantic Ridge stretches 7,000 miles (11,300 km) from Iceland in the north to the edge of the Antarctic Ocean in the south.

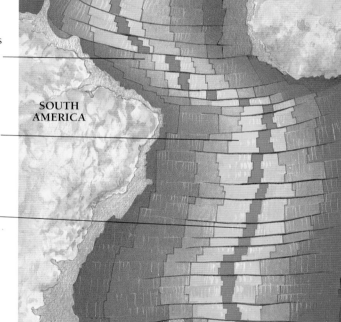

NORTH AMERICA

EUROPE

AFRICA

SOUTH AMERICA

200 million years ago (MYA) The oldest crust is nearest the land.

65–140 MYA The crust here formed in the age of dinosaurs.

20–65 MYA The Pyrenees and Himalayas grew as this crust formed.

2–20 MYA The Himalayas soared higher as this crust formed.

0–2 MYA The youngest crust is nearest the ridge.

Transform faults

The spreading ridges are in short sections across the oceans. Every few tens of miles (kilometers), the active part of the ridge is moved sideways by fractures called transform faults. These faults cut across the middle of the ridge and offset the crust into sections.

The fractures extend far beyond the transform fault, where they offset the spreading ridge

Piles of pillows

Although the outside of a pillow lava cools rapidly to a dark skin, red-hot magma still flows inside. It may break through the skin to form a new pillow, so that great heaps of pillow lavas pile up to make the uppermost part of the ocean crust.

Lifting the crust

Cracks develop as magma pushes up against the overlying continental crust, stretching and lifting it upward.

Rift valley forms

The continent begins to crack apart, and a central block sinks, forming a rift valley. Magma squeezes in to fill the cracks.

From valley to sea

Fresh cracks fringe the widening rift valley as its walls move farther apart. Seawater enters the deep basin.

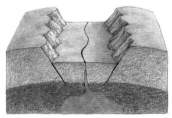

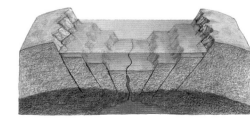

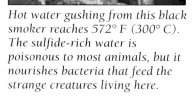

Hot water gushing from this black smoker reaches 572° F (300° C). The sulfide-rich water is poisonous to most animals, but it nourishes bacteria that feed the strange creatures living here.

BIRTH OF THE RED SEA

The Red Sea in eastern Africa formed in the same way as the Atlantic Ocean – at a spreading ridge. Today it is only about 186 miles (300 km) across, but millions of years from now it may rival the Atlantic in size. The Red Sea was born 20 million years ago as Arabia started to crack away from Africa. First, great layers of basalt lava poured out over the surrounding land through cracks in the crust, as magma rose from beneath. Later, the basalt eruptions were concentrated in the central part of the widening rift. This basalt eventually became the new ocean floor as seawater filled the valley. The Red Sea will keep getting wider as long as Arabia keeps moving away from Africa.

THE LIFE OF A RIVER

A TINY TORRENT OF WATER high up in the mountains eventually becomes a vast, placid river flowing into the sea, but it has to go through several stages and pass through many landscapes before it gets there. Streams and rivers are fed from water that runs over the surface of the ground as well as from underground water seeping out from the rock. In the great continents, rivers usually rise in mountains near one coastline. Some travel vast distances across ancient routes to a far coastline; others take their water to inland lakes or seas. The river shown on these pages is the Nile – the longest river in the world.

Course of the Nile

The Nile River flows 4,145 miles (6,670 km) northward through the Sahara Desert to the Mediterranean Sea. The shorter route eastward to the Red Sea is blocked by a range of mountains that are younger than the river course.

BIRTH OF A RIVER

In mountain regions where there is plentiful rain and melting snow, rivers are turbulent (rough). Many little rivulets flow over steep rocky landscapes, carving their pathway as they go, and cutting valleys ever steeper and deeper. Some mountain ranges today are slowly growing higher, pushed up by forces inside the Earth. River valleys in these growing mountains stay steep and full of waterfalls. The rising mountains ensure plenty of rain and snow from cooling weather clouds, which keep the rivers flowing.

Lake Victoria

Lake Victoria is the source of the upper valley of the Nile River. It lies on a recently uplifted plateau.

Kabalega Falls

The river plunges more than 130 ft (39 m) downward over this steep, clifflike waterfall, surrounded by the rising mountains of Uganda.

Rapids

A hard, rocky riverbed creates a series of rapids where the water is turbulent, tumbling in all directions as it rushes over the rocks. Rapids are often found near waterfalls.

Swamps

The Nile flows sluggishly through the reed swamps of the Sudd region. This area was once a lake.

River junction

The two main branches of the river – the White Nile and the Blue Nile – join near the city of Khartoum in Sudan.

Deep-plunge pool at base of waterfall

THE WAY TO THE SEA

The steepest part of a river's course is usually near its source in the mountains. The closer the river gets to the sea, the flatter its pathway becomes. But along the route, there may be many interruptions to this gradual change in slope. These might be lakes, where the river slowly fills in a hollow with pebbles, sand, and mud. Waterfalls form where the river runs over bands of hard rock onto softer rock.

Ancient river valleys

During the Ice Age, the climate here was wetter. Rivers from mountains near the Red Sea ran into the Nile. Today, these dried-up river valleys are called wadis.

Tributaries

The Blue Nile brings water from the Ethiopian mountains, which are hit by heavy seasonal rains. The White Nile carries water from eastern Africa. Smaller rivers that join a main river are called tributaries.

These meanders on the Darling River are cutting their way across the rocky landscape near Pooncarie in New South Wales, Australia.

MEANDERS

Where the river course runs through flat land, its path winds along in broad curves. These are called meanders. The meander curves continually get bigger and wider. This is because the water travels fastest around the outside of the curve, cutting its pathway through the riverbanks. On the inside of the curve, the water travels more slowly. Here it drops the sediment it is carrying, and forms a bank.

When it is in flood, a river can cut right through the narrow neck of land between meanders, straightening its course. The curving lake left behind is called an oxbow. An oxbow lake gradually silts up, as it is no longer part of the river.

GRAND CANYON OF THE NILE RIVER

Overall, the slope of a river's course relates to the sea level at the time. Five million years ago, the Mediterranean Sea dried up completely so that sea level, as far as the Mediterranean rivers were concerned, was 6,560 ft (2,000 m) lower than it is today. At this time, the Nile cut its pathway down to meet this deeper level. Sand and gravel carried by the river scoured away at the layers of rock, forming a steep-sided canyon.

The Nile canyon, which may have looked similar to Arizona's Grand Canyon, extended more than 620 miles (1,000 km) to Aswan. Over time, the sea level rose again, and the river dropped its sediment to fill in the canyon.

Five million years ago
The Mediterranean dried up and sea level was lower. The Nile carved a deep canyon, to try to meet the new sea level.

Present day
Later, when the sea level rose again, the canyon slowly filled in with gravel, sand, and mud from higher up the river's course.

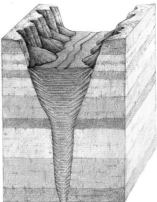

DELTAS

Rivers in flood carry along huge amounts of gravel, sand, and mud. When a river reaches the relatively calm seawater, it drops its load of sediment in layers. These layers cannot build up thicker unless the region is sinking. Instead they get carried farther out to sea. In this way, the river may build up a triangular-shaped area of new, swampy land, crisscrossed by small channels of water. This is called a delta, after the Greek letter "delta" (Δ) which is a triangle.

A satellite view of the Mississippi River delta in Louisiana shows its bird's-foot shape.

Cataracts
Where the river passes over hard granite rocks it forms great foaming rapids of white water. These are known as cataracts. There are six cataracts on the Nile; the first, at Aswan, was the first cataract that the Nile explorers met.

Sahara Desert
The Nile finds its pathway through 1,700 miles (2,375 km) of the Sahara Desert on its journey to the Mediterranean Sea. It rains very rarely in the Sahara, so there are no tributary rivers on this part of the Nile. Nowadays, it is only fed by water from the faraway mountains upstream.

Flood waters
On the broad, low-lying plain, flood water from the Nile has spread onto the land at either side, forming a strip of green, fertile land in the midst of the brown desert.

The Nile Delta
The Nile River divides into many sluggish rivers which wander over the broad fan of the delta region in Egypt.

Bumpy bed
This is a section of a cataract. The bumpy surface of the rocky riverbed at a cataract makes the yearly flood water running over it turn a foamy white.

New land
In the delta, new land is formed by the rock and mud that the river has carried from upstream. Eventually the swampy land dries.

COASTLINES

WHERE SEA MEETS LAND, the battle between the pounding waves and solid rock creates the Earth's changing coastlines. The water of the seas and oceans is continually moving, driven by the energy of waves and currents. As the waves crash one after another against the shoreline, they find weaknesses in the rock and wear their way through. Bays, for example, are carved out where coastal rock is softer. Even cliffs made of harder rock are undercut by waves. Once undermined, the cliff breaks away in occasional rockfalls. The sea builds as well as destroys. Pieces of eroded rock are sorted out by waves – smaller ones are carried away, while larger pieces stay put, building a beach. Sand and pebbles can also add new fingerlike land to the coastline. The illustrations on these pages show how the sea is continually remodeling the coastline of Dorset, England.

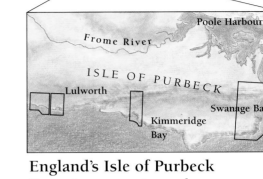

England's Isle of Purbeck
Dorset is a county in southwestern England. Its coastline stretches along the English Channel, which separates Britain from France. The area of Dorset seen on these pages is called the Isle of Purbeck.

Rocky walls
Some coasts are bordered by hard, rocky walls of granite or limestone. These walls are strong enough to resist waves and slow the rate of erosion.

Spit and tombolo
A long ridge of sand or pebbles that extends from the land into open water is called a spit. Sand is carried by drifting waves and then dropped. A tombolo is a spit between an island and land.

Hole in the roof
Waves can pound into cracks in the rock, pushing out the air inside so a spray of water rises from the rock with each wave.

Coastal rocks
The underlying rock shows why the Dorset coast has worn into an irregular shape. Headlands are found where the rock is more resistant, while bays are sculpted out of softer rock.

Layered ledges
Alternating layers of hard limestone and soft clay support a series of ledges stretching out to sea.

Hard band of limestone makes a vertical wall

Softer clay rocks behind the wall

Sea finds a weak spot in the wall and starts to wear through

A second weak spot

Soft rocks are easily eroded, and are etched away by waves to form a cove

Waves swirl into the cove and wear away its sides

The eroded rock is deposited in the bay to form a beach

BIT BY BIT
The pounding waves can eat away the land one bit at a time. Once the waves cut through the hard wall of rock, the softer rocks behind are easily worn away. First a small cove is carved out. At high tide, the sea swirls in. The waves wear away the sides of the cove, enlarging it to make a curving bay.

Two coves may open up to form a curving bay

THE DORSET COAST
The Dorset coastline is built layer by layer of soft and hard rocks that have been gently folded. The folding has broken up some of the harder rocks, making them more easily eroded by waves pounding against the coast. Other hard rock layers form walls able to resist the waves. Soft rocks make up the low ground, which is easily invaded by the sea. Dorset's beaches are made of large hard flinty pebbles called shingle. As waves break onto the shingle their energy is absorbed, rolling the pebbles. In this way, shingle protects the cliffs and landscape from being worn away by the breaking waves.

LONGSHORE DRIFT

Each incoming wave breaks at an angle to the shore. The surf picks up pebbles and sand and moves them slightly sideways up the beach, then gravity pulls the surf straight back down to the sea. As a result, pebbles move along in a zigzag known as longshore drift. To keep the pebbles from drifting so far that they fill harbors, fences called groines are built.

Spit built by pebbles carried by the drift

Waves push pebbles and sand to the shore at an angle

Fences stop pebbles traveling too far along

Gravity pulls the water back parallel to the shore, moving the pebbles along the beach

CHANGING SEA LEVELS

Sea levels change continuously. During the Ice Age, large changes of sea level took place – as much as 660 ft (200 m) over thousands of years. In a cold phase, sea level drops, as water from the oceans is locked up in glaciers. When the glaciers melt at the end of a cold phase, the water returns to the oceans, and sea level rises.

The Dart Estuary in Devon, England, is a ria – a river valley drowned by the sea.

A river spills into the sea

Rivers erode their valleys down to the sea at sea level. Their riverbed usually slopes very gently at the mouth, or estuary, where the river meets the sea.

The sea drowns the river

If sea level rises relative to the land, estuaries become drowned by seawater and are called rias. Rias are excellent natural harbors for ships.

Chalk hills

The chalky limestone underlying rocks makes a line of rolling hills farther inland.

A layer of chalk rocks underlies this area, visible in the chalk cliffs of the coastline.

A dent in the land

A bay is a curving dent in the land. The waves within are usually gentle, as the headlands at either end break up the wave energy.

Studland Bay

Old Harry Rocks

Ballard Point

Swanage Bay

Sea stacks

The Old Harry Rocks were once part of the chalk headlands. But waves cut a cave into a weak spot of the rocks, eventually breaking right through it to form an arch. The top of the arch was later worn away to form sea stacks, isolated blocks of rock left stranded by erosion.

Peveril Point

Underlying layer of clay is easily eroded

Clay beneath the bay

A bay formed here because the underlying clay rocks are softer than the chalk and limestone rocks of the headlands. The pebbly beach is made of harder rock fragments worn from the headlands.

Durlston Head

Headlands

The resistant limestone rocks stretching out from the coast are its headlands. These shelter the rest of the coastline, protecting softer rocks farther behind. The limestone breaks up the energy of the waves, causing the water to foam in white breakers.

SAND AND SHINGLE BEACHES

Rocks worn from the coastline are ground down by the pounding waves to shingle or sand, then eventually deposited in a bay or other sheltered area to form a beach. The sand or shingle doesn't stop moving once it is laid down – in fact, beaches may sometimes change radically within hours. In a storm, large, heavy waves break directly onto the beach. These can pick up and carry the beach material into deep water offshore, so a sandy beach can disappear overnight. The beach usually returns eventually after a long spell of calmer weather.

UNDERGROUND WATER

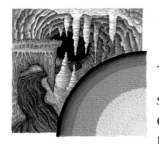

WINDING ITS WAY gently and silently through tiny spaces, water slowly travels through the rocks underground. Water is found at some depth everywhere beneath the land surface. Most of this water is rain that soaked into the ground after a shower and was not immediately used up by plant roots. Some rainwater passes through the underground rocks quickly and emerges only a few hours, days, or weeks later at a spring seeping out into a river valley. Sometimes the water stays underground for many thousands of years, either because it travels a long way or because it travels slowly. During such a long time in the rocks, water usually picks up and dissolves minerals from the rocks. In this way, the water can widen cracks in the rock until eventually an enormous underground cave forms. Underground rivers run through some caves, wearing their walls away even further. France's spectacular Gouffre Berger is shown in cross-sections on these pages.

A cross-section of the Gouffre Berger is shown here. Parts of the cave are enlarged below

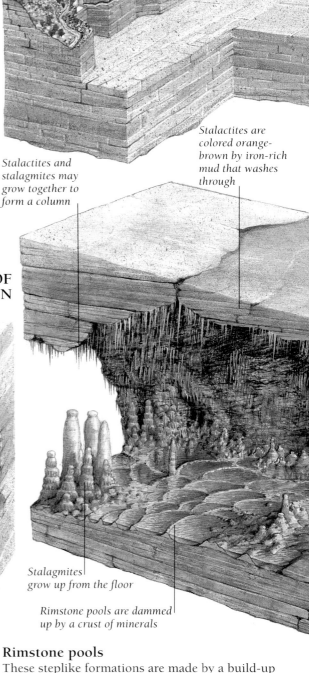

AN UNDERGROUND LABYRINTH

The Gouffre Berger (gouffre is French for "cave") is a long underground labyrinth of passageways and chambers, possibly tens of millions of years old. Its entrance is an open hole in a high limestone plateau. Today, a river runs through some parts of the cave, but others are dry. The cross-sections shown on these pages reveal some of the strangely shaped rock formations built by dripping water inside the cave. After traveling 13 miles (22 km) and dropping 3,936 ft (1,200 m), the river emerges into the light of day and joins the Furon River.

Stalactites are colored orange-brown by iron-rich mud that washes through

Stalactites and stalagmites may grow together to form a column

Gouffre Berger, France

The Gouffre Berger is near the city of Grenoble, beneath the Vercors Mountains. The limestone landscape here is honeycombed with caves and underground rivers.

The river emerges

During its passage through the cold, dark cave, the river picks up lime and other minerals and dissolves them. When the river emerges, the lime-rich water forms deposits called tufa as the bubbling spring water is warmed by the sunshine.

THE CANALS

HALL OF THIRTEEN

Stalagmites grow up from the floor

Rimstone pools are dammed up by a crust of minerals

Walls of the cave are hollowed out by water as it dissolves the limestone.

Underground river

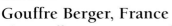

Crusts of tufa, a type of limestone

Spring water emerges from the limestone in the river valley

Submerged river

The water level of the lakes and streams within caves changes rapidly. As soon as it rains outside, the caves fill up quickly; after a prolonged dry and hot spell, the water level may drop.

Rimstone pools

These steplike formations are made by a build-up of mineral deposits at the edge of a slope. Sometimes minerals are left behind as water runs over a slope. They form a crust, trapping a pool of water that overflows to form another step.

Cavernous cave

The biggest cave so far explored in the world is the Sarawak Chamber in Borneo, a staggering 2,300 ft (700 m) long, 1,410 ft (430 m) wide, and 395 ft (120 m) high.

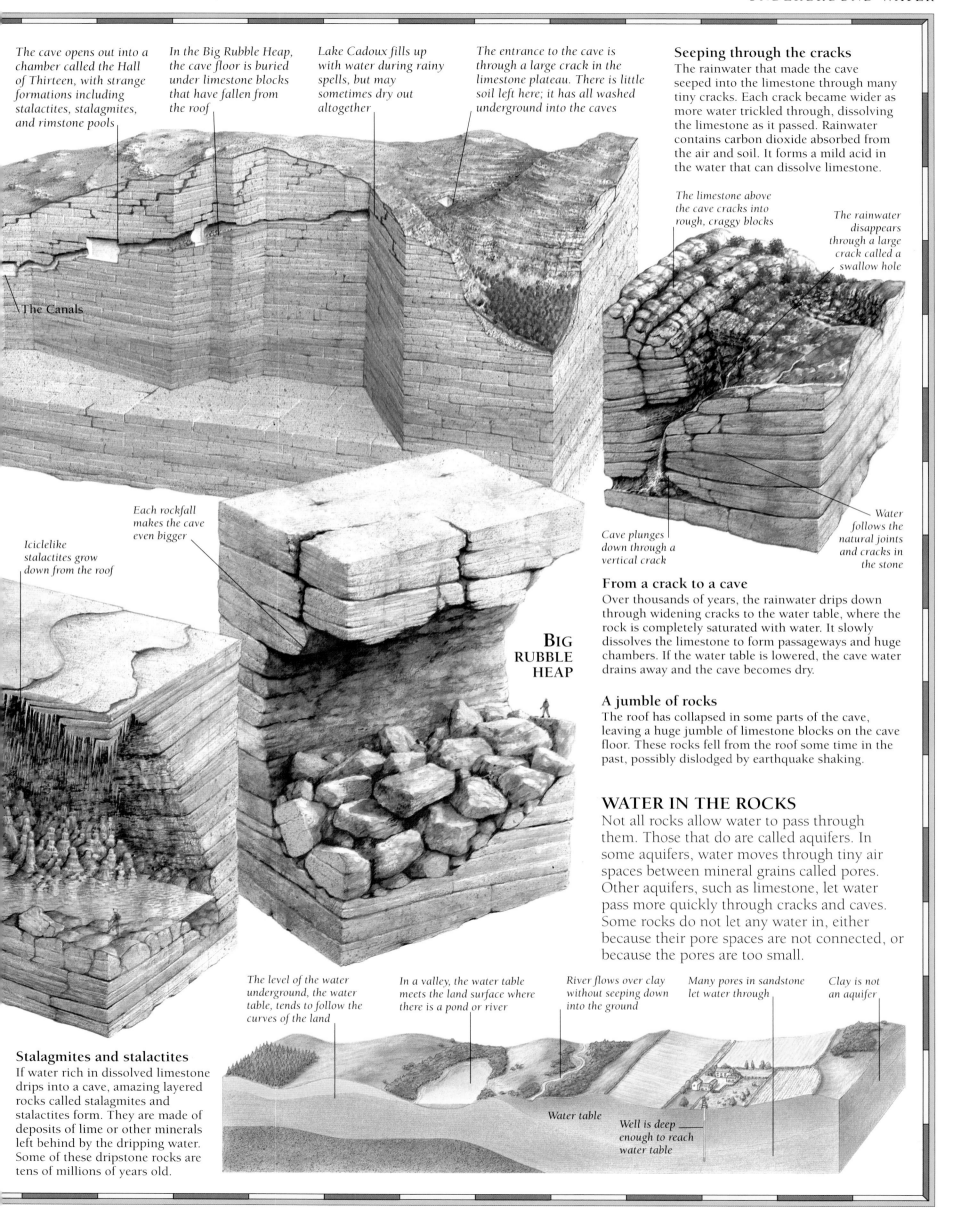

The cave opens out into a chamber called the Hall of Thirteen, with strange formations including stalactites, stalagmites, and rimstone pools

In the Big Rubble Heap, the cave floor is buried under limestone blocks that have fallen from the roof

Lake Cadoux fills up with water during rainy spells, but may sometimes dry out altogether

The entrance to the cave is through a large crack in the limestone plateau. There is little soil left here; it has all washed underground into the caves

Seeping through the cracks

The rainwater that made the cave seeped into the limestone through many tiny cracks. Each crack became wider as more water trickled through, dissolving the limestone as it passed. Rainwater contains carbon dioxide absorbed from the air and soil. It forms a mild acid in the water that can dissolve limestone.

The limestone above the cave cracks into rough, craggy blocks

The rainwater disappears through a large crack called a swallow hole

The Canals

Each rockfall makes the cave even bigger

Iciclelike stalactites grow down from the roof

BIG RUBBLE HEAP

Cave plunges down through a vertical crack

Water follows the natural joints and cracks in the stone

From a crack to a cave

Over thousands of years, the rainwater drips down through widening cracks to the water table, where the rock is completely saturated with water. It slowly dissolves the limestone to form passageways and huge chambers. If the water table is lowered, the cave water drains away and the cave becomes dry.

A jumble of rocks

The roof has collapsed in some parts of the cave, leaving a huge jumble of limestone blocks on the cave floor. These rocks fell from the roof some time in the past, possibly dislodged by earthquake shaking.

WATER IN THE ROCKS

Not all rocks allow water to pass through them. Those that do are called aquifers. In some aquifers, water moves through tiny air spaces between mineral grains called pores. Other aquifers, such as limestone, let water pass more quickly through cracks and caves. Some rocks do not let any water in, either because their pore spaces are not connected, or because the pores are too small.

The level of the water underground, the water table, tends to follow the curves of the land

In a valley, the water table meets the land surface where there is a pond or river

River flows over clay without seeping down into the ground

Many pores in sandstone let water through

Clay is not an aquifer

Water table

Well is deep enough to reach water table

Stalagmites and stalactites

If water rich in dissolved limestone drips into a cave, amazing layered rocks called stalagmites and stalactites form. They are made of deposits of lime or other minerals left behind by the dripping water. Some of these dripstone rocks are tens of millions of years old.

ICE REGIONS

AT THE ENDS OF THE EARTH, crowning the frozen continent of Antarctica and the icy ocean of the Arctic, are the polar ice caps. A vast amount of water is locked up inside the ice caps – they contain a hundred times more water than is in all the world's freshwater lakes put together. The water to make this ice has come from the global oceans. Ocean water is continually evaporating as warm atmospheric air circulates over it, forming moist clouds. The clouds drop their moisture as snow in cold or mountainous regions. This snow grows more compacted over the years and turns into glacier ice. In order for glaciers and ice caps grow larger, the rate at which the snow falls must be much greater than the rate at which it melts, so that there is snow left over at the end of each summer. During the great Pleistocene Ice Age over the last two million years, much of North America, and the whole Baltic Sea, were under ice caps. At times when there was so much ice, global sea level was much lower.

Storm waves have eroded this Arctic iceberg into pinnacles. Icebergs are not made of frozen seawater. They are broken off from the end of an ice sheet or glacier, so are composed of frozen fresh water.

THE FROZEN CONTINENT

A vast ice sheet covers much of the frozen continent of Antarctica. It has been accumulating for tens of thousands of years, and today it is over 14,800 ft (4,500 m) thick. The ice moves slowly outward and downhill, and toward the frigid seas. On the coastline, the ice is thinner, so that the summits of high mountains peek through. The sheet of ice extends out from the continental landmass, floating on the sea to form an ice shelf. At its edge great lumps of ice split off from the main mass and float away as icebergs – "berg" is a German word which means "mountain." Three sections of Antarctica are illustrated here.

Floating mountains of ice

Only a small part of an iceberg floats above the sea. Most of its mass is below sea level. The ice contains rocky boulders scraped off Antarctica as the ice sheet moved towards the coast. When large icebergs break off, or calve, from the ice sheet, they make huge waves.

Floating sea ice

The edge of the Antarctic ice sheet spreads out as shelves of sea ice. It floats because it is less dense than the ocean water, which is salty as well as very cold.

Glaciers weave their way through the nunatak mountain tops

Meteorites that fell thousands of years ago are revealed in the glacier ice

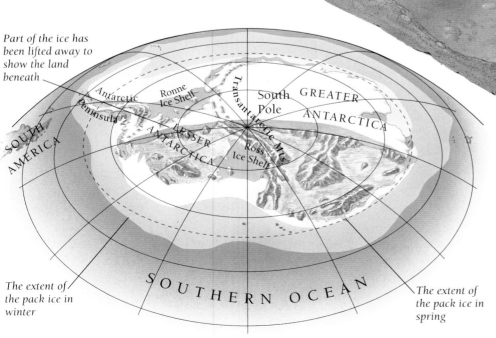

Part of the ice has been lifted away to show the land beneath

The extent of the pack ice in winter

SOUTH AMERICA

Antarctic Peninsula

Ronne Ice Shelf

LESSER ANTARCTICA

Transantarctic Mts

South Pole

GREATER ANTARCTICA

Ross Ice Shelf

SOUTHERN OCEAN

The extent of the pack ice in spring

Mounta peeking throu the glacier ice called nunat

Seabed deposits

The seabed is covered with layers of clay and sandy gravel dotted with boulders, all deposited here from melting of the icebergs.

THE ICY LAND OF ANTARCTICA

This vast continent is about one and a half times the size of the USA. Ice covers all but about five per cent of the land. Although Antarctica seems to have been near the South Pole for the last 200 million years, it was not always a frozen land. Around 35 million years ago, it became totally separated from the other continents as Pangaea split up. Perhaps it was then that the climate began to change. Once the cold Southern Ocean currents could circulate right round Antarctica, it was isolated from warm, tropical ocean currents. This may have been enough to trigger heavy snowfall, which led to the growth of ice sheets.

THE ICY WATERS OF THE ARCTIC

There is no continent at the North Pole. Instead, the region includes the Arctic Ocean, the northernmost parts of North America, Europe, and Asia, and Greenland and several smaller islands. The surface of the ocean is covered with salty sea ice, formed from frozen seawater. Pack ice, broken and crushed together again by the movement of the water, fringes the sea ice. The extent of the pack ice varies from season to season – about half of it melts in the summer. Glaciers crisscross the land in and near the Arctic. But in Siberia, some parts of Alaska, and Canada, there is too little snowfall for glaciers to form. The winter air is so cold that the water in the ground freezes to such a depth that it never completely thaws. This frozen ground is called permafrost.

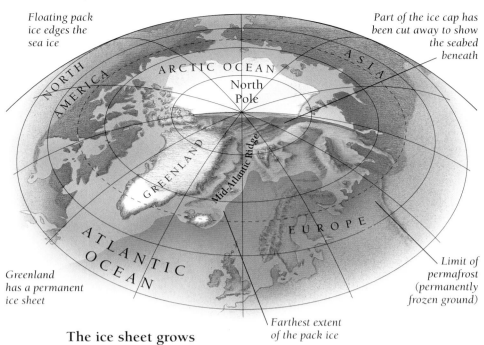

Floating pack ice edges the sea ice

North Pole

Part of the ice cap has been cut away to show the seabed beneath

NORTH AMERICA
ARCTIC OCEAN
ASIA
Greenland
Mid-Atlantic Ridge
EUROPE
ATLANTIC OCEAN

Greenland has a permanent ice sheet

Farthest extent of the pack ice

Limit of permafrost (permanently frozen ground)

Glacier ice has scraped the mountains into rugged peaks

At the South Pole, the ice sheet is 9,000 ft (2,800 m) thick. The rocky land beneath is at about sea level.

The ice sheet grows

As the ice sheet grew over Scandinavia, it spread out. But it also became thicker, so the surface of the ice grew higher. The ice also added to the weight of the land mass, which then pressed down on the squishy asthenosphere. The ice grew thicker and higher much faster than the asthenosphere was able to sink lower out of the way.

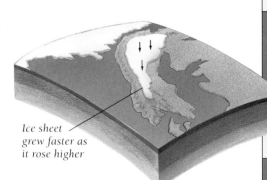

Ice sheet grew faster as it rose higher

Full press

As the ice sheet reached its full extent, at last the asthenosphere caught up and flowed away. The land level became lower. It became so low that the ice sheet was no longer high and cool enough to collect snow, and so it began to melt and shrink.

Asthenosphere material flows away sideways

Thick ice depresses the whole land mass

Frozen summits

On its way toward the sea, the ice sheet must flow around the peaks of the mountains. Cold, dry winds whip down off the high central ice plateau, whistling through the passes between the mountain summits. Because the winds are dry, they strip off and erode the upper layers of ice, revealing meteorites that fell onto the ice thousands of years ago.

Under pressure

The top of the thick ice covering Antarctica is well above sea level. But in the vast interior of the continent, the weight of the ice has pushed the rocky land below sea level. Some of the deep ice may be very old, formed by snow that fell up to a million years ago. Just as rocks recrystallize under pressure, the deep ice slowly recrystallizes under the massive weight of the overlying ice.

Land bounces back after ice melts

Lifting land

Today, the asthenosphere is still slowly flowing back, long after the ice sheet has melted away. The plate under the Baltic Sea may eventually bounce back so much that the sea becomes dry land. Many shorelines show evidence of huge isostatic uplift over recent centuries.

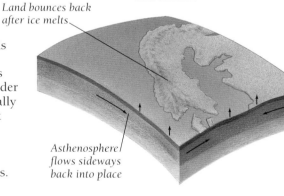

Asthenosphere flows sideways back into place

DEPRESSED BY ICE

Even though ice is not as dense as rock, the weight of an ice sheet covering a landmass is considerable. It alters the balance of the plate, which floats on the squishy asthenosphere. As the ice sheet builds up, the asthenosphere flows out of the way, and the plate sinks. If the ice melts, the asthenosphere slowly flows back and the plate rises. These changes in land level are called isostatic changes. The sequence above shows isostatic changes created by an ice sheet over Scandinavia 30,000 years ago.

Antarctica's Ross Sea (above) is fringed by an ice shelf, and is littered with icebergs calved off from the main ice sheet.

This is a raised beach on the Isle of Mull, Scotland. The land has risen, and the old shoreline is now left high and dry.

RIVERS OF ICE

GLACIERS SNAKE DOWN THE VALLEYS of many of the world's mountain ranges. These huge masses of ice are made from layers of snow that build up until the increasing weight causes solid blocks of ice to form. The ice becomes so thick and heavy that it starts to move – either outward in all directions, such as the vast domelike ice sheets of Greenland and Antarctica, or down a valley, such as the Athabasca Glacier seen here. Glacier ice travels slowly, less than 3 feet (1 meter) a day. Grinding against the surrounding valley sides, the glacier scrapes away any loosened rocks, which are carried downhill with the glacier ice. Eventually, far down the valley where the glacier melts, rocks, boulders, and fine rock dust are dumped in great heaps. At the moment, most glaciers are melting faster than new ice is forming in the high mountains. This means that glaciers are getting smaller. Glaciers have been retreating for 10,000 years.

Icy Athabasca
The Athabasca Glacier is in the Rocky Mountains of Alberta, in western Canada.

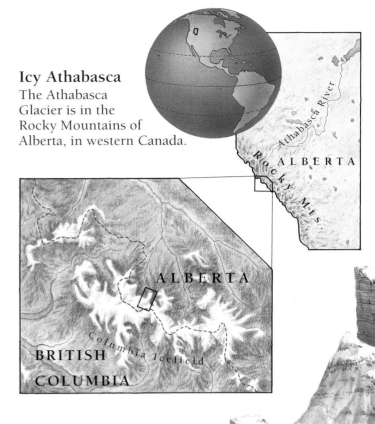

THE ATHABASCA GLACIER
The glacier flows out from an ice sheet, the Columbia Icefield, in the snowy mountains around the 12,293-ft (3,747-m-) -high Mount Columbia. The icefield was once much larger. At that time, the glaciers in the side valleys were all part of the main glacier. Today, the ice level has dropped so low that they no longer meet the main glacier. Instead, they hang isolated above the main valley. The end of the glacier is a heap of boulders and rock dust, called the terminal moraine. The glacier meltwater is the source of the Athabasca River, which flows into Hudson Bay and the Arctic Ocean, thousands of miles (kilometers) away.

Hanging valley
This valley, carved by a glacier long ago, now "hangs" above and to the side of the main valley.

A river of melted ice runs around rocks at the snout of a glacier in Norway. The rocks have been polished smooth by the action of the sandpaper-like rock dust that is frozen within the glacier.

The snout, or end, of the glacier is colored gray from all the rock fragments and dust in the ice

Glacial gravel
When glaciers advance over soft sediment, such as clay or gravel left by a previous glacier, they smooth it into long, egg-shaped hills. These streamlined hills, called drumlins, may be up to 164 ft (50 m) high and 6,562 ft (2,000 m) long. Drumlins are usually in groups, forming what is known as a "basket of eggs" landscape.

Moraine left by an earlier glacier

Long side of a drumlin is parallel to the ice flow

Loose gravel of all sizes – from large boulders to the very finest rock dust – forms a drumlin.

Rock ridges
These ridges of rock deposits are old terminal moraines, from when the glacier was longer and thicker. The gravel is now being eroded and carried away by the rivers of meltwater.

Milky rivers
Meltwater pours out from ice caves under the glacier to feed rivers. The water is milky green because it contains fine rock dust.

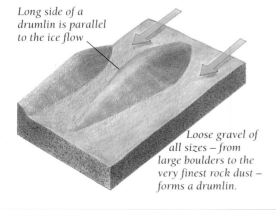

Lake filled with glacier meltwater is dammed up by the gravels of the terminal moraine.

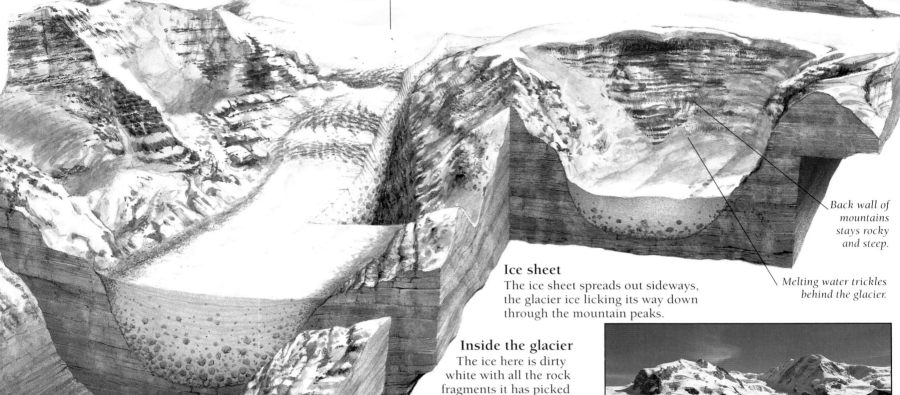

Ice on the move
When the glacier ice becomes thick enough, it starts to move under the pressure of its own weight.

Crevasses
Deep crevasses, or cracks, open up on the surface of the glacier as it travels over steep or rugged terrain.

Heavy winter snowfall "tops off" the ice dome that feeds the glacier.

Steep slope
The slope at the head of a glacier is steep because the glacier has ground rock off the mountainside.

Glued to a glacier
Melting water trickles down the rock face behind the glacier, seeping into cracks in the rock. Under the glacier, the water freezes again, "glueing" the rock to the glacier so it is dragged away.

Back wall of mountains stays rocky and steep.

Melting water trickles behind the glacier.

Ice sheet
The ice sheet spreads out sideways, the glacier ice licking its way down through the mountain peaks.

Inside the glacier
The ice here is dirty white with all the rock fragments it has picked up. The fragments grate against the valley bed.

Glacier lifted away to show how the valley beneath has been widened and gouged out to a broad U-shape.

Moraines
Rock fragments are frozen into the glacier ice in long bands called moraines. It takes thousands of years for one rock from a mountain peak to travel all the way to the glacier snout, where it is dropped in a long ridge known as the terminal (end) moraine.

As two glaciers meet in the mountains of Switzerland, their lateral (side) moraines converge to make a dark stripe down the middle, the medial moraine. Where several glaciers meet, there are many of these stripes.

Icebreaker
The mountain surface is eroded by melting snow running into cracks in the rocks. At night it freezes to ice, expanding and breaking apart the rock.

Polished smooth
The valley walls and floor are rasped smooth by the rocky ice, sometimes to a fine polished surface.

GLACIER VALLEYS
A glacier makes its valley wider and deeper as it carves away at the mountainsides. It scoops everything from rock fragments to huge boulders from the mountain by ice-plucking. This happens when water that seeps into cracks in the rock freezes, attaching the rock to the glacier. The resulting rock-laden ice scours the valley walls and floor as it grinds over them. Rock fragments dislodged from the steep, rocky mountain cliffs fall to the sides of the glacier and are carried away.

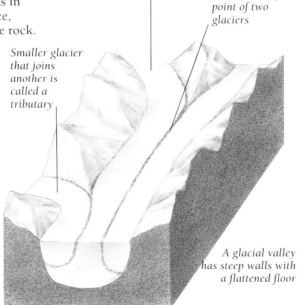

Valley filled with ice

Medial moraine at the meeting point of two glaciers

Smaller glacier that joins another is called a tributary

A glacial valley has steep walls with a flattened floor

Two glaciers flow together to make a larger glacier that fills the valley with ice. A smaller glacier from a valley to one side merges into the large glacier.

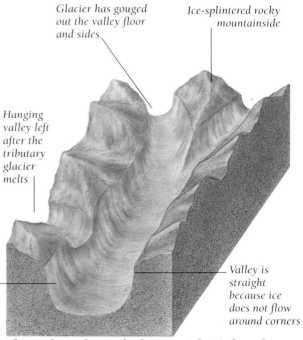

Glacier has gouged out the valley floor and sides

Ice-splintered rocky mountainside

Hanging valley left after the tributary glacier melts

Valley is straight because ice does not flow around corners

After a glacier has melted, its straight U-shaped valley is revealed. Tributary valleys hang higher above the level of the main valley.

DESERTS

AMONG THE MOST DESOLATE places on Earth are its deserts – deserted areas where almost nothing lives. Some deserts are hot and dry all year round, others are dry with intensely cold winters. The cold lands of the Arctic and Antarctic are also deserts. Deserts have thin soil or none at all, so there is little vegetation. Instead, the land is littered with stones or covered with bare rock or shifting sand dunes. The sparse plant life means few creatures can survive. Deserts have very low rainfall. Only a few inches (centimeters) might fall a year, though years may go by when no rain falls at all. The dry air over the desert means that any surface water rapidly evaporates. During the rare rainstorms, there is no vegetation to slow down the running surface water. Flash floods create lakes, which then quickly dry up leaving behind salt flats. The Earth's desert regions are shown in this map.

In the tundras of the northernmost part of North America, almost all the water is frozen beneath the surface.

Because mountains near the Pacific coast catch all the rainfall, the air inland is dry.

NORTH AMERICA

Death Valley

Sonoran

Tropic of Cancer

PACIFIC OCEAN

ATLANTIC

Equator

SOUTH AMERICA

Atacama

Cold ocean currents off South America cool the wind blowing on land. Any moisture makes fog at the coast – so very little reaches the Atacama Desert.

Tropic of Capricorn

HOT, DRY, AND LOW

Death Valley tops the lists of places with the hottest temperatures, the lightest rainfall, and the lowest elevation in North America. This inland valley is a desert because the moist winds from the Pacific Ocean drop all their rain on the mountains nearer to the coastline. There is no soil and very little vegetation. On the rare occasions when it rains, the water pours over barren rock, scouring off all loose fragments and sand. The coarse rocky material is dropped at the foot of the mountain cliffs, while sand and salty silt is spread out on the hot valley floor, where it eventually dries out. Two sections of Death Valley are illustrated below.

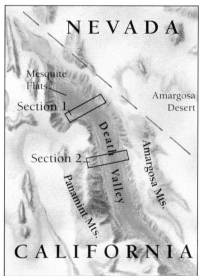

N E V A D A

Mesquite Flats

Section 1

Amargosa Desert

Death Valley

Amargosa Mts.

Section 2

Panamint Mts.

C A L I F O R N I A

This is one of the many huge playas, or dried-up lakebeds, in the Atacama Desert in Chile, probably the driest place on Earth.

California's Death Valley
Death Valley is one of hundreds of salty land-locked valleys in the western states of California, Utah, and Nevada.

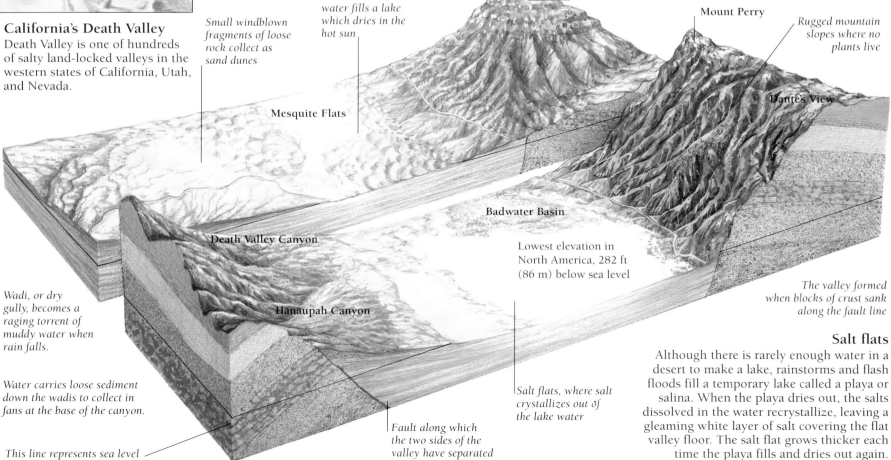

Small windblown fragments of loose rock collect as sand dunes

When it rains, the water fills a lake which dries in the hot sun

Thimble Peak

Mount Perry

Rugged mountain slopes where no plants live

Mesquite Flats

Dante's View

Death Valley Canyon

Badwater Basin

Hanaupah Canyon

Lowest elevation in North America, 282 ft (86 m) below sea level

The valley formed when blocks of crust sank along the fault line

Wadi, or dry gully, becomes a raging torrent of muddy water when rain falls.

Water carries loose sediment down the wadis to collect in fans at the base of the canyon.

This line represents sea level

Fault along which the two sides of the valley have separated

Salt flats, where salt crystallizes out of the lake water

Salt flats
Although there is rarely enough water in a desert to make a lake, rainstorms and flash floods fill a temporary lake called a playa or salina. When the playa dries out, the salts dissolved in the water recrystallize, leaving a gleaming white layer of salt covering the flat valley floor. The salt flat grows thicker each time the playa fills and dries out again.

The Sahara (the world's largest desert) and Arabian deserts are hot and dry tropical regions, north of the equator.

The Gobi and Taklimakan deserts are in the middle of a huge continent, far from any moist winds.

When the Himalayas were pushed up, they stopped moist air from reaching the interior of Asia. This is how the Gobi Desert area became so dry.

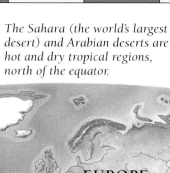

EUROPE   A S I A

Taklimakan   Gobi

Sind

Sahara

Arabian

A F R I C A

Rub Al Kali

PACIFIC OCEAN

OCEAN

I N D I A N   O C E A N

Almost two-thirds of Australia is a desert, at its driest in the flat, barren plateaus of the center.

A U S T R A L I A

Gibson   Simpson

Namib

The Namib Desert, like the Atacama in South America, is dry because of cold ocean currents nearby.

Kalahari

Underneath the sands of the Kalahari Desert is a plateau built from lava flows 65 million years ago.

S O U T H E R N   O C E A N

ANTARCTICA

Violent winds

The wind whips up dust storms which blow through deserts, removing fine silt and sand, and dumping it elsewhere. They are also known by the Arabic name haboobs, which means "violent wind."

Tropical deserts

Although seasonal rains do fall in tropical deserts, sometimes in vast downpours, these areas are so hot that they quickly lose the moisture through evaporation.

KEY TO MAP

- *Extremely arid desert regions, where there is no rain for an entire year*
- *Arid desert regions, where any rainfall evaporates quickly*
- *Semi-arid desert regions, where under 20 in (50 cm) of rain falls a year*
- *Frozen tundra desert regions, where cold dry air means there is little rain*

Frozen deserts

Although an enormous amount of water exists in the frozen regions of Greenland and Antarctica, these places are still deserts, because it is so cold that the water is all frozen into ice. It sometimes rains in Greenland, but only snow falls in Antarctica – and very little. Some places here are so dry that ice evaporates in the dry wind.

Desert dunes

When most people think of deserts, they imagine sand dunes, hills of loose sand deposited by the wind. In fact, only about 20 percent of the world's deserts are sandy. In some of these deserts, the underlying rock is covered by only a few inches (centimeters) of sand, but in others there is enough to pile into huge dunes up to 1,640 ft (500 m) tall. Even a small pile of sand is big enough to block and trap other grains drifting by, so that the dune grows larger.

These towering sand dunes rise above the Sahara Desert in Algeria.

SAND DUNES

The shape of sand dunes depends on the strength and direction of the wind. Crescent-shaped barchan dunes form where wind moves the low crescent ends faster than the high middle part of the dunes. Ridge-like seif dunes are found where the wind direction is strong and steady.

Barchan dunes

The crescent ends point downwind.

These dunes form where the desert floor is hard and flat, and wind blows regularly in the same direction.

Seif dunes

Dunes are in straight lines.

The wind spirals along, blowing sand to the sides to form long ridges.

How dunes move

Sand dunes move about 82 ft (25 m) a year. Wind blows sand up the gentle slope of a dune, and the steep slope becomes steeper and steeper until it collapses in a small avalanche. The sand comes to rest in sloping layers parallel to the avalanche tracks, called cross-bedding.

Dune moves in this direction, blown by the wind

Older dunes are covered up by newer ones

Sand of old dunes is compacted and their structure is preserved

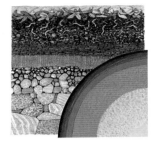

SOIL SUPPORTS LIFE

WITHOUT SOIL, there would be little life on Earth. Soil is the link between life and the rocky part of the Earth, supporting the plants that nourish people and animals. Soil is made where rocks are weathering and softening, breaking up into smaller particles, and giving up their rich store of chemicals in a form which plants can use. Soil contains mineral grains, air, and water. It is also rich in organic material, such as plant roots, fungi, beetles, and worms, as well as microorganisms such as bacteria and algae. The water and air in the soil are vital to plants. If soil becomes waterlogged, plants suffocate, and the soil becomes putrid with undecayed plant and animal remains. If there is no water, plants wilt and die and the dry soil may disappear on the wind. It takes a long time for a thick, nourishing soil to develop over the underlying rock.

Hillsides of the world
The soil profiles below are found in three different climates: temperate, arid, and tropical. The thickness and richness of soil depends on climate and many other factors: underlying rock type, the age of the soil, the landscape, the drainage, the vegetation, and the diversity of animals living in the soil and nearby.

Temperate climate soil
In a temperate climate, the soil is thicker in the valley than on the hillslopes, because rain and frost – and gravity – move soil downhill.

Roots penetrate into soil and make channels for air and water. These tree roots also help prevent soil from being washed away by heavy rain.

SOIL PROFILE
By digging down into the soil right through to the rock below, it is possible to see the entire profile of soil. Soils are made up of layers known as horizons. Each horizon has its own unique physical, chemical, and biological characteristics. The topsoil layer at the surface is rich in organic material. Below this is the subsoil, penetrated by a few roots. Deeper still is a layer of weathered rock fragments and boulders worn from the solid bedrock.

A closer look at soil
This is a section of soil viewed through a microscope. It shows the dead and decaying plant and animal material that will eventually nourish living plants growing in the soil. Air and water fill the spaces between the decaying material, along with microorganisms and tiny plants.

Topsoil
The dark, rich topsoil is matted together with plant and grass roots. Topsoil contains humus – the remains of plants and animals in the process of being broken down to simpler chemicals. Bacteria and fungi within the topsoil help this to happen.

Animal burrows, whether made by a tiny earthworm or a large rabbit or badger, let air into the soil and allow water to drain through

Subsoil
There is less organic material in the subsoil. This horizon is rich in mineral particles weathered from the solid rock beneath. These minerals contribute new plant nutrients to enrich the soil above.

Underlying rock
Bedrock is at the bottom of the soil profile. The nature of the bedrock is important to the composition of the soil above. Some rocks contain more chemicals that are useful to plants as nutrients, and therefore make richer soils.

Mat of plant roots in topsoil

Rabbit burrow

Left behind
Animals eat grass and browse the shrubs, but in turn, they leave behind their droppings, which fertilize the soil. Fallen leaves and twigs are also broken down into humus.

Humus and clay particles have large spongy surfaces, that can hold and exchange plant nutrients

Bedrock
The constant weathering of the bedrock below the soil helps to make the soil thicker. The basic texture of the soil depends to a great extent on the type of bedrock underlying it.

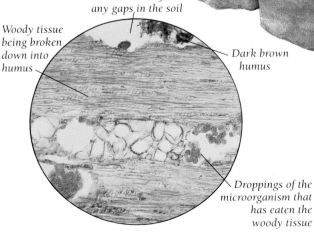

Air and water fill any gaps in the soil

Woody tissue being broken down into humus

Dark brown humus

Droppings of the microorganism that has eaten the woody tissue

SOILS ON SLOPES
Soil continually moves downhill. When hillslopes are plowed or are bare of vegetation in winter, heavy rain may wash soil into the valley below. Animals may also dislodge soil and push it slowly downhill as they walk over, or burrow through, steep slopes. With each frost, ice lifts soil particles out from the hill, then drops them lower down in the valley.

Arid climate soil

The sparse vegetation in an arid (very dry) climate cannot prevent occasional rainstorms from washing the soil away downhill. When it is dry, the wind blows the soil away. As a result, the soil is thin.

There is no soil on a rocky hilltop. Instead, the rocks are split by temperature changes between day and night, winter and summer.

Tropical climate soil

Thick, quick-growing forest shrubs and roots of trees hold the soils in place, so hillsides as well as valleys in tropical climates have thick soil.

Tropical vegetation grows quickly, and it supports many kinds of animals

In a warm, moist tropical climate, bacteria and fungi work fast to make a thick blanket of humus

A part of the southwestern U.S. known as the Dust Bowl was devastated by dust storms in the 1930s. They buried farms and roads and made farming impossible. Because the soil had been plowed up and the crops taken off, there were no longer roots to hold the soil in place. It became dry, and blew away with the wind.

Rock weathers rapidly in a tropical climate, enriching the soil with plant nutrients

How tropical soil weathers

The damp climate and rapid rock weathering means the soil becomes thicker with time. In spite of heavy rain, the soil is not washed away as long as plant roots hold it in place. When they die, plants decay and return their nutrients to the soil.

Because there is little moisture to support vegetation, there is little humus in the arid soil

Dry mineral grains are blown away because there are few roots to anchor soil

Slow weathering in a dry climate cannot keep pace with the soil blown away

Hot, wet climate and strong sunshine allow quick plant growth

As plants die, they decay and add to the soil

Fast-weathering rocks also add to the soil thickness

Rocky surface left behind has little soil

How arid soil weathers

Arid soil has few plants and roots to hold it in place. The mineral grains are easily blown away. Because weathering is so slow in an arid climate, the soil tends to be shallower and less developed than soils in warm, mosit regions.

In the valley

The moist climate and continual weathering of the underlying rocks helps maintain the rich humus in the valley, making a nourishing soil for a variety of plants.

HOW SOIL FORMS

The process of soil formation in a cold climate is shown here. Glaciers strip away all soils over which they pass. When they melt, new soil forms slowly from rock weathering. At first, there is little in the way of plant and animal life to help make humus. But mosses and scrubby bushes soon grow, and the process of breaking down the bedrock begins.

Glacier strips away the soil

Bare rock and gravel remains

Moss and scrubby bushes grow

Small trees gain a foothold and start to contribute their decaying leaves to new soil

More animals move in, and their droppings enrich the soil

The topsoil horizon grows thicker as the underlying rock weathers away

Thicker, richer soil is now able to support a mature forest

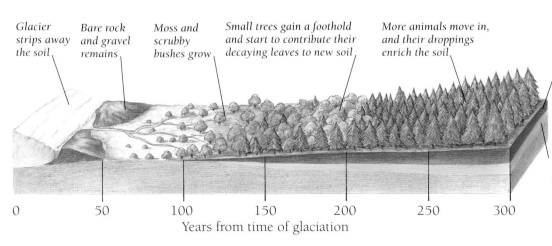

0   50   100   150   200   250   300
Years from time of glaciation

EARTH'S INGREDIENTS

MILLIONS OF STARS populating the universe long ago created the ingredients of our Earth. Each star was a factory for chemical elements, turning hydrogen and helium into other, heavier elements. Some stars exploded at the end of their lives, scattering their materials out through the universe. Then 5 billion years ago, some of this stardust clumped together to make Earth and the rest of the solar system. Since its formation, the planet Earth has shaped and regrouped the chemical elements that make it up. Its solid surface is made up of what at first seems like a bewildering variety of rocks. In fact, only a small number of different minerals make up most Earth rocks. Less than ten of the hundred or so chemical elements known on Earth are found in these rock-forming minerals. The tiny atoms that combine chemically to make up the Earth's minerals are made of even smaller particles, called protons, electrons, and neutrons.

Swirling white cloud patterns in the atmosphere

The solid rocky surface is seen in yellow and green

White cloud appears where the atmosphere contains masses of water droplets

The oceans are shown in blue

Earth and its neighbors
The Earth is one of nine planets that travel around our local star, the sun, in more or less circular orbits, or paths. Only Mercury and Venus are nearer to the fiery sun.

Colliding in space
As the planets spin, they collide with smaller fragments. Most of these fragments were swept up in the first billion years of the solar system's history. Some remain as asteroids, and others crash onto planets as meteorites.

All life on Earth depends on the light and heat of the sun

The nine planets and about 70 moons condensed from the same dust cloud as the sun

The solar system
More than 5 billion years ago, somewhere towards the end of one of the spiral arms of the Milky Way galaxy, a dust cloud began to gather. It was mostly made of hydrogen and helium, but also contained heavier elements created in previous supernova explosions. As the cloud became hotter and thicker, gravity pulled a clump of material toward the center, while the rest of the gas and dust flattened into a spinning disk. The central clump condensed to become the young sun. Smaller clumps of matter still spinning around the center became the planets of the solar system.

An exploding supernova shines brighter than a billion suns put together

BIRTH AND DEATH OF STARS
The most common chemical elements in the universe are hydrogen and helium. All the other chemical elements are made within stars. Stars have a long but definite life cycle. After a star is born, hydrogen is converted to helium in its core, as the star glows white and bright with light and heat energy. When there is no more hydrogen left, the star begins to die. Some massive stars explode as supernovae. The huge collapse which begins the death throes of the star also raises its temperature, and brings about a synthesis of new, heavier chemical elements. Seconds later an explosion follows, which blasts these new chemical elements out across the universe. In this way, the whole mix of about a hundred chemical elements are made.

PLANET EARTH

Earth's surface is unlike that of any of the other planets. Earth is surrounded by an atmosphere of gas, and nearly three-quarters of its solid surface is hidden under water. This gas atmosphere and liquid hydrosphere have separated from the solid part of the planet over thousands of millions of years. The most common element, or basic chemical, in Earth's crust is oxygen. Although oxygen is usually a gas, it is combined in the planet's rocks with the element silicon. Because the two bind strongly together, the silicate rocks they form are chemically stable.

The only planet with liquid water is the Earth – other planets are too hot or too cold

Earth's atmosphere protects life on the surface from some of the harmful rays of the sun

TABLE OF ELEMENTS

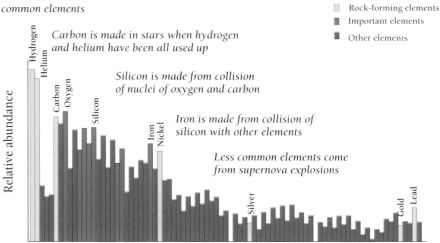

Hydrogen and helium are the most common elements

Carbon is made in stars when hydrogen and helium have been all used up

Silicon is made from collision of nuclei of oxygen and carbon

Iron is made from collision of silicon with other elements

Less common elements come from supernova explosions

Key to table
- Rock-forming elements
- Important elements
- Other elements

Relative abundance

Hydrogen, Helium, Carbon, Oxygen, Silicon, Iron, Nickel, Silver, Gold, Lead

Increasing atomic number (number of protons)

An abundance of elements

Chemical elements are basic substances that make up minerals. The table above shows the elements in the universe – so far, 109 are known, including 89 found naturally on Earth. Some elements are much more common than others. Hydrogen is the simplest and most fundamental element from which all others are made. In the intense heat of a star, for example, hydrogen nuclei collide to make helium. When all the hydrogen is used up, the star uses its helium nuclei to make carbon and oxygen, its carbon to make magnesium, then oxygen to form silicon, and finally silicon to make iron. Other, less common elements are only made in supernova explosions.

Rock ingredients

Minerals, naturally formed solids with crystalline structures, are made up of elements. Almost all rocks are made of silicate minerals, formed by a strong bond between the elements oxygen and silicon. Other common elements are iron, magnesium, aluminum, calcium, potassium, and sodium. Together, these eight elements make up most of the rocks in the Earth's crust. This serpentinite rock is especially rich in iron and magnesium, which make it dark in color.

Serpentinite rock is made from crystals of olivine and pyroxene which have been changed by adding water into their crystal structure

Gray striped crystals are feldspar minerals

Bright colors of the mineral olivine

Under the microscope

The minerals that make up rocks can be seen as individual crystals when viewed through a microscope. Most minerals are transparent when sliced thinly enough.

Mineral mixtures

There are several thousand different kinds of minerals, but only a few dozen are common. Rocks are usually made of a mixture of three or four common minerals, with a scattering of more unusual ones. The different amounts and different types of minerals present give the great variety of rocks that cover the Earth's surface – from soft sand and clay to granite, limestone, and basalt. This microscopic view shows a slice of gabbro, a rock made of three main minerals, feldspar, olivine, and pyroxene, with smaller amounts of iron oxide.

Black minerals are iron oxide

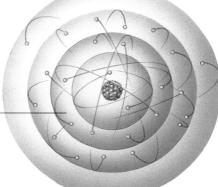

Twenty six electrons whiz around the nucleus

Structure of atoms

The smallest particle of a chemical element is an atom. Even smaller particles called protons (which have positive electrical charges) and neutrons (which are neutral) form the nucleus, or core, of an atom. Electrons (which have negative charges) whiz around in a cloud outside the nucleus. Each chemical element has a different number of each kind of particle. The number of protons and electrons controls which chemical elements combine with what others in order to make minerals. The atomic structures of three elements – hydrogen, carbon, and iron – are illustrated here.

Nucleus of one proton

Nucleus made of six protons and six neutrons

Six electrons round the nucleus

Hydrogen

Hydrogen atoms, the most abundant element in the universe, are also the simplest, with just one proton circled by one electron. Hydrogen combines with other elements to form compounds, such as water.

Carbon

This element is made in the dying stages of a star's life. The carbon in humans, trees, and rocks all came originally from stars.

Iron

In the whole Earth, iron is the most abundant element, but most of it is concentrated in its heavy metal core. Iron is common in many minerals, and it is the chemical element that adds color to most rocks. It is the heaviest element made when ordinary stars die.

IGNEOUS ROCKS

WHEN PLANET EARTH became cool enough to have a solid outer skin, igneous rocks were the first to appear on its surface. Igneous rocks are still being made today as volcanoes erupt molten magma, which cools and becomes solid. Some magma, though, does not get to the surface. Instead, it cools as igneous rock underground. Many millions of years later, the igneous rocks that cooled several miles (kilometers) down in the crust may become exposed at the Earth's surface by uplift and erosion. There are many different types of igneous rocks that crystallize from different magmas under different conditions. They are grouped by their textures and by the minerals they contain.

Basalt with amygdales
Gas bubbles in lava fill up with minerals to make amygdales.

Pegmatite
Pegmatite contains unusually large crystals.

Mica
The shiny dark flakes seen in some granites are mica. In granites with large crystals, bits of mica can be flaked off in thin sheets.

Quartz
Glassy quartz, an essential mineral in granite, may be transparent, but is sometimes a milky blue.

Feldspar
Igneous rocks are classified by the amount and type of feldspar they contain. It is one of the most common minerals in the Earth's crust.

Granite

GRANITE

If it were possible to put all the rocks of a continent in some kind of giant crushing machine, mix up the crushed rock, melt it, and then let it cool and crystallize, the result would be granite. Granite is one of the most common igneous rocks, found at the core of many mountain ranges. The first continents were made of granite-like rock. Granite contains the minerals quartz and feldspar, along with a small amount of dark minerals, such as mica. Their crystals can be seen in the granite on the left: quartz is gray, feldspar is pink or white, and mica is black.

Gabbro
Gabbro crystallized slowly like granite, but has more dark minerals and usually no quartz.

Agate
The beautiful bands of agate are formed, one layer after another, as they coat the inside of gas bubbles in volcanic rock. The outermost agate layer forms first, then in time, each layer afterward forms toward the center. Sometimes there are quartz crystals lining the inner core of the agate.

Gold
Some chemical elements, such as gold, do not crystallize easily as magma cools and hardens. These awkward elements get concentrated in the last bit of magma liquid, and finally crystallize in cracks called veins, which open up as granite cools and shrinks.

Silver
Silver, a shiny, gray-white metal, is one of the few metals that crystallizes from magma without combining with other chemical elements. These are called native metals; they need almost no processing before they are used. Other native metals include gold, platinum, and copper.

Diamond
One of the most amazing minerals is diamond, the hardest natural substance known. Its dense structure is a result of crystallizing under great pressure. Diamonds are brought to the Earth's surface by volcanic eruptions.

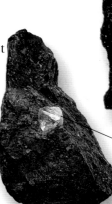

A diamond crystallizes about 62 miles (100 km) below the surface

LAVAS

Some of the rocks formed by recrystallized lava are shown here. The texture of the rocks depends on the type of lava. Some lavas are very hot when they are erupted, spreading out quickly as they cool. Others are cooler, and move only slowly, hindered by the crystals as they shape and grow.

Vesicular basalt
Volcanic gas bubbles out of magma and may be trapped as the lava solidifies. The bubbles in this rock are called vesicles.

Obsidian
This lava erupts at a low temperature, with its chemical framework already in place. This "freezes" to obsidian, which has no crystals.

Pumice
This is a glassy lava froth, and is often part of the same eruptions as obsidian. Some pumice is so frothy and bubbly that it floats on water.

Volcanic bomb
Hot basalt lava cools so fast that blobs like this, which are thrown out in explosions, have solidified by the time they land on the ground.

This is a crystal of augite, one of the minerals in the pyroxene family, embedded in an igneous rock

BASALT

Most of the solid surface of the Earth is made of basalt. All the solid ocean crust is basalt, and there are also many huge basalt lava flows on the continents. Basalt is formed by molten rock in the Earth's mantle. It is fine-grained and dark in color because of the dark minerals it contains: principally pyroxene and olivine. If basalt magma cools slowly, it grows larger crystals. Then it is called dolerite, or if the crystals are really large, gabbro.

Pyroxene
Pyroxene is a group of dark, dense minerals that makes up basalt, gabbro, and dolerite. It is rich in the chemical elements iron and magnesium.

Basalt

Ropy lava
The twists and turns in this rock are formed when hot flowing lava causes wrinkles in its cooler crust.

Feldspar
The dark, heavy rocks on this page contain calcium-rich feldspar. The lighter granites contain sodium- and potassium-rich feldspar.

Olivine
Olivine is a shiny green, heavy mineral, rich in iron and magnesium.

Sulfur is scraped from volcano craters. The workers who collect it risk their lives every day

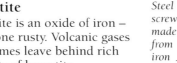

Sulfur
These lemon yellow crystals are found around many volcanic craters and hot springs. Sometimes sulfur is combined with other chemicals to make sulfates or sulfides.

Hematite
Hematite is an oxide of iron – iron gone rusty. Volcanic gases sometimes leave behind rich deposits of hematite. The metal iron is extracted from its red-brown crystals.

Steel screw made from iron

Galena
Galena is a sulfide of lead that sometimes comes in large shiny crystals. Around black smokers, it makes a powdery cloud of tiny crystals.

Copper is flexible, making it useful for bendable pipes

Lead, which comes from galena, has a low melting point, making it ideal for use in soldering wire

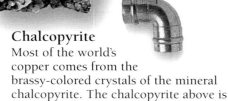

Peridotite
Peridotite is a heavy dark-colored rock, rarely found at the Earth's surface. The upper mantle may be made of peridotite.

Chalcopyrite
Most of the world's copper comes from the brassy-colored crystals of the mineral chalcopyrite. The chalcopyrite above is mixed with white quartz crystals.

SEDIMENTARY ROCKS

LAYER BY LAYER, sedimentary rocks are formed from material that previously made other rocks. This material is created by weathering, which breaks older rocks down into fragments and chemicals into solutions. Then, the grains and dissolved rock are transported by wind, rivers, and glaciers and eventually are deposited as layers, or beds, of sediment, along with any plant and animal remains trapped within. Over time, the layers are buried and squashed to become lithified, or hardened, into new rocks. Sedimentary rocks contain features that reveal their origins – the kind of rock that weathered into grains, the means of transport and deposition, and all the processes of lithification that turned loose sediment into hard rock.

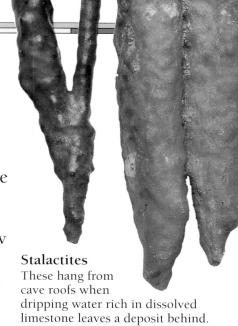

Stalactites
These hang from cave roofs when dripping water rich in dissolved limestone leaves a deposit behind.

Large, coarse pebbles   Medium-sized, coarse pebbles   Small, fine pebbles   Rock fragments   Quartz sand

GRAINS OF ROCK

Pebbles, gravel, and sand in a riverbed or on the beach are the raw materials for new sedimentary rock. As they tumble along in the water, pebbles and rock fragments may fracture by impact with each other, while continuing to be chemically weathered or dissolved. Where the grains settle, they may be buried by other layers. Water that percolates through the layers sometimes contains rock material in a solution. If this mateiral should come out of the solution to crystallize around the rock grains, the solution cements them together to make sedimentary rock.

Breccia and conglomerate

A pebble beach might become hardened and lithified (below) to make a conglomerate (below). The pebbles with sand grains between them are firmly held together by a rock cement. Breccia (right) forms in the same way, but its fragments are much rougher around the edges.

Sandstone

The grains of sand that make up sandstone tell the rock's history. Those with a polished surface may be quartz grains that have been rolled around on a beach. Sand grains with a matt surface like ground glass show the sandstone was formed in a desert.

Rounded flint pebbles in this conglomerate have been smoothed by tumbling in water

Sharp rock fragments may pile up at the bottom of a cliff to form breccia

Layered limestones and volcanic ash rocks were used for the Colosseum in Rome, Italy.

Grindstone

This grindstone for grinding corn kernels was fashioned in Roman times from a hard conglomerate made of flint pebbles. The rough surface texture of the conglomerate is perfect for the job.

Bauxite

Bauxite is a mix of aluminum minerals left behind in tropical climates when all the other rock chemicals weather away.

The metal aluminum, used in foil, is extracted from bauxite

LIMESTONE

It is easy to see grains of sand on a beach that might one day become sandstone, but limestone's chemicals are transported invisibly – they are dissolved in water. Sea creatures and plants take carbon dioxide from seawater. This changes the chemical balance of the water, and as a result, the chemicals that make limestone – calcium and magnesium carbonate – separate from the water. They are deposited in thick layers of limy mud on the seabed to make limestone. Carbonates are the chemicals that make water hard.

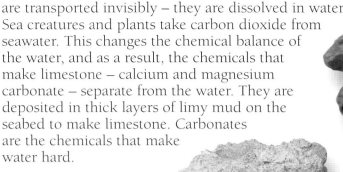

Shelly limestone

Sea creatures such as shellfish help make limestone by taking dissolved calcium carbonate from the water to make their shells. When the shellfish die, they sink into the limy ooze on the sea- or lakebed and help build up limestone.

Chalk

Chalk is a soft, pure limestone. Europe's chalk cliffs are made from the skeletons of tiny floating plants that lived in the sea more than 65 million years ago.

Clay

Tiny clay grains weathered from other rocks travel suspended in water. These are what makes river water look muddy. When river water meets the sea, the clay flakes flock together into mud (left) that may form mudstone, claystone, or shale.

Cup and saucer made from clay

Clay brick

HOW COAL IS FORMED

Tree ferns and mosses that flourished in swamps of long ago sank into swampy water when they died. They were compressed to make peat. The deeper the peat was buried, the hotter and denser it became, until it was pressed into coal. The coal buried deepest became anthracite, the hardest, purest coal.

The plants did not rot, but formed a layer of peat. The remains of the plants are still visible.

Brown coal is peat that has been compressed by burial. Most of the water has been squeezed out. Some traces of the plants can still be seen.

Opal

Vividly colored opal coats cracks and cavities in sedimentary rocks. Sometimes opal transforms fossils trapped in rocks, replacing wood and shells and preserving their structures in opal.

Opal's colors make it an attractive gem

White opal

Black opal

Colors refracted by layers of silica

Uncut opal

Sharp-edged flint arrowhead

Flint

Flint (above) is fine-grained silica, the same chemical as quartz. Flint breaks to make sharp edges, so it was ideal for making knives and arrowheads.

Black coal is hard and rich in carbon. It sometimes contains fossils of the plant matter that formed it.

The gypsum crystals in a desert rose grow in flakes that resemble rose petals

Sharp edges of gypsum crystals

Rock salt

When the sea or salty desert lakes evaporate, they leave salt, which hardens to become rock. Gypsum is one of the salts that makes up the rock.

Desert rose

When underground water in the desert evaporates, it leaves behind salts such as gypsum to crystallize. These gypsum crystals wrap around grains of sand.

Anthracite has been buried the deepest, and is the purest and cleanest coal to burn. It has a glossy surface, with few of the layers seen in black coal.

METAMORPHIC ROCKS

As PLATES MOVE and crunch together, the rocks within are stretched, squeezed, heated – and changed. Metamorphic rocks are made from preexisting rocks, whether sedimentary, igneous, or metamorphic. When a rock metamorphoses, its minerals recrystallize and its original texture changes. Usually these changes happen deep inside the Earth's crust, where it is hot enough and there is enough pressure from the overlying rocks to make rocks recrystallize without melting. The recrystallization creates larger crystals and different minerals. At the same time, the rocks may become folded or crushed, so they get a new texture in which all the mineral grains are aligned according to the pressures on the rock. Several metamorphic rocks are featured on these two pages.

Quartzite

When a sandstone that is made entirely of quartz sand grains is metamorphosed, each grain of sand grows to a different shape in response to increased pressure. The once-rounded sand grains interlock and the spaces between are filled with quartz to form a tough new metamorphic rock, quartzite. It is much harder rock than marble.

Quartzite

LIMESTONE TO MARBLE

Intense heat changes limestone into marble, an even-grained, sugary-textured rock. Most limestones contain some chemicals other than calcium carbonate. These may be caught in the limestone as grains of sand, or wisps of clay. When the calcium carbonate recrystallizes to marble, it reacts with these other chemicals to make new metamorphic minerals, which come in many colors. The colored minerals may be in layers that become folded by the pressures of metamorphism. Folds in the green striped marble, for example, show that the original sedimentary layers get both thinned and thickened as they fold.

Limestone
Muddy gray limestone can be transformed into the multicolored marbles seen here.

Marble streaked with green

Gneiss
Heat and pressure change granite to gneiss. Gneiss shows dark wispy bands of mica curling around creamy white knots of feldspar.

Banded gneiss
The bands that stripe this rock show that directional pressure was high when it recrystallized.

Granite
This igneous rock is made of quartz, feldspar, and mica crystals. These are all more or less the same size, and are randomly scattered throughout the rock.

White marble, made from pure calcium carbonate limestone, was used to build the Taj Mahal in Agra in northern India. This monument is decorated in fine patterns with colored slivers of marble and precious stones inlaid in the white.

GRANITE BECOMES GNEISS

When granite is metamorphosed, the original crystals that make it up recrystallize. If metamorphism is not very intense, the new rock still looks like granite, but it takes on a new texture if there is also directional pressure, like the squeezing that happens in a mountain range. The new rock, gneiss, has a foliated texture. This means the minerals form wispy, more or less parallel bands.

Migmatite
This rock formed in heat so intense that parts of it melted. Migmatite shows no sign of the texture of the original rock, which might have been granite. Its banding has been intricately folded.

Talc

Talc comes from the metamorphism of wet limestones containing sand. It is the softest mineral known, and has a smooth, slippery texture. Talc is the mineral used in making talcum powder.

Only deep green beryl crystals like this can be called emeralds

Beryl has the same chemical composition as emerald

Gemstones

Rocks are sometimes soaked with watery fluid during metamorphism. This helps recrystallization, so that bigger, clearer crystals grow. Many of the crystals shown here can be cut and polished as gemstones.

Ruby is colored a rich red by chromium chemicals

Sapphire is the same family as ruby, but is deep blue

Nephrite jade boulder from New Zealand formed in the high pressure of the Alpine Fault

Jadeite jade cut stones

Nephrite jade vase

Jade

Jade minerals are tough, making them suitable for gemstones. They come from the metamorphism of dark igneous rocks and are often found in fault zones. There are two types: nephrite and jadeite.

Feldspar gives the marble its pale pink color

Pink marble

The dark green pyroxene crystals in this Scottish marble were formed in a dolomite limestone.

White marble

White marble from southern Spain is recrystallized from a pure calcium carbonate limestone.

White marble (as shown in the statue above) has a grainy, regular texture that has been prized for carving since the time of the ancient Greeks.

Black slate

Cubes of brassy-colored pyrite dot this rock.

Phyllite

The mica crystals within phyllite give it a shiny look.

Garnet schist

This schist grows garnet crystals in response to higher heat and pressure.

Grossular garnet

This garnet may be orange or green. Grossular garnets are found in Sri Lanka and Brazil.

MUDSTONE TO SCHIST

A dull, gray mudstone can be transformed by metamorphism into sparkling colored crystalline rocks. At different temperatures and pressures, different new minerals appear. The rocks here are shown in a sequence from left to right. The rocks on the left have been formed at the lowest temperatures and pressures, and those on the right, at the highest.

Garnets

Garnets are a group of minerals found in metamorphic rocks. Garnet forms crystals that come in many different colors. Their color depends on the chemistry of the original rock. Almandine, for example, gets its rich brownish-red color from iron. Garnet is a dense, hard mineral, tough enough to be used as an abrasive for grinding and polishing.

Almandine

Hessonite

Pyrope

Demantoid

Gray mudstone

This is a sedimentary rock formed in seas or lakes.

Kyanite schist

Its pale blue crystals formed in the depth and heat of a mountain range.

THE AGE OF THE EARTH

PLANET EARTH IS so old that it is hard to imagine its age: 4.5 billion years old. During the first 3.5 billion years of Earth history, the events that still shape its surface occurred: the first solid crust, the first life, the origins of the continents and the atmosphere, and the beginnings of plate tectonics. These events are recorded in the rocks that formed during this time. About 570 million years ago, there was a great explosion of life, and gradually the range of different plants and animals that now populate the Earth came into being. The remains of some of these life forms are captured in the rocks as fossils. These allow geologists to build up a picture of the Earth's long history.

Fossils provide valuable clues about the origin – and extinction – of life forms on Earth. In this 19th-century engraving, geologists are excavating fossil remains of a Mosasaurus from a cavern in Holland.

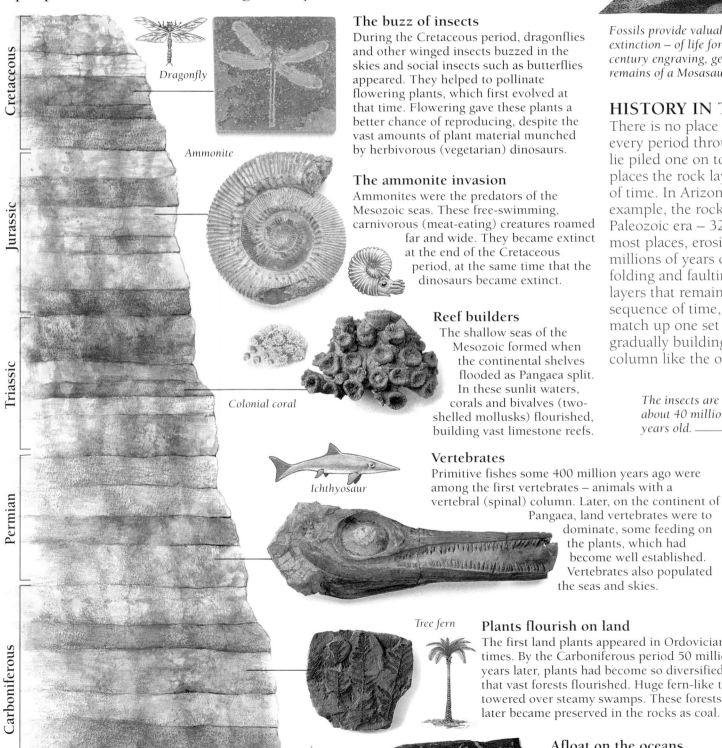

The buzz of insects

During the Cretaceous period, dragonflies and other winged insects buzzed in the skies and social insects such as butterflies appeared. They helped to pollinate flowering plants, which first evolved at that time. Flowering gave these plants a better chance of reproducing, despite the vast amounts of plant material munched by herbivorous (vegetarian) dinosaurs.

Dragonfly

Ammonite

The ammonite invasion

Ammonites were the predators of the Mesozoic seas. These free-swimming, carnivorous (meat-eating) creatures roamed far and wide. They became extinct at the end of the Cretaceous period, at the same time that the dinosaurs became extinct.

Reef builders

The shallow seas of the Mesozoic formed when the continental shelves flooded as Pangaea split. In these sunlit waters, corals and bivalves (two-shelled mollusks) flourished, building vast limestone reefs.

Colonial coral

Vertebrates

Primitive fishes some 400 million years ago were among the first vertebrates – animals with a vertebral (spinal) column. Later, on the continent of Pangaea, land vertebrates were to dominate, some feeding on the plants, which had become well established. Vertebrates also populated the seas and skies.

Ichthyosaur

Tree fern

Plants flourish on land

The first land plants appeared in Ordovician times. By the Carboniferous period 50 million years later, plants had become so diversified that vast forests flourished. Huge fern-like trees towered over steamy swamps. These forests later became preserved in the rocks as coal.

Afloat on the oceans

The oceans in Paleozoic times were populated with marine animals called graptolites. Many individual graptolites, such as these tweezer-shaped creatures, lived together in colonies, floating in the surface waters. Graptolites had already disappeared when a mass extinction at the end of the Paleozoic era wiped out several species.

Graptolite

HISTORY IN THE LAYERS

There is no place on Earth where rocks from every period throughout geological history lie piled one on top of another. In some places the rock layers represent big chunks of time. In Arizona's Grand Canyon, for example, the rocks span the whole Paleozoic era – 320 million years. But in most places, erosion has worn away millions of years of the Earth's history, and folding and faulting may have jumbled the layers that remain. To understand the whole sequence of time, geologists painstakingly match up one set of rocks with another, gradually building a stratigraphic (layered) column like the one on the far left.

The insects are about 40 million years old.

Trapped in amber

Not all fossils are found in rocks. These gnatlike insects are trapped in amber, a sticky resin that seeps from pine trees. The amber hardened, preserving their bodies.

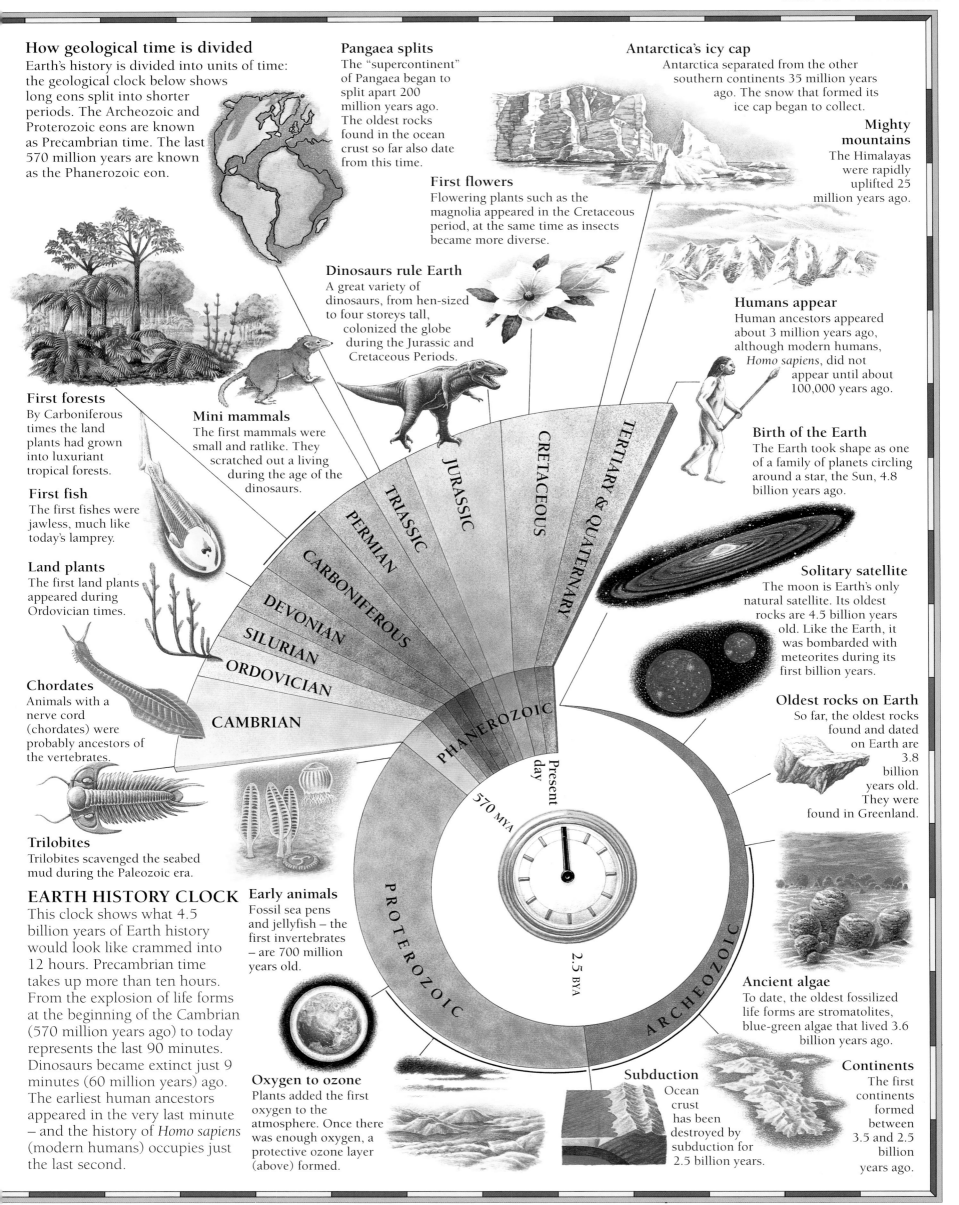

How geological time is divided
Earth's history is divided into units of time: the geological clock below shows long eons split into shorter periods. The Archeozoic and Proterozoic eons are known as Precambrian time. The last 570 million years are known as the Phanerozoic eon.

Pangaea splits
The "supercontinent" of Pangaea began to split apart 200 million years ago. The oldest rocks found in the ocean crust so far also date from this time.

Antarctica's icy cap
Antarctica separated from the other southern continents 35 million years ago. The snow that formed its ice cap began to collect.

Mighty mountains
The Himalayas were rapidly uplifted 25 million years ago.

First flowers
Flowering plants such as the magnolia appeared in the Cretaceous period, at the same time as insects became more diverse.

Dinosaurs rule Earth
A great variety of dinosaurs, from hen-sized to four storeys tall, colonized the globe during the Jurassic and Cretaceous Periods.

Humans appear
Human ancestors appeared about 3 million years ago, although modern humans, *Homo sapiens*, did not appear until about 100,000 years ago.

First forests
By Carboniferous times the land plants had grown into luxuriant tropical forests.

Mini mammals
The first mammals were small and ratlike. They scratched out a living during the age of the dinosaurs.

Birth of the Earth
The Earth took shape as one of a family of planets circling around a star, the Sun, 4.8 billion years ago.

First fish
The first fishes were jawless, much like today's lamprey.

Land plants
The first land plants appeared during Ordovician times.

Solitary satellite
The moon is Earth's only natural satellite. Its oldest rocks are 4.5 billion years old. Like the Earth, it was bombarded with meteorites during its first billion years.

Chordates
Animals with a nerve cord (chordates) were probably ancestors of the vertebrates.

Oldest rocks on Earth
So far, the oldest rocks found and dated on Earth are 3.8 billion years old. They were found in Greenland.

Trilobites
Trilobites scavenged the seabed mud during the Paleozoic era.

EARTH HISTORY CLOCK
This clock shows what 4.5 billion years of Earth history would look like crammed into 12 hours. Precambrian time takes up more than ten hours. From the explosion of life forms at the beginning of the Cambrian (570 million years ago) to today represents the last 90 minutes. Dinosaurs became extinct just 9 minutes (60 million years) ago. The earliest human ancestors appeared in the very last minute – and the history of *Homo sapiens* (modern humans) occupies just the last second.

Early animals
Fossil sea pens and jellyfish – the first invertebrates – are 700 million years old.

Oxygen to ozone
Plants added the first oxygen to the atmosphere. Once there was enough oxygen, a protective ozone layer (above) formed.

Subduction
Ocean crust has been destroyed by subduction for 2.5 billion years.

Ancient algae
To date, the oldest fossilized life forms are stromatolites, blue-green algae that lived 3.6 billion years ago.

Continents
The first continents formed between 3.5 and 2.5 billion years ago.

JURASSIC
TRIASSIC
PERMIAN
CARBONIFEROUS
DEVONIAN
SILURIAN
ORDOVICIAN
CAMBRIAN
CRETACEOUS
TERTIARY & QUATERNARY
PHANEROZOIC
PROTEROZOIC
ARCHEOZOIC

570 MYA
Present day
2.5 BYA

EARTH OR OCEAN?

IF YOU COULD JOURNEY into space and look back homeward, you might think that "Ocean" would be a more accurate name for our planet than "Earth." Over two-thirds of its surface is covered in seawater, making it the most watery planet in the solar system. The water lies in five oceans. In order of size, they are the Pacific, Atlantic, Indian, Antarctic, and Arctic. They form a continuous expanse of sea, broken up by the continents.

The tallest mountain, the deepest trench, and the longest mountain range on Earth are all found in its oceans. With this book, you can explore the oceans from shore to seafloor, and find out about the amazing landscapes and creatures under the waves.

This picture looks blue because the blue portion of light penetrates the farthest distance under water.

LETTING IN LIGHT
When sunlight hits the sea, some of the rays are reflected back up into the sky. The rest are absorbed by the water. Tiny particles in the water scatter the various colors in the light. The diagram below shows how colors are absorbed. Red is absorbed first, so it only reaches a short distance into the water. Blue is the last to be absorbed, so it reaches the farthest. Even in clear water, however, very little sunlight can reach below 820 ft (250 m).

North Sea
The North Sea is the site of many undersea oil and gas fields. The extraction of this oil and gas has been a major challenge to technology because of the depths and the treacherous seas involved.

North Atlantic Ocean
The North Atlantic has been a major shipping route between Europe and North America for centuries. It is also one of the world's main fishing grounds.

Sargasso Sea
The Sargasso Sea is a sea within a sea in a calm, warm area of the mid-Atlantic. In places it is covered with sargassum weed, a plant that floats in clumps on the surface with the help of small, air-filled bladders that look like grapes.

Atlantis
Some people believe that a fabulous, ancient city called Atlantis once existed in the middle of the Atlantic Ocean. The city was supposed to have been destroyed by a massive earthquake, and slipped beneath the waves without a trace.

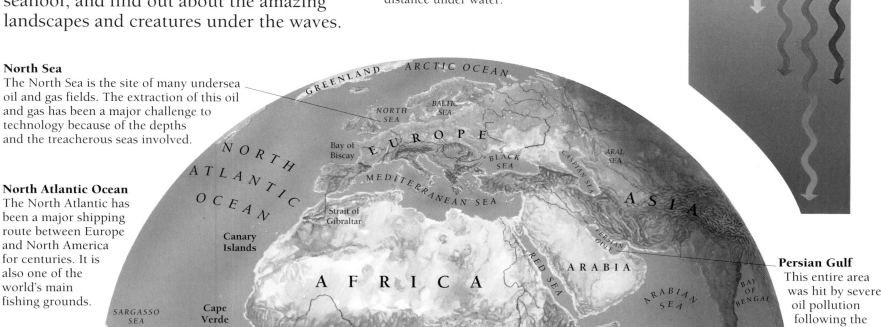

Persian Gulf
This entire area was hit by severe oil pollution following the Gulf War, in 1991. Seabirds and marine life in particular were badly affected.

Colorful seas
Not all seas appear to be blue. The Black Sea, on the borders of Europe and Asia, looks black because the mud it contains is rich in hydrogen sulfide. The Red Sea gets its name from the red plants that sometimes bloom on its surface.

Antarctic Ocean
The Antarctic Ocean surrounds the continent of Antarctica. It is home to many of the world's great whales, now in danger of extinction, and hundreds of thousands of seabirds, such as albatrosses and penguins. It is freezing cold and whipped by high winds in the winter, producing mountainous seas.

SEAWATER DENSITY

Gas

Liquid

Solid

Water
vapor

Ice

Water

Density measures how heavy something is for its size. The gas form of most substances is less dense than the liquid form, which is less dense than the solid form. If you put all three in a beaker, the gas would float on the liquid, which would float on the solid (see top beaker). But water is different. Its liquid form is denser than its solid form, ice. The solid ice floats on the liquid water, topped by the gas form, water vapor (see bottom beaker).

SALTWATER SOUP

2.2 lb (1 kg)
of seawater

The salty taste of seawater is due to the large amounts of sodium chloride, or common salt, dissolved in it. But seawater also contains smaller quantities of other "salts," including sulfate, magnesium, calcium, and potassium. The saltiness, or salinity, of seawater is measured as the number of grams of salts in 2.2 lb (1 kg) of water. This is written as ‰. The average salinity of the oceans is about 35 ‰.

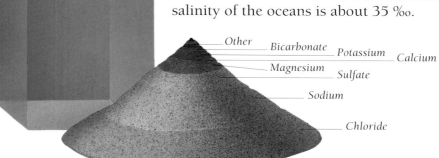

Other — Bicarbonate — Potassium — Calcium

Magnesium — Sulfate

Sodium

Chloride

Salts in 2.2 lb (1 kg) of seawater

Bering Strait
The narrow Bering Strait connects the Arctic Ocean with the north Pacific Ocean. Millions of years ago, Asia and North America were joined by a bridge of land here. Today, the land is submerged beneath the strait.

Great gulfs
A gulf is part of an ocean that "dents" the land, whether in a gentle curve such as the Gulf of Alaska, or a narrow arm such as the Gulf of California.

Volcanic islands
The Pacific Ocean floor is marked with chains of underwater volcanoes that break the surface to form island groups. There are thousands of these islands. Some, such as the Hawaiian Islands, are home to large numbers of people, while others are almost uninhabited.

Pacific Ocean
Covering an area twice the size of the Atlantic, the Pacific Ocean is the largest ocean by far. It covers about one-third of the globe. At its widest point, the Pacific reaches nearly halfway around the world.

Island eruptions
Violent volcanic eruptions are sometimes felt on the islands of the Caribbean Sea. In 1902, Mt. Pelée exploded with a shower of glowing hot gas, devastating the city of St. Pierre, Martinique, and killing all but two of its 29,000 residents.

Galápagos Islands
The Galápagos are one of the few island groups in the eastern Pacific Ocean. The six main islands in this group are inhabited by unique wildlife that has evolved in isolation, including giant tortoises and exotic marine lizards.

Great Barrier Reef
The tiny volcanic islands, or atolls, which are dotted about the Pacific Ocean are ringed with coral reefs. These reefs are built by millions of tiny coral animals, and filled with brightly colored fish, sharks, sea slugs, and other creatures. The Great Barrier Reef lies off the northeastern coast of Australia. It is the largest natural feature on Earth and is clearly visible from space.

SEA OR OCEAN?

The names "sea" and "ocean" are often used to describe the same thing. But a sea is not quite the same as an ocean. A sea is a body of saltwater that is partly or totally enclosed by land. Many seas are connected to an ocean by channels.

Map labels:
ARCTIC OCEAN
ASIA
BERING STRAIT
BERING SEA
GULF OF ALASKA
NORTH AMERICA
SEA OF OKHOTSK
SEA OF JAPAN
NORTH PACIFIC OCEAN
Hawaiian Islands
GULF OF CALIFORNIA
GULF OF MEXICO
CARIBBEAN SEA
PHILIPPINE SEA
Galápagos Islands
NEW GUINEA
Solomon Islands
TIMOR SEA
CORAL SEA
GREAT BARRIER REEF
Samoa
SOUTH PACIFIC OCEAN
Fiji
AUSTRALIA
New Caledonia
TASMAN SEA
TASMANIA
NEW ZEALAND
ANTARCTIC OCEAN
ANTARCTICA

EARTH EXPOSED

WITH ALL OF ITS WATER REMOVED, the Earth looks strange and barren. On the maps below, the enormous basins that the oceans normally fill are shown empty, exposing huge, mountainous ridges that snake across the surface, as well as great gashes, called trenches, that cut deep into the Earth's crust. In addition to these features there are giant underwater volcanoes, vast, barren areas known as abyssal plains, and flat-topped sea plateaus. All these features are the result of movements of the seafloor, including earthquakes and volcanic activity in the Earth's crust, which change the shape of the ocean basins over hundreds of thousands of years.

UNDER PRESSURE

The deeper you go underwater, the greater the weight of the water pressing on you. Air puts pressure on too. At sea level, air pressure is equivalent to 14.7 pounds pressing down on each square inch (or a 1 kg weight per each square centimeter). This measurement is known as one atmosphere.

Underwater, pressure increases by one atmosphere for every 33 ft (10 m) you descend. At 9,842 ft (3,000 m) the pressure is about 300 times as great as at sea level. Divers can only descend this far if they are protected inside thick-walled submarines or other underwater craft. Otherwise the pressure would crush them.

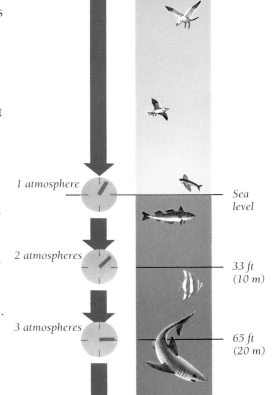

1 atmosphere — Sea level

2 atmospheres — 33 ft (10 m)

3 atmospheres — 65 ft (20 m)

Continental shelves
Both Europe and the east coast of North America are surrounded by projecting shelves of land, called continental shelves. The sea is quite shallow in these areas.

Mediterranean Basin
About seven million years ago, the Mediterranean was cut off from the Atlantic Ocean and dried up. The age of its seabed rocks indicates that the sea has actually flooded and dried up again many times.

Amazon Fan
Fans occur where a large river deposits sediment in the sea at the edge of a continent.

Mid-Atlantic Ridge
The surface of the Earth is made up of vast plates of rock. Mid-ocean ridges mark the places where two of these plates meet underwater. The Mid-Atlantic Ridge is the longest mountain chain in the world.

Basins
A huge, bowl-shaped dent in the ocean floor is called a basin.

Weddell Abyssal Plain
The floor of the Antarctic Ocean, surrounding Antarctica, is mainly vast, featureless abyssal plains. These are flat or very gently sloping areas found on the ocean floor.

Red Sea
One of the youngest and saltiest of the world's seas, the Red Sea, formed when Arabia split from Africa.

Carlsberg Ridge
This ridge is the northernmost part of the Indian Ocean ridge system, which forms a huge, inverted "Y" shape.

Ninety East Ridge
Stretching over 1,700 miles (2,735 km), this ridge gets its name because it is situated on longitude 90°E.

Kerguelen Plateau
Lonely Kerguelen Island sits on this plateau. Once a center of the whaling industry, it is now a home for seabirds and other wildlife.

UPS AND DOWNS

This chart shows relative high and low points on our planet, from the deepest depth in the Mariana Trench, to the highest height, Mount Everest. The average height of the Earth's surface, including that which is usually submerged beneath the oceans, comes out below sea level, showing just how deep the oceans really are.

Deepest depth Mariana Trench 35,827 ft (10,920 m)

Average ocean depth 12,237 ft (3,730 m)

Average height of Earth's surface 7,873 ft (2,400 m) below sea level

Average land height 2,854 ft (870 m)

Highest height Mount Everest 29,029 ft (8,848 m)

AMAZING OCEAN FACTS

❏ The Pacific Ocean holds more than half the seawater on Earth – almost as much as the Atlantic and Indian oceans combined.

❏ The Arctic Ocean is the smallest ocean. It is about 13 times smaller than the Pacific and contains just one percent of the Earth's seawater.

❏ About 97 percent of all the water on Earth is found in its oceans.

❏ Only 29 percent of the Earth is dry land. Together, Africa and Europe cover about 15,670,000 sq miles (40,600,000 sq km). Yet this is only half the size of the Atlantic, the second largest ocean.

❏ The length of the world's coastlines is about 312,000 miles (504,000 km), enough to circle the Equator 12 times.

Aleutian Trench
This is part of a gigantic series of trenches stretching into the western Pacific.

Emperor Seamounts
Seamounts are large mountains, usually formed by volcanic activity, which rise steeply from the seafloor.

The Mariana Trench
The Mariana Trench contains the deepest point on Earth, the Challenger Deep, which plunges to 35,827 ft (10,920 m).

Melanesian Basin
The Pacific Ocean floor in this area is typical of an ocean basin, gently hollowed out to form a curved dip.

South Australian Basin
South of Australia, the seafloor drops away to form a deep basin, then gradually rises towards Antarctica.

Volcanic cones
Many of the hundreds of Pacific islands are volcanic cones that rise sharply from the seafloor to break the surface of the water above. Some volcanic island chains mark the edges of the Earth's underwater crustal plates.

A steep drop
Along the west coast of North America, there is very little continental shelf and the land drops off steeply.

Fracture zones
Fracture zones dominate the East Pacific. They are cracks in the Earth's crust caused by the movement of plates.

Peru-Chile Trench
This trench, situated along the western coast of South America, is about 11,800 miles (1,900 km) long.

East Pacific Rise
The East Pacific Rise is another massive ridge system. Like the Mid-Atlantic Ridge, it marks the place where two plates meet.

MOVING PLATES

THE EARTH'S HARD, OUTER LAYER, called the crust, is cracked into seven gigantic and many smaller pieces, called plates. In 1915, the German scientist Alfred Wegener put forward a theory that millions of years ago all the land on Earth was joined together as a single continent, Pangaea. It was surrounded by a huge ocean, called Panthalassa. As the plates of crust drifted apart, Pangaea split up, forming the oceans and continents we know today.

Until the 1960s, Wegener's theory was not taken seriously. Then scientists discovered that the plates do move on the semi-molten rocks below. They also found fossil evidence that supported the idea that the continents were once linked. As the plates drifted, they opened up the ocean basins. The size and shape of these basins are still changing today.

WHERE THE WATER CAME FROM

The Earth formed about 4,600 million years ago from a cloud of hot gases and dust. As the Earth cooled and solidified, water vapor was thrown into the atmosphere by volcanoes on its surface. The water vapor condensed to form storm clouds, and torrential rain filled the first oceans. This seawater was not cool and salty as it is today, but very hot and as acidic as vinegar.

THE EARTH'S LAYERS
The Earth is made up of several layers, which fit one around the other. These layers form three main sections: the crust, the mantle, and the core. The outermost layer is a brittle shell called the lithosphere. A cross-section of the lithosphere is shown below. It is made up of the crust and the molten rocks of the upper mantle. The upper mantle wraps around the lower mantle, which in turn surrounds the outer and inner cores (see left).

Lithosphere

Upper mantle
The rocks of the upper mantle are partly melted. They flow very slowly, like thick syrup.

Lower mantle
Below about 90 miles (150 km), the rocks of the lower mantle are dense and solid.

Outer core
The outer core is made up of molten iron and nickel. Scientists know it is liquid because of the way earthquake waves pass through it.

Inner core
The center of the Earth is a solid ball of iron and nickel. Despite temperatures of up to 8,100°F (4,500°C), the inner core remains solid because of the immense pressure of the layers above it.

UPPER MANTLE
390 miles (630 km)

LOWER MANTLE
1,420 miles (2,290 km)

OUTER CORE
1,130 miles (1,820 km)

INNER CORE
995 miles (1,600 km)

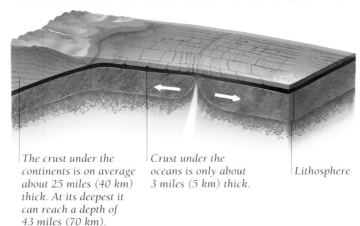

The crust under the continents is on average about 25 miles (40 km) thick. At its deepest it can reach a depth of 43 miles (70 km).

Crust under the oceans is only about 3 miles (5 km) thick.

Lithosphere

HOW THE PLATES MOVE
The plates of the crust drift on the mantle, driven by heat from deep inside the Earth. Everything on the Earth's surface – from the continents to the ocean basins – is carried along on the plates. This means that all the features on Earth are created as the plates pull apart from each other or collide. Mountains are pushed up by two plates crashing into each other. Earthquakes and volcanoes happen at the edges of plates. Where two plates pull apart, molten rock from the mantle wells up to plug the gap.

PACIFIC PLATE

Surtsey, off southwest Iceland

The surface evidence
Although it is difficult to imagine continents and oceans being carried along on gigantic plates, there is some visible evidence of plate movement. The photograph of Thingvellir, Iceland (right), shows ravines and cliffs that mark the edges of two plates: the North American Plate and the Eurasian Plate. The two plates are slowly pulling apart, cutting a rift across Iceland and causing frequent volcanoes and earthquakes. This same plate movement was also responsible for the massive undersea volcano that formed the island of Surtsey.

Earth 200 million years ago
After hundreds of millions of years, the plates settled some 300 million years ago to form Pangaea and Panthalassa, the world ocean. Pangaea began to split up about 200 million years ago.

Earth 180 million years ago
Pangaea split into two landmasses separated by the Tethys Sea about 180 million years ago: Laurasia in the north, and Gondwanaland in the south. A Y-shaped rift began to divide Gondwanaland.

Earth 65 million years ago
Further plate movements opened the Atlantic, Indian, and Antarctic oceans. Panthalassa shrank to half its original size and became the Pacific Ocean, while the Tethys became the Mediterranean Sea.

SPREADING CONTINENTS
Between 65 million years ago and the present day, Greenland split from Europe, and Australia drifted from Antarctica. The map below shows the current position of the plates. The key describes what happens where two plates meet. At a spreading ridge, the plates move apart and new crust forms to fill the gap. At a subduction zone, the plates are forced together. Crust from one of the plates is carried down (subducted) into the mantle. At transform faults, no crust is made or destroyed. Instead, the plates grind past each other, creating deep cracks.

Earth 50 million years from now
What might tomorrow's world look like? The eastern part of Africa may split off along the line of its rift valley, while the rest of the continent moves northward and closes the Mediterranean. Australia could nudge closer to Asia, and a sliver of western North America might slide up the coast.

KEY TO PLATE BOUNDARIES
- SPREADING RIDGE
- SUBDUCTION ZONE
- TRANSFORM FAULT
- UNCERTAIN BOUNDARY
- MOVEMENT OF PLATE

JUAN DE FUCA PLATE — ICELAND — **EURASIAN PLATE** — **CHINA PLATE**

NORTH AMERICAN PLATE — HELLENIC PLATE — IRANIAN PLATE — MID-ATLANTIC RIDGE

CARIBBEAN PLATE — ARABIAN PLATE — **PHILIPPINE PLATE** — **PACIFIC PLATE**

COCOS PLATE — **AFRICAN PLATE**

NAZCA PLATE — **SOUTH AMERICAN PLATE** — MID-ATLANTIC RIDGE — **INDO-AUSTRALIAN PLATE**

EAST PACIFIC RISE — SOUTHWEST INDIAN RIDGE — MID-INDIAN RIDGE — SOUTHEAST INDIAN RIDGE

ANTARCTIC PLATE — PACIFIC PLATE

Continental jigsaw
The shapes of the continents fit together like a giant jigsaw. This may be the most obvious evidence that the continents were once linked.

HOW DO WE KNOW?
Fascinating fossil finds provide evidence that the continents were once joined together. Fossils of the fern *Glossopteris* have been found in rocks from Africa, India, Australia, and South America. These places are now far apart but were once joined as Gondwanaland. *Massospondylus* fossils have only been found in Africa and North America, which were once neighboring continents.
Further proof that the southern continents were once joined comes from the matching rock types found running through South America, Antarctica, and Australia. The map on the right shows how bands of rocks from two geological ages match up when these continents are put together.

Glossopteris

Massospondylus

AFRICA

SOUTH AMERICA

INDIA

ANTARCTICA

AUSTRALIA

- PRECAMBRIAN ROCK
- PALEOZOIC ROCK

EXPLORATION

PEOPLE HAVE SAILED the seas for thousands of years in search of new homes, better trade routes, and adventure. But the detailed study of the oceans only really began in 1872, with the voyage of HMS *Challenger*. Its crew spent more than three years investigating all aspects of the oceans – their chemistry, physics, and biology. The reports written by *Challenger*'s scientists form the basis of the modern science of oceanography – the scientific study of the oceans. Modern technology has helped further this knowledge. Scientists can now investigate deeper than ever before. The latest submersibles (small, free-swimming, underwater vehicles) and ROVs (remote-operated vehicles) are expanding our knowledge of the oceans, and new discoveries are being made all the time.

EXPLORATION TODAY

Until recently scientists had very little idea about what the ocean floor looked like. After 1945, however, major advances were made in exploration techniques. The greatest steps forward came in the 1960s with the development of modern submersibles and unmanned ROVs. Both operate from research and support ships on the surface. Some of the newer equipment, such as GLORIA, shown below, has been developed by the U.K.'s Institute of Oceanographic Sciences.

MAPPING WITH SOUND

Scientists use sonar (sound) to make maps of the deep-sea floor, indicating features such as volcanoes and trenches. Sonar instruments give out pulses of sound. These hit parts of the seabed and send back echoes. The echoes are recorded, and their pattern traced on paper to build up a "sound image" of the features.

Box corer
Box corers are used for taking samples of the seabed. These are analyzed to give scientists information about the seabed and its creatures.

Benthic sled
The sled is lowered to the sea bottom, where its nets collect samples of sea animals. It also carries a camera.

Seismic profiling
To explore for oil, explosions are set off underwater. The shock waves hit seabed rocks and are reflected off them. From the reflected waves, scientists can tell which sort of rock they have hit.

Moored buoy
Moored buoys can carry instruments for measuring temperature, pressure, and currents.

GLORIA
GLORIA (Geological Long-Range Inclined Asdic) is a sonar device that scans the seabed on either side. It is towed along by a surface ship.

Wooden diving bell

Air-filled hood allowed divers to walk on the seabed.

Waterproof air-filled barrels supplied fresh air to the bell when the trapped surface air ran out.

Lead weight

Leather air hose

HALLEY'S DIVING BELL

The astronomer Sir Edmond Halley built his famous "diving bell" in 1690. It allowed divers to work on the seabed. Air was trapped inside the bell at the surface and was used by the divers below. Diving bells are still used today, but with modern self-contained air supplies.

Ballast weight keeps buoy in position.

A fan-shaped beam of sound maps features on the seabed.

Sonar blind spot

The spade digs into the seabed.

Nets made of fine and coarse mesh collect bottom-living creatures.

Cone-shaped drogues help keep the instrument on a level tow path.

Camera sled
Camera sleds carry video and still cameras and take photographs and videos of the seabed. They have powerful lights to pierce the darkness.

Powerful lights

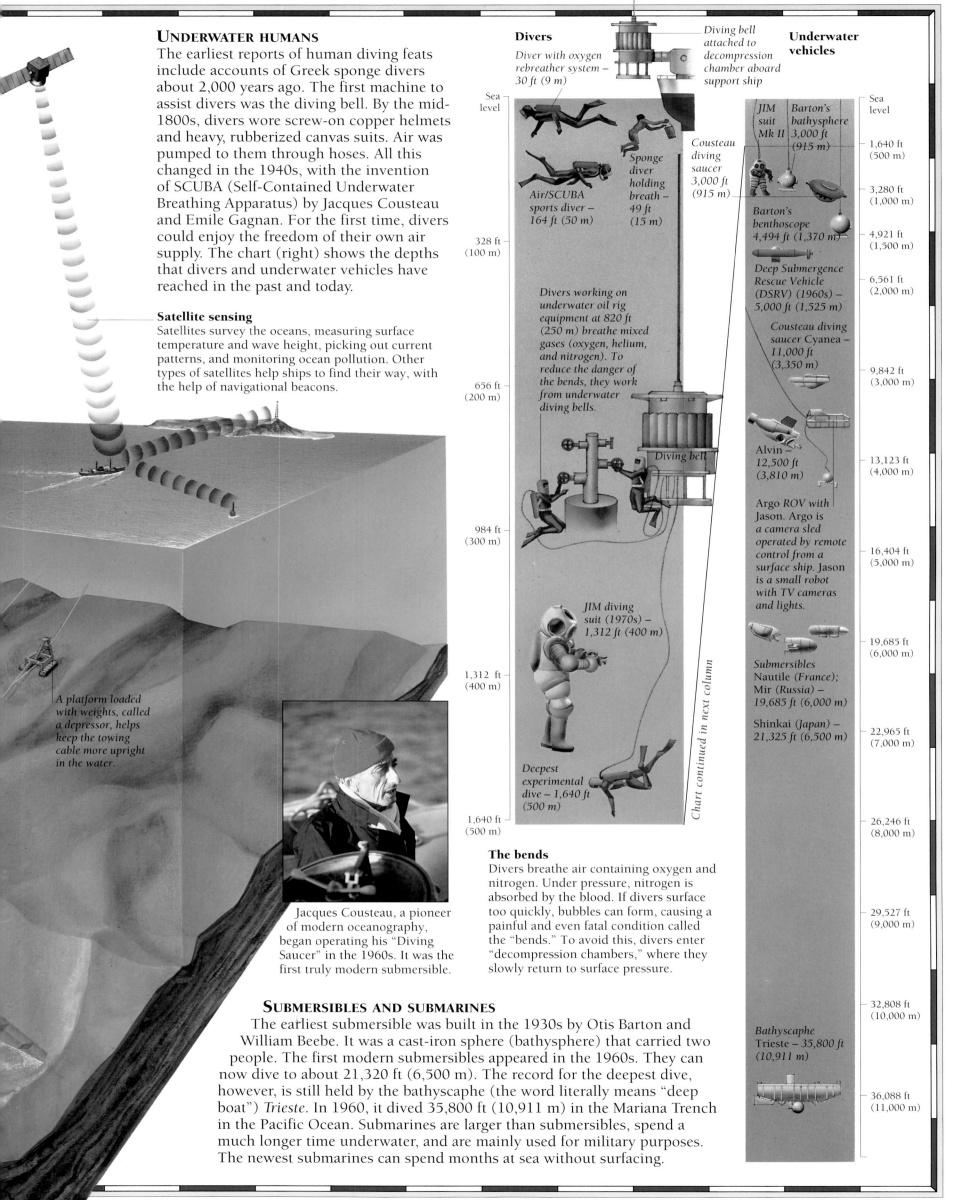

UNDERWATER HUMANS

The earliest reports of human diving feats include accounts of Greek sponge divers about 2,000 years ago. The first machine to assist divers was the diving bell. By the mid-1800s, divers wore screw-on copper helmets and heavy, rubberized canvas suits. Air was pumped to them through hoses. All this changed in the 1940s, with the invention of SCUBA (Self-Contained Underwater Breathing Apparatus) by Jacques Cousteau and Emile Gagnan. For the first time, divers could enjoy the freedom of their own air supply. The chart (right) shows the depths that divers and underwater vehicles have reached in the past and today.

Satellite sensing

Satellites survey the oceans, measuring surface temperature and wave height, picking out current patterns, and monitoring ocean pollution. Other types of satellites help ships to find their way, with the help of navigational beacons.

A platform loaded with weights, called a depressor, helps keep the towing cable more upright in the water.

Jacques Cousteau, a pioneer of modern oceanography, began operating his "Diving Saucer" in the 1960s. It was the first truly modern submersible.

Divers

Diver with oxygen rebreather system – 30 ft (9 m)

Diving bell attached to decompression chamber aboard support ship

Underwater vehicles

Sea level

Air/SCUBA sports diver – 164 ft (50 m)

Sponge diver holding breath – 49 ft (15 m)

Cousteau diving saucer 3,000 ft (915 m)

JIM suit Mk II

Barton's bathysphere 3,000 ft (915 m)

Sea level

1,640 ft (500 m)

3,280 ft (1,000 m)

Barton's benthoscope 4,494 ft (1,370 m)

4,921 ft (1,500 m)

328 ft (100 m)

Divers working on underwater oil rig equipment at 820 ft (250 m) breathe mixed gases (oxygen, helium, and nitrogen). To reduce the danger of the bends, they work from underwater diving bells.

Deep Submergence Rescue Vehicle (DSRV) (1960s) – 5,000 ft (1,525 m)

6,561 ft (2,000 m)

Cousteau diving saucer Cyanea – 11,000 ft (3,350 m)

9,842 ft (3,000 m)

656 ft (200 m)

Diving bell

Alvin – 12,500 ft (3,810 m)

13,123 ft (4,000 m)

Argo ROV with Jason. Argo is a camera sled operated by remote control from a surface ship. Jason is a small robot with TV cameras and lights.

16,404 ft (5,000 m)

984 ft (300 m)

JIM diving suit (1970s) – 1,312 ft (400 m)

19,685 ft (6,000 m)

Submersibles Nautile (France); Mir (Russia) – 19,685 ft (6,000 m)

Shinkai (Japan) – 21,325 ft (6,500 m)

22,965 ft (7,000 m)

1,312 ft (400 m)

Chart continued in next column

Deepest experimental dive – 1,640 ft (500 m)

26,246 ft (8,000 m)

1,640 ft (500 m)

The bends

Divers breathe air containing oxygen and nitrogen. Under pressure, nitrogen is absorbed by the blood. If divers surface too quickly, bubbles can form, causing a painful and even fatal condition called the "bends." To avoid this, divers enter "decompression chambers," where they slowly return to surface pressure.

29,527 ft (9,000 m)

SUBMERSIBLES AND SUBMARINES

The earliest submersible was built in the 1930s by Otis Barton and William Beebe. It was a cast-iron sphere (bathysphere) that carried two people. The first modern submersibles appeared in the 1960s. They can now dive to about 21,320 ft (6,500 m). The record for the deepest dive, however, is still held by the bathyscaphe (the word literally means "deep boat") Trieste. In 1960, it dived 35,800 ft (10,911 m) in the Mariana Trench in the Pacific Ocean. Submarines are larger than submersibles, spend a much longer time underwater, and are mainly used for military purposes. The newest submarines can spend months at sea without surfacing.

32,808 ft (10,000 m)

Bathyscaphe Trieste – 35,800 ft (10,911 m)

36,088 ft (11,000 m)

THE WEB OF LIFE

THE OCEANS FORM THE LARGEST environment for living things on Earth. A huge variety of plants and animals live in the sea – both in the surface water and at every depth. As on land, they are linked together by what they eat. Every ocean food chain begins with marine plants because of the plants' ability to photosynthesize. This is the process by which plants use the energy from sunlight to combine water and carbon dioxide into food. In a simple food chain, the plants are eaten by herbivores (plant-eaters), which, in turn, are eaten by carnivores (meat-eaters). But food chains are rarely simple. They are usually linked to create the more complex food webs shown below in which the plants and animals are dependent on each other. If one link is destroyed, the rest of the web is affected.

THE LIGHTED REALM

Most sea animals live in the top 500 ft (150 m) of the sea, in the lighted, or euphotic, zone. The water is warm and sunny here and plants can grow in abundance. Three areas make up the euphotic zone – estuaries, rocky coasts, and the open ocean.

MARINE PLANTS

By far the most abundant plants in the sea are the microscopic, single-celled phytoplankton which drift on the surface of the water. They are algae, the simplest types of plant. Larger algae grow along the shore and in shallow water. These are the seaweeds, the biggest of which can grow to more than 164 ft (50 m) in length. There are relatively few flowering plants living in or near the sea. Among them are seagrasses and mangroves.

About half of all phytoplankton is made up of microscopic diatoms (shown magnified many times above). There may be a million of these tiny plants in one quart (one liter) of seawater.

Dinoflagellate (half plant, half animal)

Diatoms

HERBIVORES AND CARNIVORES

In the first part of a simple food chain, the phytoplankton is eaten by tiny herbivores, the zooplankton. They, in turn, are eaten by carnivores, which fall prey to larger carnivores, and so on. In the second part of the chain, the dead bodies and waste from the animals higher up sink and are fed upon by the decomposers (waste-eaters).

Rocky coasts

Seaweeds grow well along rocky coasts and provide food for large numbers of grazing animals, which include small snails and sea urchins. Other creatures, such as barnacles and sea squirts, feed on the phytoplankton. Some coastal seabirds have beaks specially adapted for prying open mollusks.

Oystercatcher

Sea squirts

Toothy grin
Wolf fish eat sea urchins, which they crush with their large teeth.

Sea urchin

Bladder wrack

Periwinkles
Periwinkles and other small snails are eaten by seabirds such as gulls and oystercatchers.

Barnacles
When submerged, barnacles extend their long feathery feeding arms in search of food.

Oarweed

Dog whelk

Snail tales
Periwinkles feed on bladder wrack and other sea plants, while snails such as whelks feed on barnacles and periwinkles.

Herring gull

Life in estuaries
Estuaries form where rivers meet the sea. Some of an estuary's food supply is made up of plant debris washed off the land by the rivers. At low tide, an estuary may look lifeless, but there are hundreds of animals hidden in the mud. They provide food for seabirds such as gulls and plovers.

Plant debris washes off the land into the mud.

Ringed plover

Ragworm

Lugworm

Cockle

Shore crab

Pass the debris
Shore worms and small snails eat debris in the soft mud.

Plants in the sea
Phytoplankton cannot grow below about 500 ft (150 m) because there is no sunlight for photosynthesis. On the surface, however, the phytoplankton may drift in vast numbers.

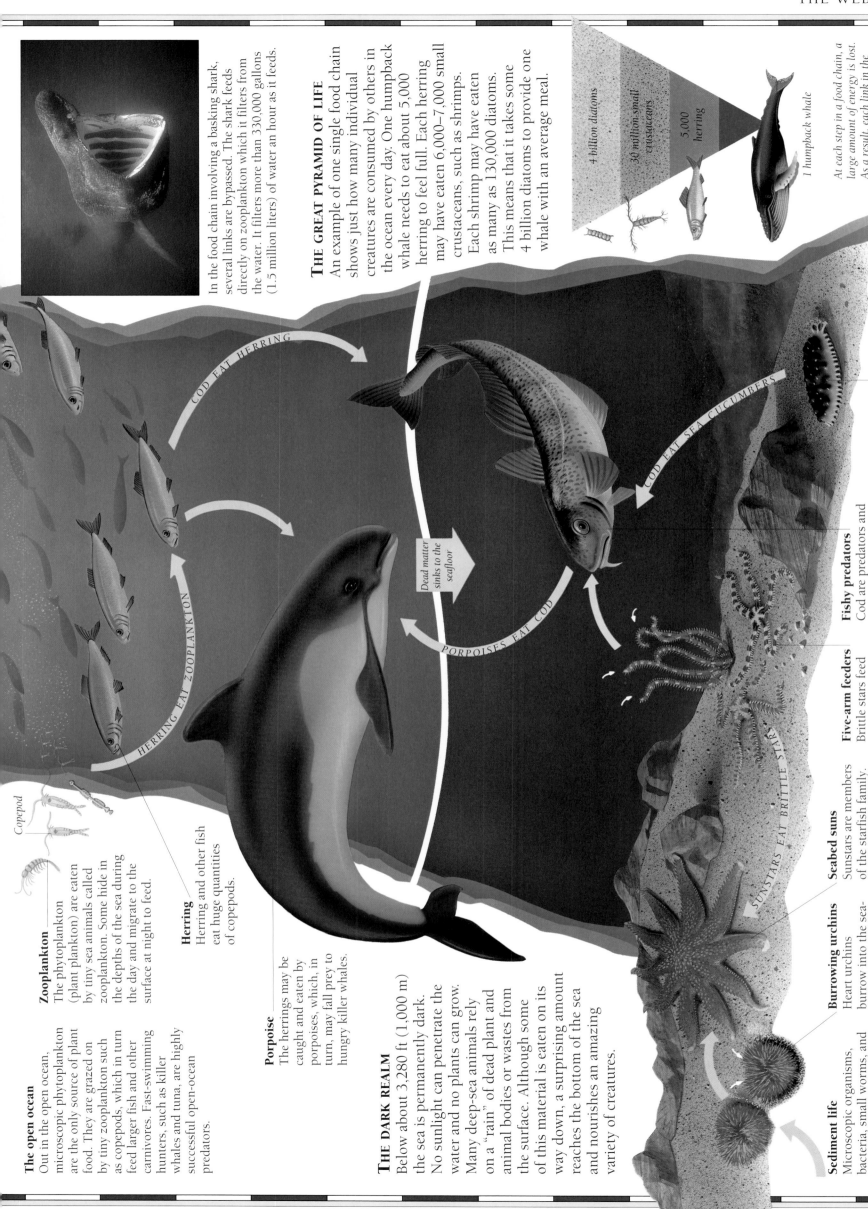

In the food chain involving a basking shark, several links are bypassed. The shark feeds directly on zooplankton which it filters from the water. It filters more than 330,000 gallons (1.5 million liters) of water an hour as it feeds.

THE GREAT PYRAMID OF LIFE

An example of one single food chain shows just how many individual creatures are consumed by others in the ocean every day. One humpback whale needs to eat about 5,000 herring to feel full. Each herring may have eaten 6,000–7,000 small crustaceans, such as shrimps. Each shrimp may have eaten as many as 130,000 diatoms. This means that it takes some 4 billion diatoms to provide one whale with an average meal.

4 billion diatoms

30 million small crustaceans

5,000 herring

1 humpback whale

At each step in a food chain, a large amount of energy is lost. As a result, each link in the chain is larger in size and less numerous than the one before, creating a food pyramid.

COD EAT HERRING

COD EAT SEA CUCUMBERS

HERRING EAT ZOOPLANKTON

Dead matter sinks to the seafloor

PORPOISES EAT COD

SUNSTARS EAT BRITTLE STARS

Cucumber meal
Sea cucumbers feed on food from the surface of the seafloor.

Fishy predators
Cod are predators and scavengers, feeding on both smaller fish and dead organic matter.

Five-arm feeders
Brittle stars feed on dead organic matter suspended in the water.

Seabed suns
Sunstars are members of the starfish family. They are predators, feeding on various forms of bottom life.

Burrowing urchins
Heart urchins burrow into the sea-bed, feeding on tiny creatures hidden in the sediment.

Sediment life
Microscopic organisms, bacteria, small worms, and crustaceans are filtered from the sediment by many bottom-living creatures.

The open ocean
Out in the open ocean, microscopic phytoplankton are the only source of plant food. They are grazed on by tiny zooplankton such as copepods, which in turn feed larger fish and other carnivores. Fast-swimming hunters, such as killer whales and tuna, are highly successful open-ocean predators.

Zooplankton
The phytoplankton (plant plankton) are eaten by tiny sea animals called zooplankton. Some hide in the depths of the sea during the day and migrate to the surface at night to feed.

Copepod

Herring
Herring and other fish eat huge quantities of copepods.

Porpoise
The herrings may be caught and eaten by porpoises, which, in turn, may fall prey to hungry killer whales.

THE DARK REALM

Below about 3,280 ft (1,000 m) the sea is permanently dark. No sunlight can penetrate the water and no plants can grow. Many deep-sea animals rely on a "rain" of dead plant and animal bodies or wastes from the surface. Although some of this material is eaten on its way down, a surprising amount reaches the bottom of the sea and nourishes an amazing variety of creatures.

THE ATLANTIC OCEAN

THE ATLANTIC OCEAN is the world's second largest ocean, after the Pacific. It covers an area of about 31,660,446 sq miles (82,000,000 sq km) – about one-fifth of the Earth's surface. It stretches from the Arctic Ocean in the north to the Antarctic Ocean in the south. Its western boundary is formed by the continents of North and South America, and its eastern boundary by Europe and Africa. At its widest point, it measures 5,965 miles (9,600 km). But it is still spreading sideward at a rate of ¾–1½ in (2–4 cm) a year along the Mid-Atlantic Ridge, the great underwater mountain range that splits the ocean down the middle. The ocean is divided into the North and South Atlantic areas by the Equator. The Atlantic is a relatively young ocean, only about 150 million years old. It has an average depth of 12,000 ft (3,660 m) and is 28,374 ft (8,648 m) deep at its deepest point.

Continental shelf
The continental shelf is the shallow area next to the land. In the Atlantic, it is a large source of fish and minerals. About 90 percent of all the fish caught for food come from the continental shelves. There are important fisheries off the coast of eastern Canada and northwestern Europe. There are also large deposits of minerals, such as oil, gas, gravel, and shell sand. But the shelf area is being polluted by sewage, oil, chemicals, and debris, especially around built-up areas on the east coast of the United States, such as New York.

Puerto Rico Trench
The Puerto Rico Trench is the deepest point in the Atlantic, at 28,374 ft (8,648 m). It lies to the north of Puerto Rico and is the result of movement between the Caribbean and American plates.

NORTH ATLANTIC OCEAN
The North Atlantic stretches from the tropical Equator to the icebound Arctic. In the north, high winds, waves, fog, and icebergs can make conditions hazardous for ships. The North Atlantic is bordered by some of the world's most industrialized countries and is one of the busiest areas for shipping. It also has some of the world's richest fishing grounds along its continental shelves. More than 3 million tons (3.1 million tonnes) of fish are caught there each year.

Many of the icebergs seen in the North Atlantic have broken off from the ice sheet that covers Greenland. This breaking-off process is called "calving." The bergs are then carried south by the current.

The *Titanic* was the largest ship of its time and thought to be unsinkable. Here it leaves its builders, Harland and Wolff of Belfast, Northern Ireland, in 1912.

DISCOVERING THE TITANIC
On April 14, 1912, the luxury ocean liner *Titanic* hit an iceberg in the North Atlantic and sank. Nearly 1,500 people died in the tragedy. The wreck was discovered 73 years later by an expedition led by Dr. Robert Ballard. A towed camera system, *Argo*, spotted it at 13,123 ft (4,000 m) at the base of the continental shelf, as indicated below.

Site of the sunken wreck of the Titanic

NEWFOUNDLAND

GREENLAND

CONTINENTAL SHELF

LABRADOR BASIN

CONTINENTAL SHELF

NEWFOUNDLAND

Site where the Titanic was discovered

REYKJANES RIDGE

ICELAND

Faeroe Islands

BRITISH ISLES

IRELAND

EUROPE

AFRICA

Azores

Site of project FAMOUS exploration

Canary Islands

Cape Verde Islands

MID ATLANTIC RIDGE

LINE OF CROSS-SECTION

B

Cuba

ANTILLES

Hispaniola

Puerto Rico

CENTRAL AMERICA

NORTH AMERICA

SOUTH

A

Mid-Atlantic Ridge

The Mid-Atlantic Ridge runs for some 7,000 miles (11,300 km) down the middle of the Atlantic Ocean, from north of Iceland to Bouvet Island on the edge of the Antarctic Ocean. Most of the ridge lies underwater, but it rises to the surface in Iceland and Ascension Island. Along the ridge, molten rock seeps up from deep inside the Earth and creates new seabed rock.

This photograph was taken from the submersible Alvin. It shows newly formed lava on the Mid-Atlantic Ridge.

SOUTH ATLANTIC OCEAN

The South Atlantic Ocean stretches from the warm water of the tropics to the cold waters of the Antarctic Ocean. It is the site of some of the most isolated islands in the world. Bouvet Island lies 1,050 miles (1,700 km) off the east coast of Antarctica. Tristan da Cunha is the world's most isolated inhabited island. Its people's nearest neighbors live on St. Helena, 1,300 miles (2,120 km) away.

On the shelf

The continental margin is made up of the continental shelf, slope, and rise. The margin is wider in the Atlantic than in the Pacific. The Atlantic shelf alone is up to 932 miles (1,500 km) wide, although it narrows along the west coast of Africa. The slope is up to 62 miles (100 km) wide.

Magnificent mountains

The mountains that make up the Mid-Atlantic Ridge are up to 13,123 ft (4,000 m) high. Their tips lie about 6,561 ft (2,000 m) below the sea. Part of the ridge was studied intensively by the FAMOUS (French-American Mid-Ocean Underwater Study) project in the 1970s.

Undersea earthquakes often rumble through the Sandwich Trench region.

Caribbean Sea

The Caribbean Sea covers an area of about 1,019,311 sq miles (2,640,000 sq km). Its deepest point is the Cayman Trench, at 25,216 ft (7,686 m). The sea is bordered in the east and west by subduction zones. About 14 percent of the world's coral reefs are found in the Caribbean Sea.

Common eel

Massive migrations

The Sargasso Sea is the spawning ground of the remarkable European and American eels. Every autumn the adult eels leave their river homes and swim across the Atlantic to the Sargasso Sea. They gather in the millions to lay their eggs deep in the water, then they die. The young eels, or elvers, drift on the ocean currents back to the same rivers their parents came from. The journey takes two years for the European eels and one year for the American eels.

THE SARGASSO SEA

The Sargasso Sea is a huge area of calm, still water in the western North Atlantic. It is famous for the green-brown weed, called sargassum weed (right), which covers its surface. Portuguese sailors named the weed after a type of grape, because the air-filled bladders that keep it afloat look like grapes. The sea is home to some unique animals, including fish and crabs that are camouflaged to blend in with the weed.

ATLANTIC CROSS-SECTION

The chart below shows a cross-section through the Atlantic from Central America to Africa between points A–B, marked on the map above.

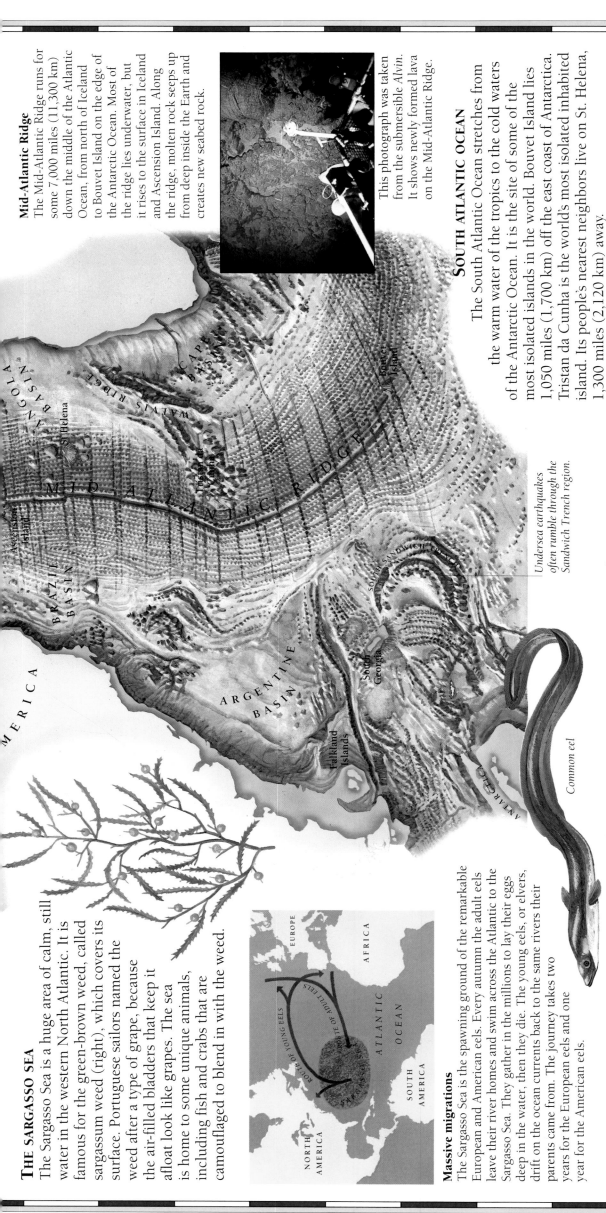

Sea level
6,561 ft (2,000 m)
19,685 ft (6,000 m)
32,808 ft (10,000 m)

CENTRAL AMERICA
CUBA
HISPANIOLA
PUERTO RICO
WEST INDIES
CARIBBEAN SEA
ATLANTIC OCEAN
MID-ATLANTIC RIDGE
CAPE VERDE ISLANDS
AFRICA
A
B

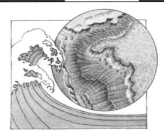

CONTINENTAL MARGINS

AROUND THE EDGES OF THE CONTINENTS, the land slopes from the shore into the deep sea. These coastal areas are called continental margins. A margin is usually made up of three parts – the continental shelf, the continental slope, and the continental rise. Each varies in width, steepness, and depth around the different continents.

There are two basic types of continental margins, called Atlantic and Pacific, although they do not only occur in these two oceans. Atlantic-type margins, such as the one around northern Europe shown here, have broad continental shelves and rises. The continent and seafloor form part of the same crustal plate so there is little or no volcanic or earthquake (seismic) activity. Pacific-type margins have narrow shelves, steep slopes, and deep trenches in place of continental rises. The continent and seafloor are on different plates. There is lots of seismic activity because the seafloor is subducted under the continent.

Atlantic margins
This map shows the continental shelf around northern Europe. The shelf is wide, like those in all Atlantic-type margins. The picture below shows the same region, but looking towards the British Isles from the mid-Atlantic. The arrow on this map shows the viewpoint for the main picture.

Continental shelf
The continental shelf slopes gently out to sea, like a huge shelf of submerged land. On average, shelves are 43 miles (70 km) wide. Off the north coast of Siberia, however, the shelf reaches a width of 559 miles (900 km). The edge of a shelf is marked by a steeper slope, called the shelf break.

Continental slope
The continental slope reaches from the shelf break to the continental rise. It is steeper, deeper, and narrower than the shelf, ending about 8,200 ft (2,500 m) below the surface, and with an average width of 12 miles (20 km). The slope is often cut by submarine canyons.

Continental rise
The continental rise is a thick wedge of sediment (sand and mud) which stretches from the slope down to the deep-sea floor, more than 13,123 ft (4,000 m) below the surface. The sediment is carried down from the continental shelf and slope by underwater avalanches called turbidity currents.

The diagram below shows the continental shelf, slope, and rise on a typical Atlantic margin, and the biological zones that correspond to them.

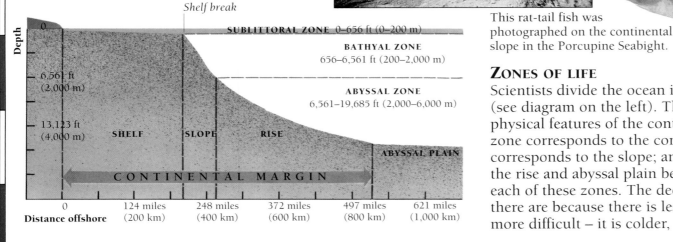

This rat-tail fish was photographed on the continental slope in the Porcupine Seabight.

Shelf break

Depth		
0		**SUBLITTORAL ZONE** 0–656 ft (0–200 m)
		BATHYAL ZONE 656–6,561 ft (200–2,000 m)
6,561 ft (2,000 m)		
		ABYSSAL ZONE 6,561–19,685 ft (2,000–6,000 m)
13,123 ft (4,000 m)	**SHELF** **SLOPE** **RISE**	
		ABYSSAL PLAIN
	CONTINENTAL MARGIN	

| Distance offshore | 0 | 124 miles (200 km) | 248 miles (400 km) | 372 miles (600 km) | 497 miles (800 km) | 621 miles (1,000 km) |

ZONES OF LIFE
Scientists divide the ocean into a number of depth zones (see diagram on the left). These zones roughly match the physical features of the continental margin. The sublittoral zone corresponds to the continental shelf; the bathyal zone corresponds to the slope; and the abyssal zone corresponds to the rise and abyssal plain beyond. Different creatures live in each of these zones. The deeper you go, the fewer creatures there are because there is less food to live on, and conditions are more difficult – it is colder, darker, and the pressure is crushing.

SUBMARINE CANYONS

Submarine canyons are huge, deep valleys cut into the floor of the continental margin. Eroded and widened by avalanches of water and sediment, they start life on the continental shelf, often at the point where a large river runs into the sea. Many submarine canyons are V-shaped, like river valleys on land. They may be more than 3,280 ft (1,000 m) deep. The canyons act as passageways for loads of sediment that continue to flow down the continental slope into the deep sea.

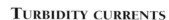

Submarine canyon

Sediment is transported down the canyon to the abyssal plain by a turbidity current.

At the mouth of the canyon, the sediment is deposited as a deep-sea fan.

Submarine canyon

The continental shelf off the coast of Spain and Portugal is quite narrow, and there is a steep drop to the ocean floor below.

Shelf break

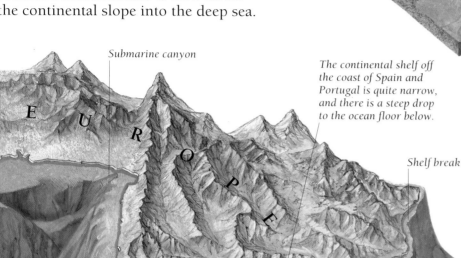

EUROPE

BISCAY ABYSSAL PLAIN

Underwater seamounts

TURBIDITY CURRENTS

Turbidity currents are underwater avalanches of water and mud that carry huge quantities of sediment from the continental shelf down the continental slope. They may be triggered by earthquakes, floods, or other disturbances. At first, these currents flow very quickly, sometimes with such speed and power that they have been known to snap underwater cables in two. As the slope gets gentler, the currents slow down and deposit their load on the deep-sea floor.

DEEP-SEA FANS

Deep-sea fans form at the bottom of submarine canyons, where a turbidity current deposits its load of sediment. The sediment spreads out in a wide fan shape on the relatively flat seafloor. These fans are only found on Atlantic-style continental margins. On a Pacific-style margin, where there is a trench next to the continental slope, the sediment is deposited into the trench and a fan cannot form.

The Amazon fan

The Amazon River flows into the Atlantic Ocean on the northeast coast of South America (see map on the left). Every hour, the Amazon pours about 170 billion gallons (773 billion liters) of water into the Atlantic. A massive amount of clay, mud, and silt is suspended in the water, carried along by its powerful flow. Some of this sediment forms a delta at the mouth of the river, but most is swept out to sea, and has formed the deep-sea fan shown below.

Deep-sea fan

Amazon

SOUTH AMERICA

In this aerial view of part of the Amazon delta, the gray areas are deposits of sediment. Other sediment is washed out over the continental shelf and eventually forms a deep-sea fan.

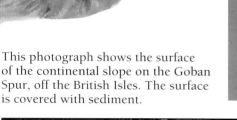

This photograph shows the surface of the continental slope on the Goban Spur, off the British Isles. The surface is covered with sediment.

Sediment is carried into the ocean from the Amazon River.

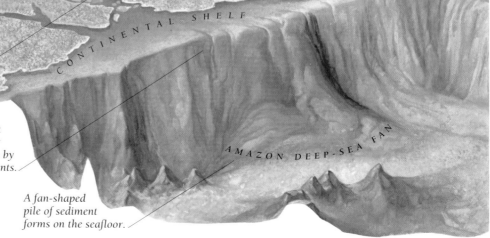

SOUTH AMERICA

Amazon River

CONTINENTAL SHELF

AMAZON DEEP-SEA FAN

Some sediment is washed over the shelf break by turbidity currents.

A fan-shaped pile of sediment forms on the seafloor.

ABYSSAL PLAINS

THE ABYSSAL PLAINS begin where the continental margins end. They are found at depths of 13,123–19,685 ft (4,000–6,000 m) below the surface of the sea. Only the deep-sea trenches plunge farther down. The abyssal plains are not only the flattest but also the most featureless places on Earth. Many of the hills and hollows in the underlying seabed crust were buried long ago under the thick layer of sediment that carpets the plains. The gradient (or steepness) of the plains is only 1:1,000. This means that for every one mile (1.6 km) you walked, you would only climb a slope 5 ft 2 in (1.6 m) high.

Until about a hundred years ago, no one believed that anything could live on the abyssal plains. We now know differently. Modern research has shown that, despite the pitch-blackness of the water, the freezing cold, and the crushing pressure, some amazing and bizarre creatures have adapted to life in the depths of the sea.

Where abyssal plains are found
Abyssal plains cover almost half of the deep-sea floor. They lie between the edges of the continental margins and the mid-ocean ridges, and are 125–1,250 miles (200–2,000 km) wide. Abyssal plains exist in all of the oceans, but are more common in the Atlantic and Indian Oceans and quite rare in the Pacific. The shaded areas on the map above show the location of the major abyssal plains.

Halosaur
The halosaur is another type of bottom-dwelling fish. It is about 6 ft 6 in (2 m) long, with a sharply pointed snout and a tapering body. The halosaur is thought to use its snout to dislodge invertebrates from the seabed. It also eats deep-sea squid.

THE ABYSSAL BENTHOS
The "abyssal benthos" is the term used to describe the animals that live in, on, or close to the deep-sea floor of the abyssal plains. The vast majority of these creatures live buried in the sediment, hidden from view. They range from tiny, single-celled animals to larger worms and shrimps. Other animals, such as starfish, sea cucumbers, and sea urchins, live on the surface of the seafloor. A few creatures can swim up off the bottom. These include deep-sea shrimps, prawns, and some extraordinary fish.

Tripod fish
The tripod fish gets its name from the three extra-long fins extending from its body. It uses these like stilts to stand on the bottom, keeping its body just above the surface of the seafloor. Then it sits and waits to ambush any passing prey. When the prey comes within range, the tripod fish pounces on it.

Tripod fish standing on seafloor

Swimming tripod fish

Sea cucumber

Venus flower basket (type of glass sponge)

Glass sponges
Tulip-shaped glass sponges grow to about 16 in (40 cm) high and are raised off the seafloor by long stalks of twisted silica. The silica "skeletons" are just like fiberglass.

Starfish
The echinoderms are the most common group of larger animals found on the abyssal plains. They include sea urchins, sea cucumbers, brittle stars, and starfish. The word "echinoderm" means "spiny skinned."

Sea cucumber
Despite the fact that they are soft and slimy, sea cucumbers are echinoderms like starfish. These creatures flourish on the abyssal plains. Most sea cucumbers crawl slowly across the deep-sea floor, feeding on the remains of animals and plants found in the mud and ooze. This is called detritus feeding.

Giant sea spider
The giant sea spider is found at depths of about 16,404 ft (5,000 m). It moves over the soft ooze of the deep-sea bed on its very long legs. It feeds on the juices of worms and other soft-bodied invertebrates, which it sucks out with its proboscis (feeding tube).

ABYSSOPELAGIC ANIMALS

Creatures that live in the water above the abyssal plains are known as "abyssopelagic" animals. This group includes some remarkable fish, squid, and prawns. The fish are almost always black, for camouflage. They are usually carnivores, with huge mouths armed with sharp teeth, and stretchy stomachs. These enable them to take full advantage of any food they are lucky enough to find, even if their prey is two or three times larger than they are.

SEEING IN THE DARK

Many of the fish that live in the dark sea depths make their own light. They do this either by means of special chemicals, called luciferins, or through luminous bacteria that live in their bodies. The fish use light to attract prey and to identify one another.

Gulper eel
The gulper eel has huge, pouchlike jaws. These can open wide enough, and its stomach stretch far enough, for it to swallow fish much bigger than itself.

Angler fish
The deep-sea angler fish has a long fishing-rod fin hanging down over its mouth, with a blob of light at the end. Small fish mistake the light for food and swim straight toward it – right into the angler fish's huge, wide-open mouth.

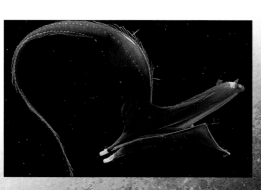

The gulper eel (left) can unhinge its jaws, opening its cavernous mouth even wider.

Halosaur

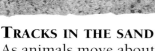
Sea urchin

Brittle star

TRACKS IN THE SAND

As animals move about over the abyssal plain, they leave a crisscross of marks or tracks behind. These marks are called *Lebensspuren*, which is German for "traces of life." It can take a long time for them to be covered by sediment and disappear.

Sea pen
Sea pens are soft corals, related to stony, reef-building corals. They are named after old-fashioned quill pens. Sea pens can reach a height of 5 ft (1.5 m).

SEABED SEDIMENTS

The layer of sediment that carpets the plains is usually 984–1,640 ft (300–500 m) thick. This map shows the different types of sediment that are found in the Atlantic Ocean. The sediment has taken millions of years to accumulate, at a rate of less than ½ in (or 1–15 mm) every thousand years. Some of it has been washed into the sea from the land by rivers. Most has rained down slowly from the surface waters. It contains the remains of countless millions of tiny plants and animals, such as those shown below.

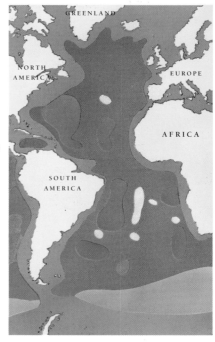

■ Clay

■ Globigerina ooze

■ Radiolarian ooze

■ Pteropod ooze

■ Diatom ooze

Globigerina

Radiolarian

Pteropod

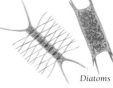
Diatoms

THE PACIFIC OCEAN

THE PACIFIC OCEAN is the biggest ocean – by a very long way. It is twice as large as its closest rival, the Atlantic, and covers a third of the Earth's surface.

It stretches from the Arctic in the north to the Antarctic in the south, and from the Americas to Australia and Asia. At its widest point, the Pacific Ocean measures about 11,000 miles (17,700 km) and reaches almost halfway around the Earth. The Pacific is also the deepest of the oceans. On average, its water is 13,800 ft (4,200 m) deep. But it drops to 35,827 ft (10,920 m) in the Mariana Trench. This is the deepest part of the ocean and the deepest point on Earth.

The first people to explore the Pacific were the Polynesians, some 2,000 years ago. They used stick maps, the stars, and cloud formations to find their way. Today, the Pacific is of particular interest to oceanographers because it contains many different seafloor features. These include trenches, mountain ridges, and thousands of volcanic and coral islands.

THE EAST PACIFIC RISE

The East Pacific Rise is an underwater mountain range that runs from north to south down the Pacific Ocean. It marks the boundary of the Pacific crustal plate and the Nazca crustal plate. The East Pacific Rise is a spreading ridge, where volcanic eruptions are constantly pushing the existing seafloor apart and creating areas of new ocean crust. As a result, the floor of the Pacific is getting 4–6 in (12–16 cm) wider each year. The East Pacific Rise is 6,561–9,842 ft (2–3,000 m) high and up to 2.5 miles (4 km) wide. It lies about 10,800 ft (3,300 m) underwater.

Fracture zones

There are long, narrow cracks in the Pacific seafloor, particularly around the East Pacific Rise. These are called fracture zones. The zones stretch from east to west, at right angles to the spreading ridges.

The San Andreas Fault

The San Andreas Fault in the U.S. lies on the border between the Pacific Plate and the North American Plate. It stretches for 270 miles (435 km) across California. This area suffers terrible earthquakes, caused by the two plates slipping and sliding past each other.

Section of the East Pacific Rise at the line A–B above. The vertical scale (height of the section) has been exaggerated to make the features clearer.

Direction of moving plate

Depth

6,561 ft (2,000 m)

13,123 ft (4,000 m)

SOUTH AMERICAN PLATE

NORTH AMERICAN PLATE

COCOS PLATE

NAZCA PLATE

PACIFIC PLATE

EAST PACIFIC RISE

NORTH AMERICA

SAN ANDREAS FAULT

GULF OF ALASKA SEAMOUNT PROVINCE

ALEUTIAN BASIN

Aleutian Islands

ALEUTIAN TRENCH

EMPEROR SEAMOUNTS

MENDOCINO FRACTURE ZONE

MURRAY FRACTURE ZONE

MOLOKAI FRACTURE ZONE

CLARION FRACTURE ZONE

CLIPPERTON FRACTURE ZONE

GALAPAGOS FRACTURE ZONE

MIDDLE AMERICA TRENCH

Galapagos Islands

PERU

SOUTH

Hawaiian Islands

HAWAIIAN RIDGE

Line Islands

LINE OF CROSS SECTION

NORTHWEST PACIFIC BASIN

Marshall Islands

CENTRAL PACIFIC BASIN

Marquesas Islands

Tuamotu Arch.

Tuvalu

Caroline Islands

Solomon Islands

KURIL TRENCH

JAPAN TRENCH

MARIANA TRENCH

PHILIPPINE TRENCH

JAPAN

PHILIPPINES

NEW GUINEA

INDONESIA

ASIA

A

B

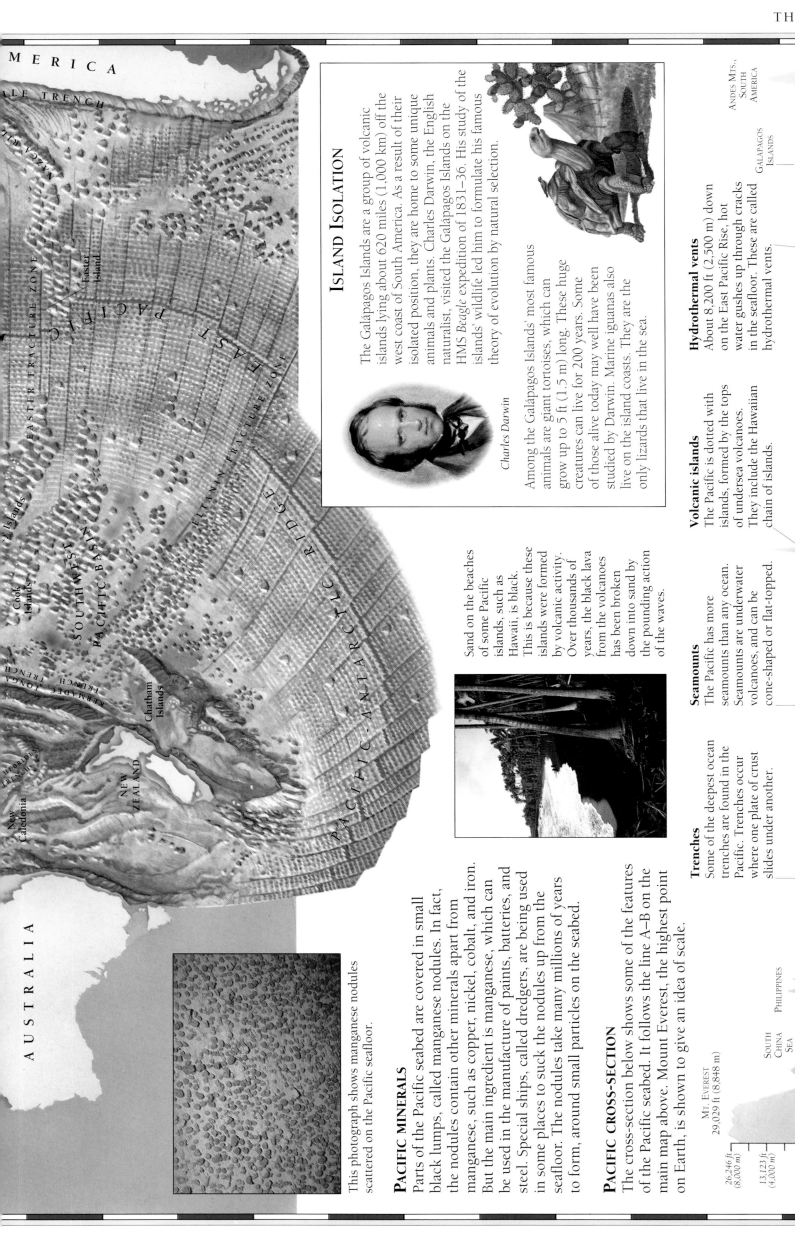

Island Isolation

The Galápagos Islands are a group of volcanic islands lying about 620 miles (1,000 km) off the west coast of South America. As a result of their isolated position, they are home to some unique animals and plants. Charles Darwin, the English naturalist, visited the Galápagos Islands on the HMS *Beagle* expedition of 1831–36. His study of the islands' wildlife led him to formulate his famous theory of evolution by natural selection.

Charles Darwin

Among the Galápagos Islands' most famous animals are giant tortoises, which can grow up to 5 ft (1.5 m) long. These huge creatures can live for 200 years. Some of those alive today may well have been studied by Darwin. Marine iguanas also live on the island coasts. They are the only lizards that live in the sea.

Sand on the beaches of some Pacific islands, such as Hawaii, is black. This is because these islands were formed by volcanic activity. Over thousands of years, the black lava from the volcanoes has been broken down into sand by the pounding action of the waves.

Pacific Minerals

Parts of the Pacific seabed are covered in small black lumps, called manganese nodules. In fact, the nodules contain other minerals apart from manganese, such as copper, nickel, cobalt, and iron. But the main ingredient is manganese, which can be used in the manufacture of paints, batteries, and steel. Special ships, called dredgers, are being used in some places to suck the nodules up from the seafloor. The nodules take many millions of years to form, around small particles on the seabed.

This photograph shows manganese nodules scattered on the Pacific seafloor.

Pacific Cross-section

The cross-section below shows some of the features of the Pacific seabed. It follows the line A–B on the main map above. Mount Everest, the highest point on Earth, is shown to give an idea of scale.

Volcanic islands
The Pacific is dotted with islands, formed by the tops of undersea volcanoes. They include the Hawaiian chain of islands.

Seamounts
The Pacific has more seamounts than any ocean. Seamounts are underwater volcanoes, and can be cone-shaped or flat-topped.

Trenches
Some of the deepest ocean trenches are found in the Pacific. Trenches occur where one plate of crust slides under another.

Hydrothermal vents
About 8,200 ft (2,500 m) down on the East Pacific Rise, hot water gushes up through cracks in the seafloor. These are called hydrothermal vents.

The vertical scale (height of the section) has been exaggerated to make the features stand out.

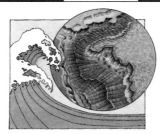

VOLCANIC ISLANDS

VOLCANOES OCCUR where hot, molten rock, called magma, from deep inside the Earth rises up through cracks or holes in the Earth's crust and solidifies. Thousands of volcanoes grow from the seafloor, many stretching to vast heights that would dwarf even the largest volcanoes on land. In some places, volcanoes grow so tall that their tops break the surface of the sea and form islands. The Hawaiian Islands, shown in the main illustration, are the tops of enormous volcanoes that have grown higher through millions of years of lava eruptions.

It has only recently been possible for scientists to study and map underwater volcanoes, thanks to great advances in technology. They now use instruments such as acoustic mapping systems, powerful cameras, deep-diving research submersibles, and ROVs (remote-operated vehicles).

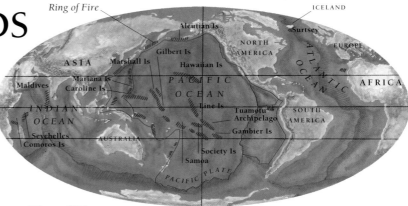

Ring of Fire
The map above shows the position of the world's volcanic islands. Most of these are found in the so-called "Ring of Fire" that circles the edge of the Pacific Plate. Devastating earthquakes, as well as frequent volcanic eruptions, give this ring its name. Chains of islands in the middle of the ring were formed over hot spots (see right).

Older and smaller
Samples taken from lava flows along the Hawaiian island chain show that the islands in the northwest are older than those in the southeast. Samples from Kauai are about five million years old; those from Hawaii are less than a million years old. This is evidence that the Pacific Plate moves like a giant conveyor belt over the fixed hot spot. Erosion has worn away the tops and sides of the oldest, inactive volcanoes.

Island arc   *Hot spot volcano*   *Mid-ocean ridge volcano*

Magma forced up   *Plate slides under*   *Column of magma*   *Plates move apart*

THREE TYPES OF VOLCANO
Volcanic islands form in one of three ways. Curving arcs of islands are created where one crustal plate slides under another in the subduction process. "Hot spot" volcanoes form over a column of magma rising like a fountain beneath the crust. Volcanic islands can also form along mid-ocean ridges, where two plates of crust move apart and magma oozes up to fill the gap. This process is known as seafloor spreading.

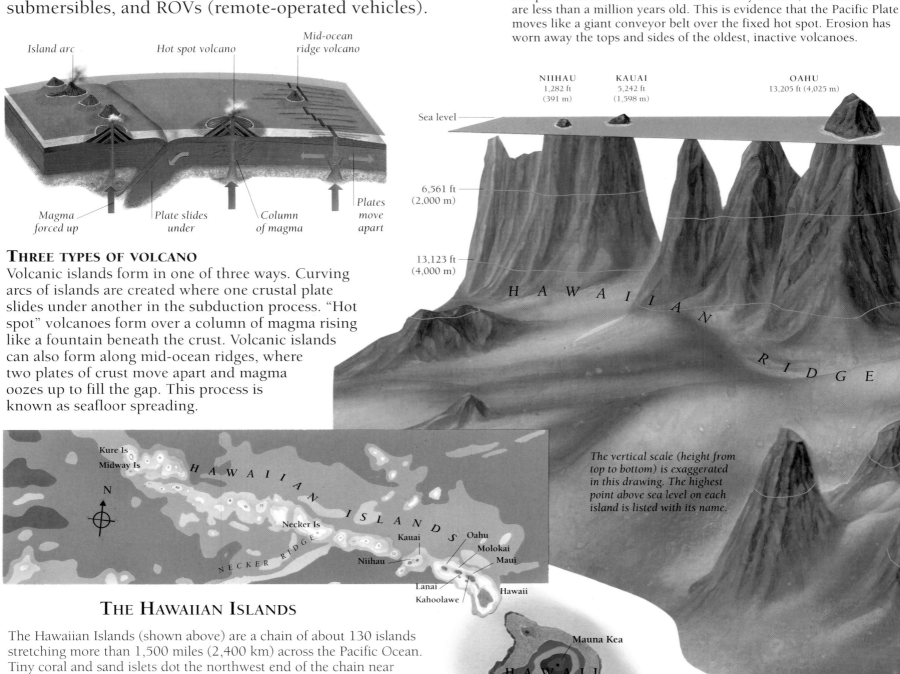

NIIHAU 1,282 ft (391 m)   KAUAI 5,242 ft (1,598 m)   OAHU 13,205 ft (4,025 m)

Sea level

6,561 ft (2,000 m)

13,123 ft (4,000 m)

HAWAIIAN RIDGE

The vertical scale (height from top to bottom) is exaggerated in this drawing. The highest point above sea level on each island is listed with its name.

THE HAWAIIAN ISLANDS

The Hawaiian Islands (shown above) are a chain of about 130 islands stretching more than 1,500 miles (2,400 km) across the Pacific Ocean. Tiny coral and sand islets dot the northwest end of the chain near Kure and Midway Islands, with rocky islets in the center and the eight largest islands (shown in the 3-D view on the right) at the southeast end. The entire chain is only a small part of the massive Hawaiian Ridge–Emperor Seamount Chain, which stretches all the way from the "big island" of Hawaii to the Aleutian Trench near Japan.

This view from above Hawaii shows three of the volcanoes that formed the island. Mauna Kea, now extinct, is Hawaii's highest point.

HOT SPOT VOLCANOES

Thousands of volcanic islands have formed over so-called hot spots in the oceans. These are isolated areas of volcanic activity where plumes of magma rise up through the seafloor. As a plate of the Earth's crust moves across a hot spot, a volcano erupts and a new island is born. The Hawaiian Islands are examples of hot spot volcanoes. Some hot spots have been creating volcanoes for more than 70 million years.

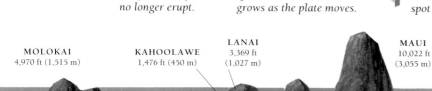

Active volcano

Direction of plate movement

Extinct volcano

1 *Volcano erupts over stationary hot spot, forming a new island.*

2 *Plate carries active volcanoes away, and they no longer erupt.*

3 *The chain of extinct volcanoes grows as the plate moves.*

Hot spot

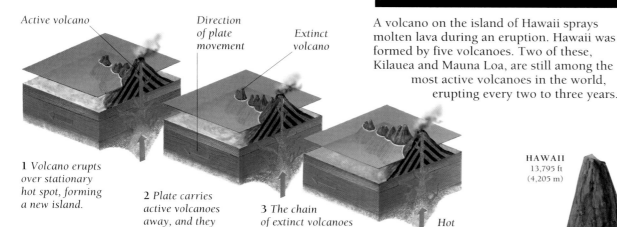

A volcano on the island of Hawaii sprays molten lava during an eruption. Hawaii was formed by five volcanoes. Two of these, Kilauea and Mauna Loa, are still among the most active volcanoes in the world, erupting every two to three years.

AN ISLAND IS BORN

In 1963, a new volcanic island was created off the south coast of Iceland. It was named Surtsey after an ancient Icelandic god of fire. The island grew quickly. Within four days, it was more than 1,970 ft (600 m) long and 197 ft (60 m) high. Eighteen months later, green plants were found growing on it, and by 1968 Surtsey was home to 40 species of insects and birds. The island stopped erupting in 1967.

Steam and smoke billow from Surtsey as it emerges from the sea off Iceland.

MOLOKAI
4,970 ft (1,515 m)

KAHOOLAWE
1,476 ft (450 m)

LANAI
3,369 ft (1,027 m)

MAUI
10,022 ft (3,055 m)

HAWAII
13,795 ft (4,205 m)

Loihi
Loihi is an active volcano in the Hawaiian chain. Its summit is now 2,950 ft (900 m) below sea level. Scientists think it will break the surface in 10,000–100,000 years' time.

Loihi seamount

Hawaiian hot spot
No one knows the exact size of the hot spot under the island of Hawaii, although it must be large enough to supply the active volcanoes along the chain. Some scientists estimate that the pool of magma is nearly 200 miles (322 km) across. Narrow tunnels feed the magma to each of the volcanoes.

SEAMOUNTS

TOWERING ABOVE the ocean floor are huge submerged mountains known as seamounts. Their peaks rise more than 3,280 ft (1,000 m) above the seabed but do not break the surface of the sea. Most seamounts are cone shaped, often with steeply sloping sides. Those with pointed summits are known as sea peaks. Those with flattened summits are called guyots. Although many seamounts appear to rise randomly from the ocean floor, most are found in groups or linear chains, such as the Emperor Seamount Chain shown on these pages. The largest single seamount is the Great Meteor Tablemount in the northeast Atlantic Ocean. It is 13,123 ft (4,000 m) high and more than 62 miles (100 km) wide at its base. Most types of seamounts are formed in the same way as volcanic islands, to which they are related (see previous pages).

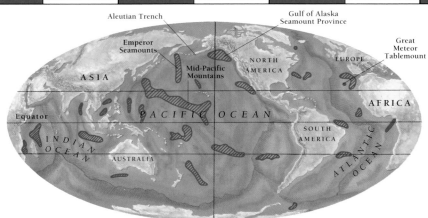

Where seamounts are found
There are hundreds of seamounts in all of the oceans, although they are most plentiful in the Pacific Ocean. The shaded areas on the map above show where groups of seamounts are found. Scientists estimate that there are more than 10,000 seamounts and guyots. The actual number may be twice as high as this. Because seamounts are similar to volcanic islands, they are found in areas where underwater volcanic activity is common.

THE EMPEROR SEAMOUNTS
Stretching northward in a vast arc across the Pacific Ocean, the Emperor Seamount Chain is one of the longest seamount ranges. The chain begins at the western tip of the Hawaiian Islands and disappears near the Aleutian Trench, nearly 3,700 miles (6,000 km) away. Scientists believe that it is a continuation of the Hawaiian chain. This is because the age of each island and seamount increases as the chain stretches northward, indicating that the entire chain formed over the same hot spot.

Age of the seamounts
The seamount closest to the Aleutian end of the chain (number one on the view below) is millions of years older than the seamount that is closest to Hawaii (number eight). The numbers correspond to those on the smaller map (below left).

Sea level

3,280 ft (1,000 m)

6,561 ft (2,000 m)

9,842 ft (3,000 m)

13,123 ft (4,000 m)

16,404 ft (5,000 m)

19,685 ft (6,000 m)

❶ ❷ ❸ ❹ ❺

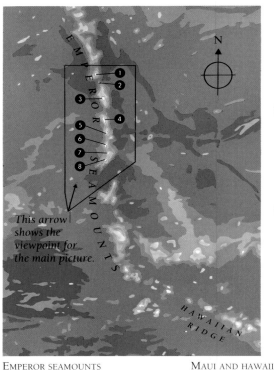

This arrow shows the viewpoint for the main picture.

Seamounts rise abruptly from the seafloor, indicating that their bases may be buried by sediment.

EMPEROR SEAMOUNTS   MAUI AND HAWAII

Sea surface

Comparative profiles of seamounts (left) and islands

Looking from above and underneath the sea
The part of the Emperor Seamount Chain in the box on the small map (left) is shown in the big picture, on the right. The height has been exaggerated to show how sharply the seamounts rise from the flat seafloor. The diagram on the lower left shows the difference in profile between the Emperor Seamounts and two of the biggest Hawaiian islands. Over millions of years, the two volcanic islands of Hawaii and Maui may erode and sink below the surface of the sea to become submerged like the seamounts.

GUYOTS

Guyots are the sunken remains of ancient islands, whose tops have been flattened by the erosive action of the waves. They are particularly common in the North Pacific, where they often form large clusters. At some time in the past, these seamounts were close to the surface of the sea. They sank as the seafloor beneath them subsided. Most are now some 3,280–6,561 ft (1,000–2,000 m) below the surface. Guyots were named after the eighteenth-century Swiss geologist Arnold Guyot.

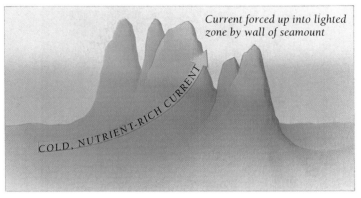

Current forced up into lighted zone by wall of seamount

COLD, NUTRIENT-RICH CURRENT

The diagram on the left shows what happens when deep-sea currents meet the submerged walls of a seamount. The current surges over the walls, or collects in eddies behind them.

Nutrient-rich waters attract feeding fish. Small fish often live in groups, because it is more difficult for a predator to catch a single fish in a large group.

TEEMING WITH LIFE

By comparison with the surrounding deep-sea floor, the upper parts of seamounts and guyots are particularly rich in marine life. This is partly because they are shallower and receive more food from the surface waters. But it is also because, due to their height, seamounts can change the flow of deep-ocean currents. The seamount may lie in the path of a current, forcing the cold, nutrient-rich waters to flow over and around the seamount. Many marine animals take advantage of the food surge and make seamounts their feeding places. Other nutrient-rich currents collect in eddies in the lee of (behind) seamounts.

Pratt Guyot
The gigantic Pratt Guyot rises nearly 8,858 ft (2,700 m) from the floor of the Gulf of Alaska, in the northern Pacific Ocean. This computer-created image shows its size and shape.

11 miles (17 km) / 31 miles (50 km) / Sea level / 3,280 ft (1,000 m)

Black coral
Antipatharians, or black corals, are related to reef-building corals. Instead of stony skeletons, however, they have skeletons of black horny material. Like most corals, they are made up of many small individuals called polyps.

Black coral / *Gorgonian coral*

FILTER FEEDERS

The currents swirling around a seamount encourage filter-feeding animals, such as the corals and sponges shown below. These creatures attach themselves to the sides of the seamount and sift food particles from the water flowing past. The currents also carry nutrients. These help phytoplankton to grow which, in turn, provide food for tiny sea animals and larger fish.

Gorgonian growth
Gorgonians, or horny corals, are sometimes found 500 ft (150 m) down on the sides of seamounts. They often grow into large fan shapes spread out across the currents. This gives these filter-feeding animals the best access to food particles in the water. The discovery of huge populations of gorgonians on several seamounts in the Emperor Chain in the 1970s caused a crash in the price of precious corals on the world market.

Sponges
Sponges attach themselves to the sides of seamounts. The outsides of their bodies are covered with many small holes called pores. Sponges take in water through these pores and filter it for food. They expel the filtered water and wastes through one or a few larger holes.

DEEP-SEA TRENCHES

DEEP-SEA TRENCHES are the deepest parts of the seabed, and the deepest points on planet Earth. They occur at the edges of two oceanic plates, or of an oceanic and a continental plate, where one plate melts back into the Earth by a process called subduction. Subduction balances out the effects of seafloor spreading (see page 37). Without it, the Earth would have increased its size by half in the last 200 million years.

The trenches are long, narrow, V-shaped seabed valleys. Some plunge to depths of 26,246–32,808 ft (8,000–10,000 m). Even 50 years ago no one imagined the oceans could reach such depths. The trenches lie 6,561–13,123 ft (2,000–4,000 m) below the rest of the seafloor. They are pitch black and freezing cold, with massive underwater pressures. Underwater earthquakes (seaquakes) and volcanic eruptions are common in deep-sea trenches because of the moving crust.

HOW TRENCHES ARE FORMED

Deep-sea trenches form when the Earth's crustal plates collide, and one is forced beneath the other. When an oceanic plate collides with a continental plate, the seabed is subducted under the land. This forms a trench and also pushes up a range of volcanic mountains on land. When two oceanic plates collide, the subducted plate melts back into the Earth.

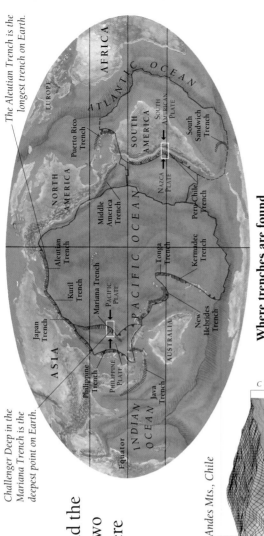

The Aleutian Trench is the longest trench on Earth.

Challenger Deep in the Mariana Trench is the deepest point on Earth.

Where trenches are found

The majority of trenches are found at the boundaries of the plates which form the Pacific Ocean seafloor. There are some smaller trenches in the Atlantic and Indian Oceans. The map above shows both the positions of the two trenches featured on these pages – the Peru-Chile Trench and the Mariana Trench – as well as the edges of their adjacent crustal plates.

This photograph of some of the unusual creatures that live around a hydrothermal vent was taken from the submersible Alvin (part of which can be seen), in an area near the Mariana Trench.

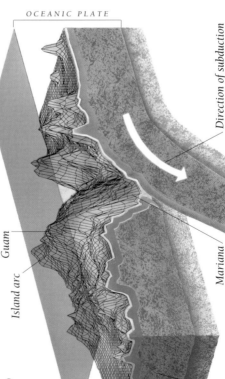

Sea anemone

Sea cucumber

Polycheate worm

Ocean and continent collide

The Andes Mountains were pushed up about 80 million years ago by subduction along the coast of Chile. The deepest point of the resulting Peru-Chile Trench is 25,050 ft (7,635 m).

CONTINENTAL PLATE

Andes Mts., Chile

Continental crust

Lithosphere (crust and upper mantle)

Subduction of oceanic plate

Peru-Chile Trench

Lithosphere

Oceanic crust

OCEANIC PLATE

LIFE IN THE HADAL ZONE

Oceanographers divide life in the sea into zones, by depth. The deep-sea trenches form the hadal zone, the deepest habitat of all. At a depth of more than 19,685 ft (6,000 m) below the surface, the amazing animals of the hadal zone have to cope with crushing pressure, darkness, and freezing water. They include sea cucumbers, anemones, crustaceans, polycheate worms, and some mollusks.

Oceanic plates collide

The Mariana Trench in the Pacific (shown in this diagram) formed when two oceanic plates collided. The subduction process also pushed up an arc of volcanic islands, including the island of Guam.

OCEANIC PLATE

Direction of subduction

Mariana Trench

Guam

Island arc

Oceanic crust

Lithosphere

OCEANIC PLATE

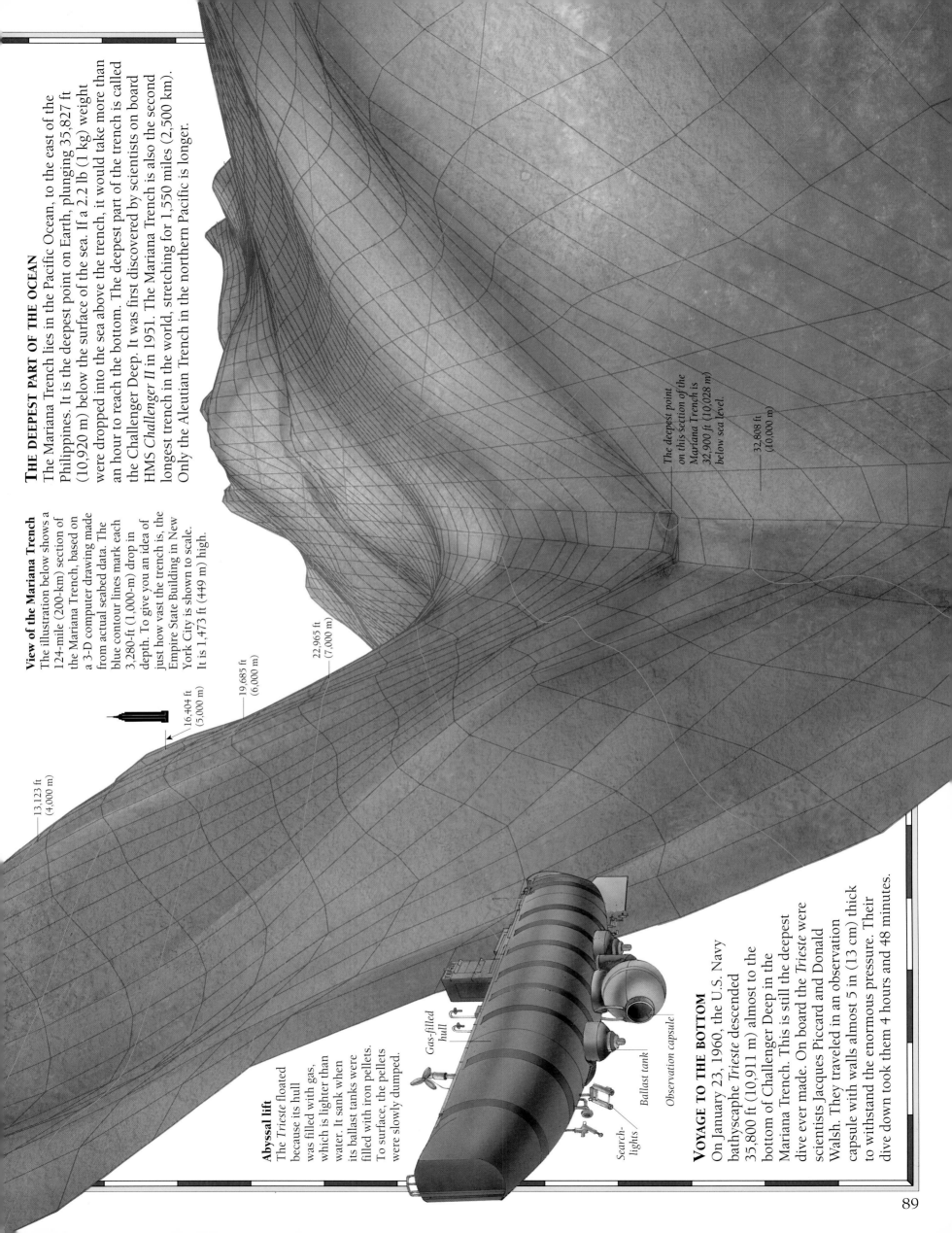

THE DEEPEST PART OF THE OCEAN

The Mariana Trench lies in the Pacific Ocean, to the east of the Philippines. It is the deepest point on Earth, plunging 35,827 ft (10,920 m) below the surface of the sea. If a 2.2 lb (1 kg) weight were dropped into the sea above the trench, it would take more than an hour to reach the bottom. The deepest part of the trench is called the Challenger Deep. It was first discovered by scientists on board HMS *Challenger II* in 1951. The Mariana Trench is also the second longest trench in the world, stretching for 1,550 miles (2,500 km). Only the Aleutian Trench in the northern Pacific is longer.

View of the Mariana Trench
The illustration below shows a 124-mile (200-km) section of the Mariana Trench, based on a 3-D computer drawing made from actual seabed data. The blue contour lines mark each 3,280-ft (1,000-m) drop in depth. To give you an idea of just how vast the trench is, the Empire State Building in New York City is shown to scale. It is 1,473 ft (449 m) high.

13,123 ft (4,000 m)

16,404 ft (5,000 m)

19,685 ft (6,000 m)

22,965 ft (7,000 m)

The deepest point on this section of the Mariana Trench is 32,900 ft (10,028 m) below sea level.

32,808 ft (10,000 m)

Abyssal lift
The *Trieste* floated because its hull was filled with gas, which is lighter than water. It sank when its ballast tanks were filled with iron pellets. To surface, the pellets were slowly dumped.

Gas-filled hull

Ballast tank

Observation capsule

Search-lights

VOYAGE TO THE BOTTOM

On January 23, 1960, the U.S. Navy bathyscaphe *Trieste* descended 35,800 ft (10,911 m) almost to the bottom of Challenger Deep in the Mariana Trench. This is still the deepest dive ever made. On board the *Trieste* were scientists Jacques Piccard and Donald Walsh. They traveled in an observation capsule with walls almost 5 in (13 cm) thick to withstand the enormous pressure. Their dive down took them 4 hours and 48 minutes.

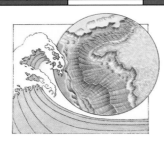

BLACK SMOKERS

SCIENTISTS INVESTIGATING volcanoes deep under the Pacific Ocean made a remarkable discovery in 1977. Hot, mineral-rich water shooting up from cracks in the seabed provides a home for huge colonies of extraordinary animals. Many of these had never been seen before. At 8,200 ft (2,500 m) below the surface, the deep sea is usually dark, deserted, and very cold. The water around these cracks, or hydrothermal vents, however, can reach temperatures of over 572°F (300°C). Sulfur, dissolved in the water, is heated by rocks in the crust below, and gushes up. This mixture is poisonous to most creatures, yet it is the only reason vent animals can survive. Clumps of bacteria use it for nourishment and they, in turn, provide food for the other creatures.

Where vents are found
Hydrothermal vents are mainly found along spreading seabed ridges. Vent sites in the Pacific Ocean include areas around the Galápagos Islands and the East Pacific Rise off Mexico. Other sites lie on the Mid-Atlantic Ridge and in the northwest Pacific Ocean.

TUBE WORM GIANTS

The most amazing members of the vent community are the giant tube worms, *Riftia*. They grow in great clusters around the vents. They have neither mouths nor digestive organs, so they cannot feed on any rare fragments of food falling from the surface. Instead, they rely on thick colonies of bacteria living inside their bodies. The worms supply hydrogen sulfide, which they extract from the sulfur-rich water around them. The bacteria use the hydrogen sulfide to make food for themselves and the worms.

A tube worm can be more than 10 ft (3 m) long – much longer than a person.

Tube worms at the Galápagos vent site, photographed from a submersible. The object on the left is a probe to measure the temperature of the gushing hot water.

The ends of the worms protrude from their tubes.

White crabs

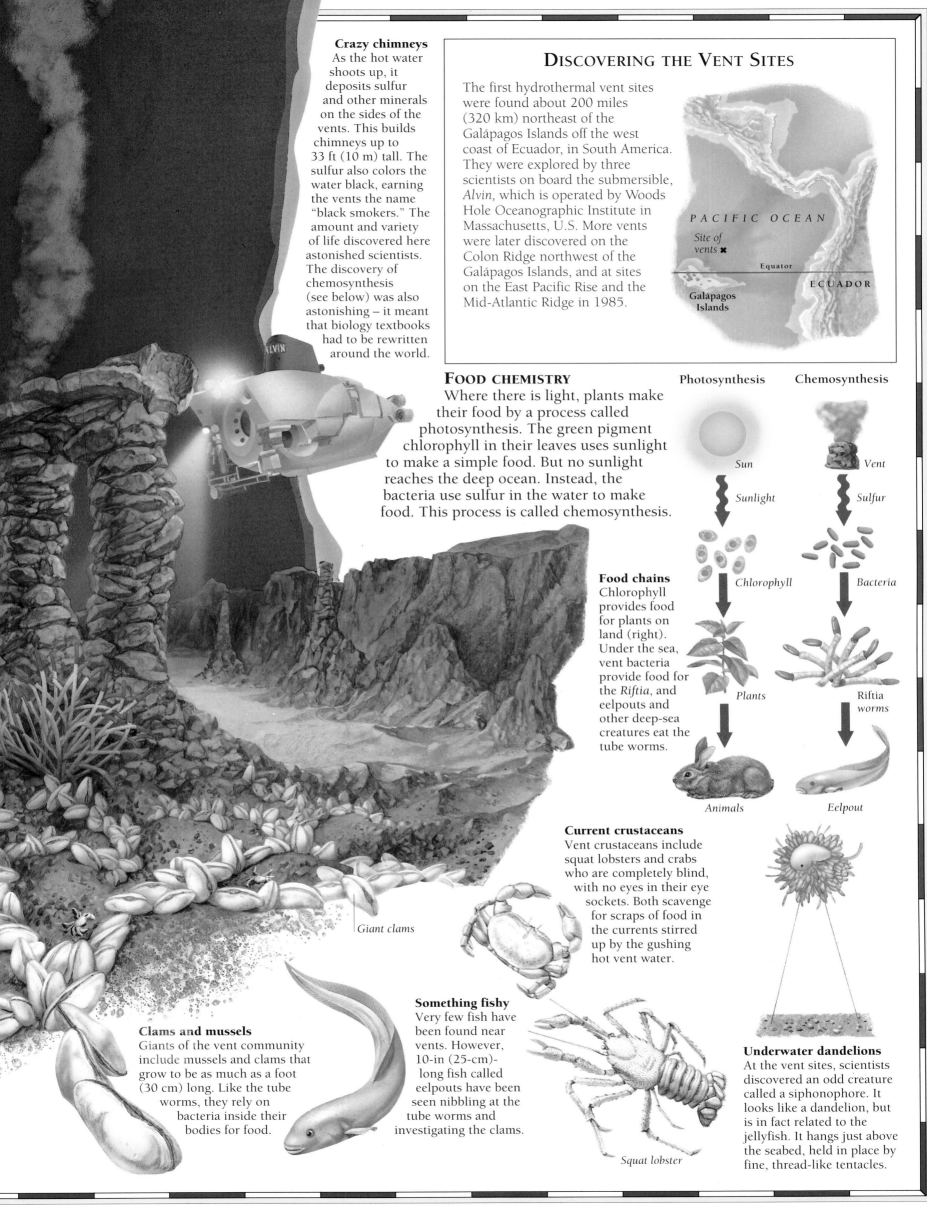

Crazy chimneys
As the hot water shoots up, it deposits sulfur and other minerals on the sides of the vents. This builds chimneys up to 33 ft (10 m) tall. The sulfur also colors the water black, earning the vents the name "black smokers." The amount and variety of life discovered here astonished scientists. The discovery of chemosynthesis (see below) was also astonishing – it meant that biology textbooks had to be rewritten around the world.

DISCOVERING THE VENT SITES

The first hydrothermal vent sites were found about 200 miles (320 km) northeast of the Galápagos Islands off the west coast of Ecuador, in South America. They were explored by three scientists on board the submersible, *Alvin,* which is operated by Woods Hole Oceanographic Institute in Massachusetts, U.S. More vents were later discovered on the Colon Ridge northwest of the Galápagos Islands, and at sites on the East Pacific Rise and the Mid-Atlantic Ridge in 1985.

PACIFIC OCEAN

Site of vents ✖

Equator

ECUADOR

Galápagos Islands

FOOD CHEMISTRY
Where there is light, plants make their food by a process called photosynthesis. The green pigment chlorophyll in their leaves uses sunlight to make a simple food. But no sunlight reaches the deep ocean. Instead, the bacteria use sulfur in the water to make food. This process is called chemosynthesis.

Photosynthesis

Chemosynthesis

Sun

Vent

Sunlight

Sulfur

Food chains
Chlorophyll provides food for plants on land (right). Under the sea, vent bacteria provide food for the *Riftia*, and eelpouts and other deep-sea creatures eat the tube worms.

Chlorophyll

Bacteria

Plants

Riftia worms

Animals

Eelpout

Giant clams

Current crustaceans
Vent crustaceans include squat lobsters and crabs who are completely blind, with no eyes in their eye sockets. Both scavenge for scraps of food in the currents stirred up by the gushing hot vent water.

Clams and mussels
Giants of the vent community include mussels and clams that grow to be as much as a foot (30 cm) long. Like the tube worms, they rely on bacteria inside their bodies for food.

Something fishy
Very few fish have been found near vents. However, 10-in (25-cm)-long fish called eelpouts have been seen nibbling at the tube worms and investigating the clams.

Underwater dandelions
At the vent sites, scientists discovered an odd creature called a siphonophore. It looks like a dandelion, but is in fact related to the jellyfish. It hangs just above the seabed, held in place by fine, thread-like tentacles.

Squat lobster

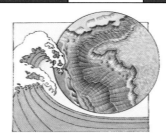

CORAL REEFS

CORAL REEFS ARE often described as underwater tropical rain forests or gardens. Like the rain forests, they are full of color and life. They swarm with brilliantly colored fish, starfish, giant clams, and sea slugs. In fact, nearly one-third of all the world's species of fish live in coral reefs. Coral reefs can cover vast areas – often thousands of square miles (kilometers) – yet they are built by tiny creatures called polyps. Most polyps grow in partnership with tiny plants called algae. For that reason, coral can grow only in warm, shallow water where there is plenty of sunlight that the algae need to make food. There have been coral reefs on Earth for more than 450 million years. Coral is formed very slowly. It takes about 20 years for a colony the size of a basketball to build up.

Reefs around the world
There are about 230,000 sq miles (600,000 sq km) of coral reefs in the world. They grow only in shallow seas, in water temperatures of 68°F (18°C) and above. Major reefs are found in the Pacific and Indian oceans.

Coral sand
The white sand commonly found in coral reefs is partly made of ground-up shells and corals. It is also produced by algae growing on the reef.

Sea level
Coral is very sensitive to changes in sea level. It can grow only in shallow water. If the sea level rises too much, it may die.

Continuous barrier
Barrier reefs form on the sea-facing side of long, narrow lagoons. They follow the contours of the coastline.

WHAT IS CORAL?
Coral is formed from the hard outer skeletons of tiny animals called polyps. Until about 200 years ago, people thought that coral polyps were plants. In fact, they are related to sea anemones and jellyfish. Most polyps are only about ¼ in (5 mm) across. Reef-building hard corals live in huge colonies. Soft corals and the closely related gorgonian, or horny, corals do not have stony outer skeletons.

A polyp expands to catch its food, using the tentacles around its mouth. The tentacles contain stinging cells to stun or kill prey.

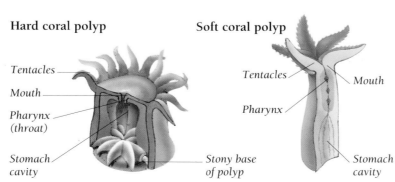

Hard coral polyp

Tentacles
Mouth
Pharynx (throat)
Stomach cavity
Stony base of polyp

Soft coral polyp

Tentacles
Mouth
Pharynx
Stomach cavity

A LIVING STONE
The stony, cuplike casings built by hard coral polyps protect their soft bodies. The cups are made from chemicals that the polyp extracts from seawater. Only the top surface of the reef is alive. The tiny, one-celled algae that live inside the polyps' bodies help them secrete limestone. This cements the reef together.

DIFFERENT KINDS OF CORAL REEFS

In 1842, the British naturalist Charles Darwin described the types of coral reefs. His definitions are still used today. There are three main types of reef. Fringing reefs grow in shallow water along the shore on rocky coastlines. Barrier reefs also grow along the shore, but they are separated from it by lagoons (shallow saltwater lakes) or straits. Atoll islands begin as reefs growing on the slopes of volcanoes. The volcanoes then sink, leaving the atoll behind. Atolls surround deeper lagoons.

Seaward edge
On the reef's seaward edge, the waves throw up debris, which forms ridges full of pools and holes. These are home to thousands of fish.

AUSTRALIA'S GREAT BARRIER REEF

The Great Barrier Reef stretches for 1,260 miles (2,028 km) off the coast of Queensland in northeastern Australia. It is the world's largest coral reef and the biggest structure ever made by living things. It covers an area of more than 80,000 sq miles (207,000 sq km) – twice as big as Iceland. The reef is not a single barrier, but consists of 210 separate reefs. The Great Barrier Reef began to grow about 18 million years ago. Recently, the reef has been threatened with destruction by tourism and pollution. In 1983, it was declared a marine park. Special zones are set aside for recreation, fishing, and snorkeling.

The Dingo Reef complex is situated in the south-central part of the Great Barrier Reef.

FANTASTIC FORMATIONS

Corals grow in an amazing variety of beautiful shapes and patterns. Some look like miniature trees. Others resemble mushrooms, dinner plates, or feathers. Reef-building coral grows in layers. The way a coral grows depends on its species, how it copes with the battering of waves, and how much it has to compete with its neighbors for space and sunlight. The color of coral is only "skin-deep." It is produced by the top, living layer of coral. The dead coral beneath is white.

Gorgonian fan coral
Orange-yellow fan coral often grows in deeper water in the Atlantic and Pacific oceans.

Gorgonian coral
This coral has a flexible, horny skeleton, not a rigid casing. It often grows in thickets under ledges or on the roofs of caves in the reef.

Staghorn coral
This hardy branching coral can grow again from just a tiny broken piece. Its branches allow it to grow upward toward the sunlight.

Brain coral
Brain coral gets its name because it looks like a human brain. Its polyps grow in ridges. This coral can grow to more than 6 ft 6 in (2 m) across.

Daisy coral
Many corals look like exotic flowers. Daisy corals are hard corals with brilliant colors.

How branching coral grows

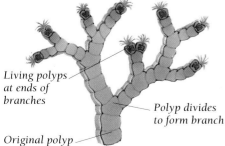

Living polyps at ends of branches

Polyp divides to form branch

Original polyp

How mound coral grows

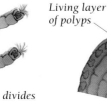

Living layer of polyps

Original polyp

MARINE LIFE OF REEFS

CORAL REEFS TEEM with wildlife. Every nook and cranny is used as a hiding place or shelter. Fish dart among the branches of coral and hide in small caves. Predators, such as moray eels, lurk in larger caves, on the lookout for passing prey.

The reefs are successful habitats because every available source of nourishment is used and recycled through a series of food chains. Each chain begins with microscopic plants called algae. Some float free in the water, while others live in the bodies of the corals. Fish and starfish graze on the coral itself. In turn, these creatures are preyed on by reef hunters, such as barracudas and sharks.

A coral reef is a finely balanced habitat, and a fragile one. All over the world, reefs are under threat from divers, shell and coral collectors, companies exploring for oil and other minerals, and from pollution.

CREATURES OF THE CORAL REEF

The warm, sunny waters of a reef are home to a huge variety of creatures, who present a dazzling display of colors, shapes, and sizes. The richest reefs contain thousands of species of fish and coral, together with starfish, giant clams, and sea slugs. In the densely packed reef, the brilliant colors of creatures such as the butterfly fish act as identity tags. They enable the fish to recognize their own species among the crowd.

Lionfish (below)
The lionfish's bright colors act as a warning. Hidden behind its fins, the fish has spines that can inject a deadly poison into an attacker.

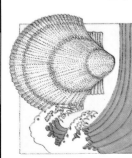

Reef shark
Sleek reef sharks patrol the reef edge after dark. They can sense the movements made by sick or injured fish and swim straight in for the kill.

Sea turtle
At breeding time, female sea turtles leave the water and lay their eggs on the sandy beaches of coral islands. The baby turtles have a dangerous journey to the sea. Many are eaten by crabs and seagulls.

Manta ray
Manta rays swim by flapping their huge wings. Some have wingspans of up to 20 ft (6 m). They sometimes make spectacular leaps out of the water.

Black noddy
These seabirds dip to the surface to feed. They also catch flying fish in midair.

Frigate bird
Frigate birds are pirates, stealing fish from other seabirds. The male has an unusual courtship display. He inflates his bright-red throat pouch like a balloon to attract a mate.

Lion's mane jellyfish
The lion's mane jellyfish gets its name from its thick manelike mass of tentacles and its tawny color. The stinging tentacles may be up to 33 ft (10 m) long.

Coral trout
The coral trout lurks among the coral, looking half asleep. Until, that is, a small fish strays from its school. Then the trout lunges and gobbles it up.

Sea snake (below)
There are about 50 species of sea snake in the tropical oceans. All of them are venomous and use poison to kill their prey. Among their adaptations for life in the sea are flattened tails for swimming.

Barracuda
Barracudas are fierce hunters of the coral reef, often more feared than sharks. They have jaws full of razor-sharp teeth, and powerful streamlined bodies for swimming fast after prey. They often hunt in large schools.

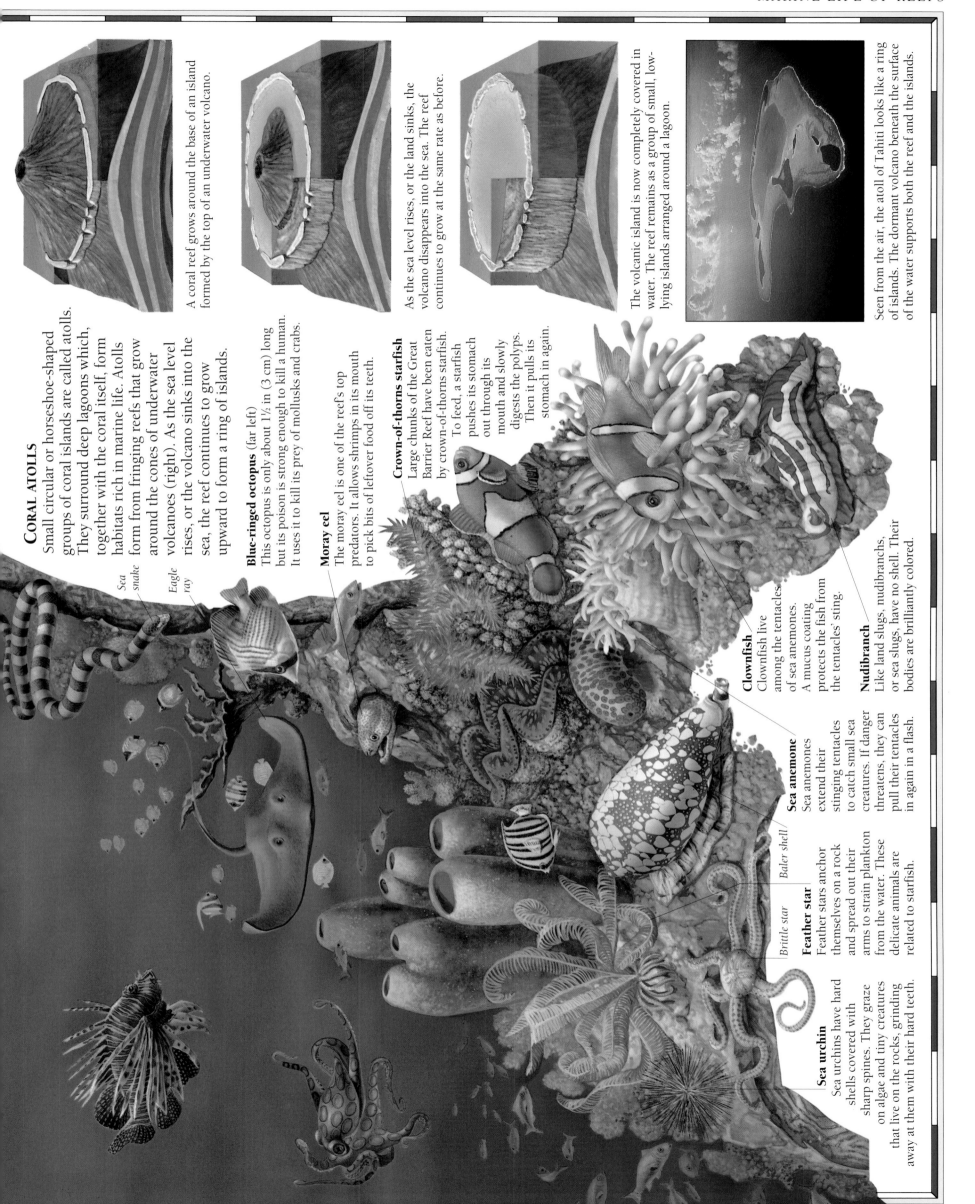

A coral reef grows around the base of an island formed by the top of an underwater volcano.

As the sea level rises, or the land sinks, the volcano disappears into the sea. The reef continues to grow at the same rate as before.

The volcanic island is now completely covered in water. The reef remains as a group of small, low-lying islands arranged around a lagoon.

Seen from the air, the atoll of Tahiti looks like a ring of islands. The dormant volcano beneath the surface of the water supports both the reef and the islands.

CORAL ATOLLS

Small circular or horseshoe-shaped groups of coral islands are called atolls. They surround deep lagoons which, together with the coral itself, form habitats rich in marine life. Atolls form from fringing reefs that grow around the cones of underwater volcanoes (right). As the sea level rises, or the volcano sinks into the sea, the reef continues to grow upward to form a ring of islands.

Blue-ringed octopus (far left)
This octopus is only about 1½ in (3 cm) long but its poison is strong enough to kill a human. It uses it to kill its prey of mollusks and crabs.

Moray eel
The moray eel is one of the reef's top predators. It allows shrimps in its mouth to pick bits of leftover food off its teeth.

Crown-of-thorns starfish
Large chunks of the Great Barrier Reef have been eaten by crown-of-thorns starfish. To feed, a starfish pushes its stomach out through its mouth and slowly digests the polyps. Then it pulls its stomach in again.

Clownfish
Clownfish live among the tentacles of sea anemones. A mucus coating protects the fish from the tentacles' sting.

Nudibranch
Like land slugs, nudibranchs, or sea slugs, have no shell. Their bodies are brilliantly colored.

Sea anemone
Sea anemones extend their stinging tentacles to catch small sea creatures. If danger threatens, they can pull their tentacles in again in a flash.

Feather star
Feather stars anchor themselves on a rock and spread out their arms to strain plankton from the water. These delicate animals are related to starfish.

Sea urchin
Sea urchins have hard shells covered with sharp spines. They graze on algae and tiny creatures that live on the rocks, grinding away at them with their hard teeth.

Sea snake

Eagle ray

Brittle star

Baler shell

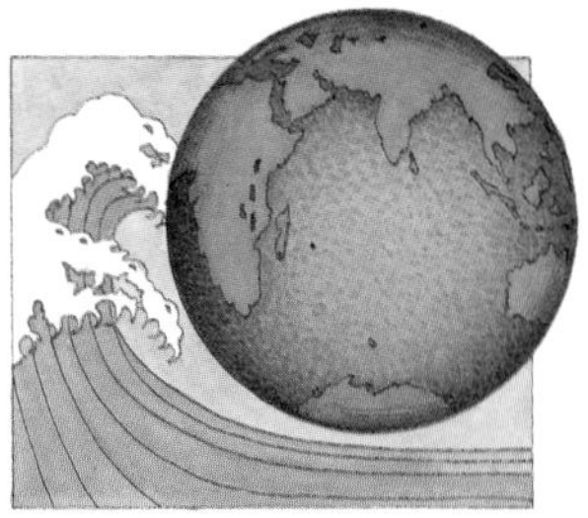

THE INDIAN OCEAN

THE INDIAN OCEAN IS THE THIRD largest of the world's oceans. It covers an area of some 28,350,000 sq miles (73,426,000 sq km), about a fifth of the total area covered by the oceans. It has an average depth of 12,762 ft (3,890 m). Its deepest point is at 24,441 ft (7,450 m) in the Java Trench. The Indian Ocean formed about 140 million years ago, when the ancient continent of Gondwanaland (see page 9) began to break up, separating India and Antarctica from Africa.

One of the features that distinguishes the Indian Ocean from the other oceans is the pattern of its currents. In the other oceans, the currents follow the same path all year. In the northern Indian Ocean, however, they change course twice a year. Blown by the monsoon winds, they flow toward Africa in winter, then in the opposite direction toward India in summer. The Indian Ocean is also unique because it contains the saltiest sea (the Red Sea) and the warmest sea (the Persian Gulf) on Earth.

THE STORY OF THE COELACANTH

Fossil evidence convinced many scientists that a fish called the coelacanth became extinct about 60 million years ago. In 1938, however, they were amazed when South African fishermen caught a living coelacanth in the Indian Ocean. In fact, the fish was well known to people living on the Comoros Islands, who used its rough scales as sandpaper. This bulky, bluish gray fish spends its time drifting just above the ocean floor. Unlike most fish, which lay eggs, the coelacanth gives birth to live young.

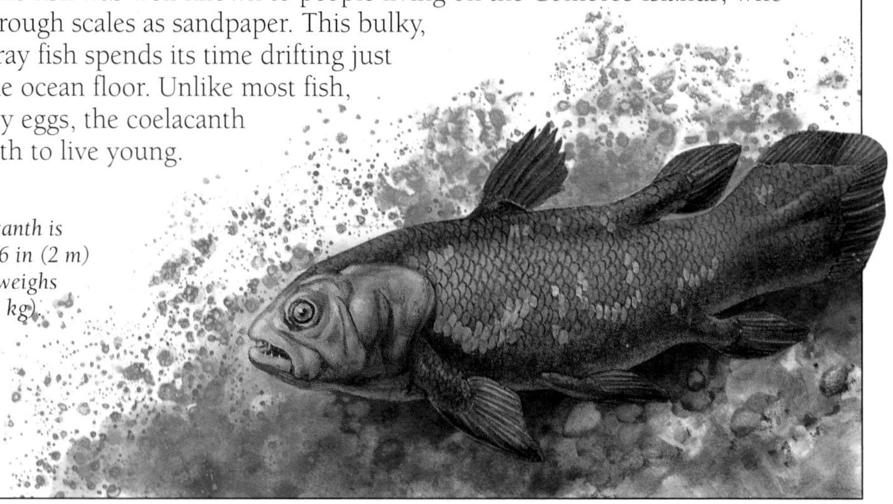

The coelacanth is about 6 ft 6 in (2 m) long, and weighs 126 lb (57 kg).

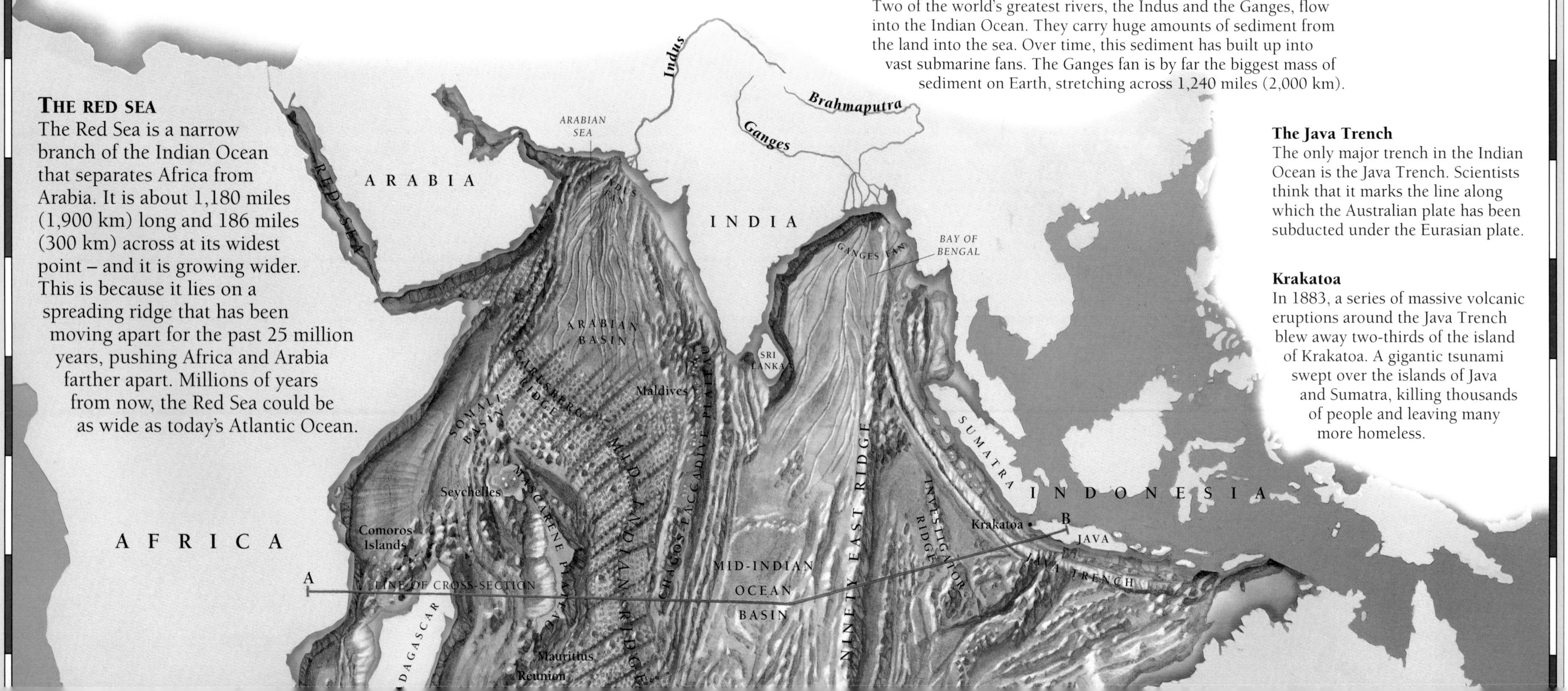
ARABIA
RED SEA
ARABIAN SEA
Indus
INDUS FAN
Brahmaputra
Ganges
INDIA
BAY OF BENGAL
GANGES FAN
SRI LANKA
ARABIAN BASIN
CARLSBERG RIDGE
SOMALI BASIN
Maldives
CHAGOS-LACCADIVE PLATEAU
MID-INDIAN RIDGE
Seychelles
MASCARENE PLATEAU
Comoros Islands
AFRICA
A
LINE OF CROSS-SECTION
MADAGASCAR
Mauritius
Réunion
MID-INDIAN OCEAN BASIN
NINETY EAST RIDGE
INVESTIGATOR RIDGE
SUMATRA
INDONESIA
Krakatoa
B
JAVA
JAVA TRENCH

THE RED SEA
The Red Sea is a narrow branch of the Indian Ocean that separates Africa from Arabia. It is about 1,180 miles (1,900 km) long and 186 miles (300 km) across at its widest point – and it is growing wider. This is because it lies on a spreading ridge that has been moving apart for the past 25 million years, pushing Africa and Arabia farther apart. Millions of years from now, the Red Sea could be as wide as today's Atlantic Ocean.

The Ganges and Indus fans
Two of the world's greatest rivers, the Indus and the Ganges, flow into the Indian Ocean. They carry huge amounts of sediment from the land into the sea. Over time, this sediment has built up into vast submarine fans. The Ganges fan is by far the biggest mass of sediment on Earth, stretching across 1,240 miles (2,000 km).

The Java Trench
The only major trench in the Indian Ocean is the Java Trench. Scientists think that it marks the line along which the Australian plate has been subducted under the Eurasian plate.

Krakatoa
In 1883, a series of massive volcanic eruptions around the Java Trench blew away two-thirds of the island of Krakatoa. A gigantic tsunami swept over the islands of Java and Sumatra, killing thousands of people and leaving many more homeless.

AUSTRALIA

SOUTHEAST INDIAN RIDGE

KERGUELEN PLATEAU

Kerguelen

SOUTHWEST INDIAN RIDGE

AGULHAS BASIN

Island of Mahé, Seychelles

EXOTIC ISLANDS

The Indian Ocean is littered with clusters of coral islands. Among the best known are the Seychelles and the Maldives. The Maldive Islands lie to the southwest of Sri Lanka and consist of more than a thousand islands, three-quarters of which are uninhabited. The coral reefs that fringe the islands teem with brightly colored clownfish and damselfish, sea anemones, and prowling reef sharks.

THE SEABED IN PROFILE

The cross-section on the right follows the line A–B on the map above, from the east coast of Africa to the west coast of Java. The section shows a profile of the major plateaus, ridges, and basins of the Indian Ocean seabed. Its plateaus are unusually shallow. They may be the remains of small microcontinents, stranded and left to subside when the large continents drifted apart.

THE MID-OCEAN RIDGE SYSTEM

The most striking feature of the Indian Ocean seabed is the huge, upside-down-Y-shaped mid-ocean ridge. One arm of the Y runs around Africa and joins the Mid-Atlantic Ridge. The other runs around the south of Australia to meet the East Pacific Rise. The ridge runs north through the Indian Ocean, then west toward the Red Sea, where it is known as the Carlsberg Ridge.

Huge seagrass beds, like these off the west coast of Australia, provide an ample food supply for sea turtles, sea snakes, and dugongs. They also help to protect the coastline from erosion.

Dugong

Mascarene Plateau

The rocks in this plateau point to its origins as a microcontinent. They are not volcanic, like most rocks found in ocean basins. Instead, they are similar to those rocks that form the continents.

Mid-Indian Ocean Basin

The mid-ocean ridges divide the ocean bed into several basins. The remote Mid-Indian Ocean Basin contains smooth, almost level plains. These are among the flattest places on Earth.

Ninety East Ridge

The Ninety East Ridge is some 1,700 miles (2,735 km) long. Deep-sea drilling has shown that the ridge was once close to the surface of the sea but sank as the seafloor spread.

INDIAN OCEAN LIFE

The warm tropical waters of the Indian Ocean provide the ideal environment for a rich variety of marine life. Some 4,000 species of fish live near the shores, many of these unique to the Indian Ocean. Farther out to sea, the fish include flying fish, sunfish, marlin, and tuna. There are also rich mangrove forests and seagrass beds. Large, rare sea mammals, called dugongs, browse among the seagrass meadows, particularly off the west coast of Australia.

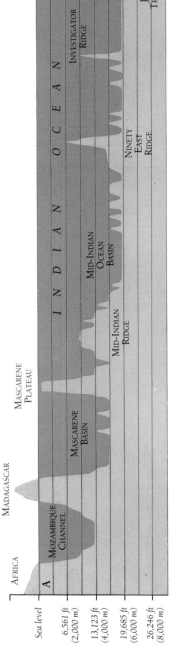

	JAVA	B
		INVESTIGATOR RIDGE
		MID-INDIAN OCEAN BASIN
MASCARENE PLATEAU		NINETY EAST RIDGE
MADAGASCAR	MASCARENE BASIN	MID-INDIAN RIDGE
AFRICA	MOZAMBIQUE CHANNEL	JAVA TRENCH
A		INDIAN OCEAN

Sea level	
6,561 ft (2,000 m)	
13,123 ft (4,000 m)	
19,685 ft (6,000 m)	
26,246 ft (8,000 m)	

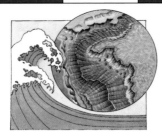

MID-OCEAN RIDGES

THE LONGEST MOUNTAIN RANGE on Earth is submerged deep beneath the sea. It is formed by the mid-ocean ridges, interconnected chains of mountains that twist and branch through each of the world's oceans. Together, they span a distance of some 4,038 miles (6,500 km). These mountain ranges are formed by lava that oozes up from the seabed, cools, and then hardens. Some break the surface to form islands, such as Iceland. The longest individual ridge is the Mid-Atlantic Ridge. It runs the entire length of the Atlantic Ocean, splitting it in two.

Mid-ocean ridges are centers of seafloor spreading, a process by which new ocean crust is made. Seafloor spreading and subduction (see pages 8-9) are the two forces responsible for changing the size and shape of the oceans – something that is happening all the time. New crust is made at the ridges, and swallowed up (subducted) at the deep-sea trenches.

Where mid-ocean ridges are found
The map below shows the "centers" of the mid-ocean ridges and the areas of fracture zones (see next page) around them. It also shows the location of the three ridge sections featured on these pages – the Carlsberg Ridge in the Indian Ocean, the East Pacific Rise in the Pacific, and the Mid-Atlantic Ridge in the Atlantic.

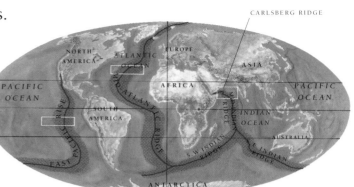

THE CARLSBERG RIDGE
A mid-ocean ridge runs through the Indian Ocean in the shape of a huge, upside-down letter Y. One arm goes around southern Africa and joins the Mid-Atlantic Ridge. The second arm bends around Australia. The central branch forms the Carlsberg Ridge in the northern part of the ocean. This ridge swings west to join up with the Red Sea. The main picture shows this part of the Carlsberg Ridge.

Ocean ridges span huge widths, from 310–3,100 miles (500–5,000 km). All the ridges put together cover about 20 percent of the Earth's surface.

Millions of lumps of pillow lava like the ones above pile up alongside the mid-ocean ridges.

PILLOW LAVA
The rock most commonly found in the crust of the seafloor is a type of lava called basalt. It forms ridges and seamounts and lies underneath the sediment-covered abyssal plains. When basalt erupts underwater and cools quickly, it forms large, round, pillow-shaped lumps, hence its name.

The age of the ocean floor
Although no part of the seafloor is more than 200 million years old, it is youngest at the mid-ocean ridges. The age of the seafloor on either side of the ridge increases as the distance from the ridge increases.

SEAFLOOR SPREADING

At the mid-ocean ridges, hot, molten lava oozes up at the boundary of two plates of crust. The lava cools and solidifies to form new ocean crust. As it does so, it pushes the older crust away to either side of the ridge. This process is known as seafloor spreading. New ocean crust is being made all the time. Over millions of years, it has been layered and pushed up to form the mountains of the mid-ocean ridges. With all this crust being made, you might expect the Earth to get bigger each year. But it does not, because ocean crust is constantly being destroyed at subduction zones, to balance things out.

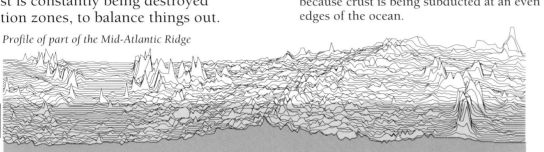

This profile of part of the East Pacific Rise shows the gentle slopes formed by runny lava.

Sea level
6,561 ft (2,000 m)
13,123 ft (4,000 m)

Fast-spreading ridges

Ridges usually spread equally on either side, but some spread more quickly than others. The East Pacific Rise spreads about 5–6 in (12–16 cm) a year, one of the fastest spreading rates of any ridge. But the Pacific Ocean is actually getting smaller, not bigger. This is because crust is being subducted at an even faster rate along the edges of the ocean.

Profile of part of the Mid-Atlantic Ridge

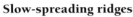

Sea level
7,800 ft (2,400 m)
15,700 ft (4,800 m)

Slow-spreading ridges

The Carlsberg Ridge and the Mid-Atlantic Ridge spread at a much slower rate than the East Pacific Rise, at a speed of less than an inch (about 2 cm) a year. But over many years this makes quite a difference – when Christopher Columbus sailed across the Atlantic in 1492, the ocean was some 65 ft (20 m) narrower than it is today. The Mid-Atlantic Ridge is marked by a steep valley that runs down its center.

Slow-spreading ridges are much steeper and more jagged than those that spread quickly. The crust is also much thicker.

Fast-spreading ridges are usually quite low-lying. The runny lava builds a thinner crust than that found at slow-spreading ridges.

Transform fault

Fracture zone

PLATE A
PLATE B
Ocean ridge
PLATE A
PLATE B
Ocean ridge

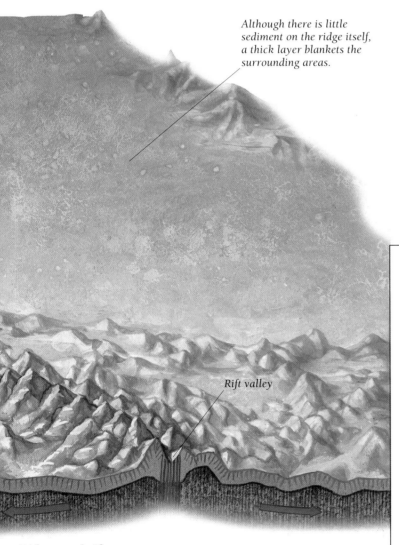

Although there is little sediment on the ridge itself, a thick layer blankets the surrounding areas.

Rift valley

TRANSFORM FAULTS AND FRACTURE ZONES

As the mid-ocean ridges spread out, they cause collisions between the plates of the Earth's crust. Some collisions are head-on. Others occur at an angle, as the plates try to slide and scrape past rather than over each other. This slipping and sliding causes deep cracks, called transform faults and fracture zones, to appear in the ocean crust. Transform faults usually run at right angles to the center line (axis) of the ridge. Earthquakes are commonplace along them. Fracture zones are the remains of old, inactive transform faults.

THE SAN ANDREAS FAULT

The San Andreas Fault in California is a good example of a transform fault. It lies at an angle to an ocean ridge and forms the boundary where two plates are trying to slide past each other. In this case, the Pacific Plate is moving northwestward past the North American Plate. The movement of the plates triggers off frequent earthquakes. In 1906, the city of San Francisco was hit and largely destroyed by a particularly violent earthquake. In 1989, another terrible earthquake shook the city. No one knows when the next one will strike.

Box shows location of San Andreas Fault

NORTH AMERICA

NORTH AMERICAN PLATE

PACIFIC PLATE

Huge rock cracks mark the fault line, which is clearly visible from the air.

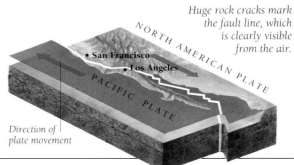

NORTH AMERICAN PLATE
San Francisco
Los Angeles
PACIFIC PLATE

Direction of plate movement

Ridges and rifts

The lava rising underneath a ridge is so hot that it melts some of the crust above it. This molten mass pushes upward, helping to open a deep crack called a rift along the middle of the ridge. Rifts run down the center of all mid-ocean ridges, marking the line of active seafloor spreading.

THE ARCTIC OCEAN

THE SMALLEST AND SHALLOWEST of the world's
oceans is the Arctic Ocean. It covers an area of
about 5,440,000 sq miles (14,089,600 sq km) and
has an average depth of 4,265 ft (1,300 m), with a maximum depth
of 17,880 ft (5,450 m) on the Pole Abyssal Plain. The Arctic Ocean
is the only ocean to be almost entirely surrounded by land – Europe,
Asia, Greenland, and North America. For most of the year, and
particularly in the freezing winter months, its waters are covered by
a thick sheet of ice. The North Pole, therefore, lies in the middle of
a raft of ice, not on top of solid land. The ice cover has long been a
challenge to ships. As a result, comparatively little is known about
the area's oceanography. Despite its harsh conditions, people, such
as the Inuit in Greenland, have lived
around the edges of the Arctic
Ocean for centuries.

The continental shelf
The Arctic Ocean has unusually wide areas
of continental shelf. They lie under about a
third of the whole ocean. Off the coasts of
Greenland and North America the shelf is
50–124 miles (80–200 km) wide – about
average. But to the north of Asia, where the
shelf reaches its widest point, it is 994 miles
(1,600 km) wide.

The Arctic Mid-Ocean Ridge
One of the major features of the Arctic
seafloor is the Arctic Mid-Ocean Ridge.
It is the northernmost extension of the
Mid-Atlantic Ridge, located on the
Asian side of the Pole Abyssal Plain,
the deepest part of the ocean. It is one
of three major ridges in the Arctic, and
an active site of seafloor spreading.

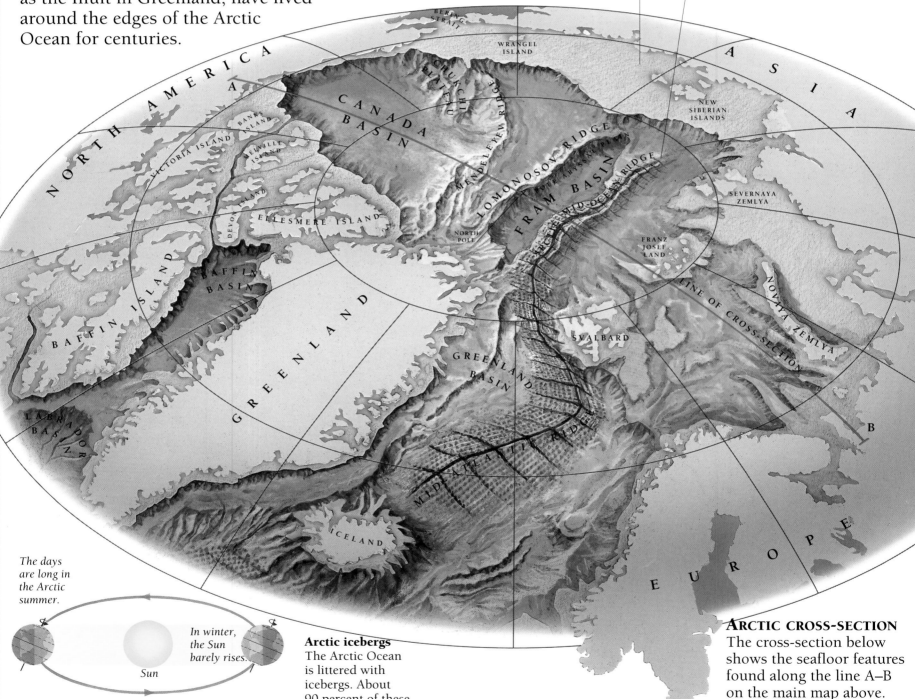

*The days
are long in
the Arctic
summer.*

*In winter,
the Sun
barely rises.*

Sun

The coldness of the Poles
At the Poles, the Sun's rays hit the Earth at
a low angle. Their heat has to spread over a
much larger area than it would at the Equator.
Depending on the season, one or the other
pole may be tilted away from the Sun, and can
remain dark for months. Parts of the Arctic
spend January and February in total darkness.

Arctic icebergs
The Arctic Ocean
is littered with
icebergs. About
90 percent of these
have broken off
the glaciers on the
coasts of Greenland.
Greenland itself
lies under a huge ice
cap, up to 1.8 miles
(3 km) thick
in some places.

ARCTIC CROSS-SECTION
The cross-section below
shows the seafloor features
found along the line A–B
on the main map above.

NORTH AMERICA		FRAM BASIN		FRANZ JOSEF LAND	ASIA/ EUROPE
	CANADA BASIN		NANSEN BASIN		
				BARENTS SEA (continental shelf below)	
		LOMONOSOV RIDGE	ARCTIC MID-OCEAN RIDGE		

Sea level

A

13,123 ft
(4,000 m)

26,246 ft
(8,000 m)

B

This map shows
the farthest extent
of pack ice. About half
the ice melts in summer.

Polar ice (on the right)
is usually flat, with
raised edges. When the
ice begins to thaw in
summer, the water
gnaws away at the
underside of the
edges. This creates
the ragged shapes
and deep cracks
shown here.

THE FROZEN SEA

The ice covering the Arctic Ocean is
called sea ice, because it forms from
frozen seawater. There are three
types of sea ice: polar ice, pack ice,
and fast ice. Most of the ocean is
covered in polar ice, which can be
up to 164 ft (50 m) thick but melts
to 6 ft 6 in (2 m) in summer. Pack
ice forms around the edges of the
ocean. Its maximum thickness is
6 ft 6 in (2 m). In winter, fast ice
forms between the shore and the
pack ice. It is called "fast" because
it is attached firmly (or fast) to the
shore. At its farthest extent, pack
ice covers about 451,740 sq miles
(11,700,000 sq km) of the ocean.

Arctic pack ice is broken and crushed
together again by the endless movement of
the water. This can result in fantastic ice
formations such as those shown above.

Nansen
designed the
Fram (right)
to drift
with the ice
without being
crushed by it.

EXPLORING THE ARCTIC

In 1893, Norwegian scientist Fridtjof
Nansen led an expedition to investigate
claims that there was a solid continent
of land at the Arctic. They took
provisions to last five years. It was a
wise precaution – their ship, the Fram,
soon found itself frozen firmly into the
ice near the New Siberian Islands. The
ship drifted with the ice for three years,
covering more than 994 miles (1,600
km) before breaking free. In 1958, a
submarine, the USS Nautilus, traveled
right under the ice cap, finally proving
that there is no Arctic continent.

ARCTIC WILDLIFE

There is little wildlife in the middle of the Arctic Ocean, but
around the edges it's a different story, especially in the summer
when the ice melts. Then the algae that live in and under the
sea ice bloom, providing food for fish such as the Arctic cod.
The fish, in turn, are eaten by seabirds, seals, and some
whales. Some animals, such as polar bears, are
permanent residents. Others, such as blue
whales, visit the Arctic in summer
to feed and breed.

Map of migration route of Arctic tern

Arctic tern
This well-traveled
bird makes the longest
migration of any animal. It breeds in the
Arctic during the brief summer. When winter
comes, it flies to the opposite pole, to take
advantage of summer in the Antarctic. Then
during the Antarctic winter, it flies back to
the Arctic – a round trip of more than
25,000 miles (40,000 km) each year.

Walrus
Walruses gather in huge herds off the Arctic coast to
breed. The males are enormous, with bristly whiskers
and tusks up to 3 ft 3 in (1 m) long. They use these
for self-defence, to root out shellfish, and to haul
themselves out of the sea onto land.
Walruses are insulated from the icy
cold by a layer of blubber just
beneath their tough skin.

Polar bear
Roaming across
the ice and snow in search of its
prey, the polar bear lives a
nomadic life.

A fully grown male
narwhal may be
20 ft (6 m) long,
without the tusk.

Beluga whales can swim
under the pack ice. If
trapped, they sometimes
break through by ramming
their heads against the ice.

Narwhal
This small whale lives in groups. A male narwhal
(above) has a long, spiral tusk – actually a twisted,
overgrown tooth – which may grow up to 8 ft 10 in (2.7 m)
long. Although they catch their food underwater, narwhals,
like all sea mammals, must surface for air. Once at the surface,
the male can rest by laying his tusk on the edge of the ice.

Beluga whale
Adult beluga whales are
pure white in color. They
swim in small herds, hunting for
fish. These beautiful creatures are
nicknamed "sea parrots" because they
make so many chirping, clicking, and
whistling noises. Unlike other whales,
they can turn their necks to look around them.

THE ANTARCTIC

AT THE OTHER END of the world from the Arctic lies the frozen continent of Antarctica, covered by a vast ice cap and surrounded by the freezing seas of the Antarctic Ocean. The Antarctic Ocean, which includes all the waters lying south of latitude 55°S, is the fourth largest of the world's oceans, covering an area of some 13,500,000 sq miles (35,000,000 sq km). In winter, more than half the Antarctic Ocean is covered with ice and littered with icebergs, which break off from the ice shelves at the edges of the continental ice cap. Even at the height of summer, Antarctica is fringed with sea ice. Unlike the Arctic, Antarctica is a continent of solid land. It has the coldest, windiest climate on Earth. Average winter temperatures along the coast are a bitter -22°F (-30°C); the temperature only rises above freezing in the brief southern summer, from December to March. Winds can reach more than 190 mph (300 km/h).

Pack ice in October

Pack ice in March

This map shows the seasonal extent of the pack ice ringing Antarctica.

LAND UNDER THE ICE

The outline on the map of Antarctica shows the edge of the ice cap that covers the land, not the land itself. The illustration below shows what the continent would look like if the ice cap were to be pulled away. The massive weight of the ice pushes much of the land below sea level, although the peaks of the Transantarctic Mountains break through the ice.

The edge of the ice forms the "coastline" in many areas.

New sea ice forms in flat, round pieces called "pancake ice." A "pancake" may be up to 10 ft (3 m) in diameter.

THE DOME OF ICE

The vast sheet of ice that covers all but about five percent of the Antarctic continent is one and a half times the size of the US and up to 9,842 ft (3,000 m) thick. The ice cap, formed from frozen snow, has taken tens of thousands of years to accumulate, and contains an amazing 90 percent of all the ice on Earth. Without the weight of the ice, Antarctica would rise by 656-984 ft (200-300 m).

ANTARCTIC OCEAN CROSS-SECTION

The cross-section above shows a profile of some of the features on the Antarctic Ocean seafloor. It is taken along the line A–B on the main illustration.

ANTARCTIC WILDLIFE

The frozen wastes of Antarctica are largely deserted, but the Antarctic Ocean teems with life. This is made possible by the vast amount of plant plankton that grows in the icy sea in spring. It begins a food chain that links together krill, fish, seals, whales, and penguins. All of these have adapted to life in the world's freezer. Many Antarctic fish, such as plunderfish and other icefish, have a natural antifreeze in their blood.

Icefish

Marble plunderfish

Krill

Krill are tiny shrimplike creatures, about 1½ in (4 cm) long. Despite their size, krill are the primary food source for a great number of species, including Antarctic whales, seals, squid, fish, and penguins. In summer, they form huge swarms, which appear as giant red patches on the ocean.

Each gulp of water is filtered for krill, then squeezed out.

Blue whale

In summer, a blue whale may eat up to 4.1 tons (4 tonnes) of krill a day. It filters seawater through baleen, the fringed plates hanging from the sides of its mouth. Blue whales are the largest animals alive today, weighing up to 132 tons (130 tonnes). Other Antarctic Ocean whales include humpback, sperm, and killer whales.

The South Sandwich Islands were built by volcanoes. Some of the volcanoes are still active.

Ocean basins
Beyond the continental shelf around Antarctica is a ring of deep ocean basins, which are divided to correspond with the three neighboring oceans.

Ice shelves, floating slabs of thick land ice, border the edges of the ice cap. The gigantic Ross Ice Shelf is about twice the size of France.

The Antarctic's continental shelf is narrower than those of most continents. It is also much deeper, perhaps due to the massive weight of the ice cap.

Adélie penguins (right) live and breed in huge colonies on the edges of the pack ice.

Penguins
Although penguins cannot fly through the air, they move through water as if they are flying. They have thick feathers and a layer of blubber under their skins to keep them warm. Emperor penguins are the biggest and heaviest penguins. They are also among the hardiest. They need to be – they breed on the ice in the middle of the winter.

Crabeater seal

Emperor penguin

Adélie penguin

King penguin

Seals
The Antarctic is home to a variety of seals. They include the Weddell seal, the most southerly living mammal, and the crabeater seal, the most abundant seal in the world. About 15 million crabeater seals live along and around the coasts of Antarctica. They feed almost solely on krill, straining them from the water through specially adapted teeth.

ANTARCTIC CURRENT
The East Wind Drift current flows counterclockwise around Antarctica. To its north, the Antarctic Circumpolar Current flows clockwise, carrying more water than any other ocean current – enough to fill the Great Lakes in two days. This mighty current eventually sweeps the freezing Antarctic waters all the way to the deep basins of the southern Atlantic, Pacific, and Indian oceans.

WINDS AND WAVES

THE WATER IN THE OCEANS and the air in the atmosphere are closely linked. Wind is moving air, caused by differences in temperature and pressure around the Earth. The Sun's heat drives the winds, which, in turn, affect the surface of the sea. Surface currents (see page 46) are powered by the wind. It is the wind, too, that creates waves, the ripples of water that flow through the sea and break on the shore. The diagram on the right shows the general pattern of winds that blow over the Earth. Some winds were of special significance to sailors of the past. The doldrums, for example, are an area of very light winds near the Equator. Sailing ships could be stranded there for weeks on end. The trade winds, on either side of the Equator, were far more welcome. They blow strongly and constantly in the same direction.

WORLD WINDS

At the Equator, the warm, light air rises, leaving an area of low pressure behind. Meanwhile at the Poles, cold, heavy air is sinking. It creates an area of high pressure. Air moves from high to low pressure, and this is what makes the wind blow. It does not blow in a straight line, however. It is swung to the side by the Coriolis Effect.

Direction of travel

Direction of Earth's rotation

60° N

30° N

Winds in Northern Hemisphere bend to right of direction of travel.

0°

30° S

Winds in Southern Hemisphere bend to left of direction of travel.

Direction of travel

THE CORIOLIS EFFECT

The direction that winds, currents, and weather systems travel is altered by the Earth spinning on its axis. This is called the Coriolis Effect. It causes winds, currents, and weather systems to swing to the right of the direction of travel in the Northern Hemisphere and to swing to the left of the direction of travel in the Southern Hemisphere.

HEAT BALANCE

The Sun heats some parts of the Earth's surface more than others. The Earth is hottest at the Equator where the Sun's rays strike directly and are concentrated in strength. The Poles are the coldest places on Earth because the Sun's rays strike at an angle and are, therefore, weaker. If nothing happened to correct the heat balance, the Equator would get hotter and hotter and the Poles colder and colder. Nothing would be able to survive in these regions. But the winds and ocean currents help to spread the heat out more evenly.

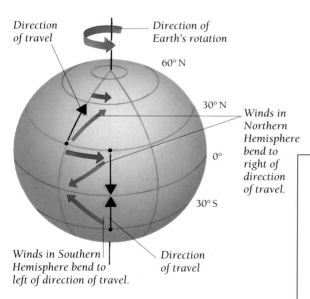

Winds here blow from the polar high to the low at 60° N.

Polar easterlies

At the Poles, the Sun's rays slant in at an angle to the land surface and are weaker than at the Equator.

Halfway between the Equator and the North Pole, winds blow from the subtropical high at 30° N to the low at 60° N.

LOW

60° N

Sun's rays

Westerlies

At the Equator, the Sun's rays strike the land surface directly and are stronger.

Warm air rises, then cools and sinks.

SUBTROPICAL HIGH OR HORSE LATITUDES

30° N

Northeast trade winds

EQUATORIAL LOW OR DOLDRUMS

Equator

Sun's rays

Winds blow from the subtropical highs at 30°N and 30°S to the low known as the doldrums at the Equator.

Southeast trade winds

SUBTROPICAL HIGH OR HORSE LATITUDES

30° S

Westerlies

LOW

60° S

ATMOSPHERE

Here the winds blow from the subtropical high at 30° S to the low at 60°S.

At the South Pole, winds blow from the polar high to the low at 60°S.

Polar easterlies

Why the horse latitudes?

Spanish sailors sailing to the Americas were often stranded without winds for weeks in the 30° latitudes. Without food, their horses starved, died, and were thrown overboard, giving the name "the horse latitudes" to this region.

LAND AND SEA BREEZES

Near the coast, the wind blows off the sea during the day and off the land at night. This is because during the day the land heats up more quickly than the water (top picture). Warm air rises and cooler air from out at sea blows in to take its place. At night, the pattern is completely reversed because the land cools down more quickly than the sea (bottom picture). Now the breeze blows off the land and out to sea. Land and sea breezes are the form of heating and cooling most easily experienced by anyone, as they occur on such a local scale.

Afternoon

Onshore breeze

Warm air rises off land

Night-time

Warm air rises off sea

Offshore breeze

WAVES

Waves are caused by the action of the wind blowing across the surface of the sea. Their steady progress across the open ocean is only broken when they reach the shore. The power of the waves lapping or pounding against the shore and the grinding action of any stones and pebbles they carry are constantly changing the shape of the world's coastlines. Wave height is measured from a wave's trough (lowest point) to its crest (highest point). Wave height is the vertical distance between the trough and the crest. Wavelength is the horizontal distance between two crests.

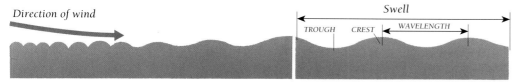

Direction of wind

Swell

TROUGH   CREST   WAVELENGTH

Open ocean The wind blowing across the open sea sets small, rounded waves in motion. If the wind continues to blow, these waves become longer and steeper. If the wind stops blowing, they form a steady swell.

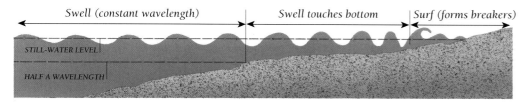

Swell (constant wavelength)   *Swell touches bottom*   *Surf (forms breakers)*

STILL-WATER LEVEL

HALF A WAVELENGTH

Surf zone As the waves near the shore, the water becomes shallower. When it is less than half a wavelength deep, the waves pile up. Then they topple over and "break" on the shore.

WAVE SIZES

The size of a wave depends on the wind speed, the length of time the wind blows (wind duration), and the distance over which the wind blows (the fetch). The stronger the wind and the longer it blows, the bigger the waves it creates. The highest recorded wave was 112 ft (34 m) high.

Fetch of wind (distance over which wind blows) affects size of waves

DIRECTION OF WIND

WATER IN WAVES

The particles of water that make up a wave do not move forward with the wave. The wave moves through the water, like a ripple passing through a rope if you give it a shake. As a wave passes, each particle of surface water moves in a circle, then returns to its original position. An object such as a bottle will bob up and down, but only slowly move in any direction. Farther down in the water, particles move in smaller and smaller circles, stopping at a depth equal to half a wavelength.

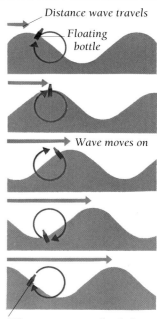

Distance wave travels

Floating bottle

Wave moves on

When wave passes, bottle has only moved a short distance.

Headlands

Wave action on rocky coasts can cause the erosion of headlands and produce caves and arches in the cliffs.

Refraction

If waves hit the shore at an angle, they may be bent so that they break almost parallel to the coast. This process is called refraction.

Wave refraction

Surf

As waves near the shallow water of the coast, they slow down and bunch together. Wavelength gets shorter but wave height increases. When the waves are steep enough, they break on the shore in a rush of surf. Surf waves are called breakers, and come in three main types: spilling, plunging, and surging. Which type of breaker forms depends on the wind direction and kind of coastline.

Waves pile up, topple over, and break on beach.

Hawaii is famous for its spilling breakers, which attract surfers. Spilling waves are formed when incoming waves pile up over a gently sloping bottom, then break slowly on the beach over a wide area.

THE HAZARDOUS SEA

THE OCEANS PLAY A CRUCIAL PART in the world's weather and are the site of some of the most dramatic and destructive of all weather events. Immense, circular storms called hurricanes are born over warm, tropical seas. Huge waterspouts hang down from clouds, like small tornadoes. They were once mistaken for sea monsters by alarmed sailors. Other natural phenomena make the sea an even more hazardous place. Tsunamis race across the ocean faster than express trains, rearing up when they reach land to drown harbors and islands. Toward the North and South Poles, ice patrols keep a lookout for icebergs and disintegrating pack ice. Sea fog is another problem as it can reduce visibility and make navigation difficult.

HURRICANES

The name hurricane is taken from the Carib Indian word *hurrican*, which means evil spirit. Hurricanes are gigantic, spinning storms up to 298 miles (480 km) wide with winds blowing from 75 mph (120 km/h) to extremes of 145 mph (233 km/h). Hurricanes form over tropical seas. Warm, moist air is drawn upward and condenses to form rain. As it does so, it releases huge quantities of heat energy which fuel the hurricane. The warm air spins as it rises because of the Earth's twist. Cold air rushes in below to replace it. As the cold air is heated, it too rises and spins.

Rings of cumulonimbus clouds form around the center of a hurricane.

The eye of the hurricane is a calm area surrounded by a wall of clouds and whirling winds.

FLORIDA

BAHAMAS

Eye of the hurricane

CUBA

Direction of hurricane

Winds rotate counterclockwise and spiral around the eye of the storm.

CARIBBEAN SEA

JAMAICA

LESSER ANTILLES

Martinique

Direction of strong surface winds

SOUTH AMERICA

THE BEAUFORT WIND SCALE

The Beaufort Scale was invented by Admiral Sir Francis Beaufort of the British Royal Navy in 1805. It was intended as a means of calculating wind speeds at sea. The scale was later modified for use on land.

Scale	Wind description	Conditions at sea
0	Calm	Smooth as a mirror
1	Light air	Ripples form
2	Light breeze	Small, short wavelets
3	Gentle breeze	Large wavelets; some foam
4	Moderate breeze	Small waves; white horses
5	Fresh breeze	Medium waves; some spray
6	Strong breeze	Larger waves; more foam crests can be seen
7	Strong wind	Sea heaps up; foam blown into streaks by wind
8	Fresh gale	Longer, higher waves; thick streaks of foam
9	Strong gale	High waves; crests of waves start to topple over; spray
10	Storm	Very high waves; sea looks white; poor visibility
11	Violent storm	Extremely high waves hide small ships from view; foam and froth cover sea surface
12	Hurricane	Air filled with driving spray and foam; violent waves

ASIA

NORTH AMERICA

EUROPE

Tropic of Cancer

AFRICA

INDIAN OCEAN

PACIFIC OCEAN

CARIBBEAN SEA

Equator

SOUTH AMERICA

AUSTRALIA

Tropic of Capricorn

ATLANTIC OCEAN

Where hurricanes occur and why

Hurricanes are powered by heat, so they can only form over warm seas where the water temperature is at least 81°F (27°C) – roughly the area between the Tropics of Cancer and Capricorn. The storms run out of steam as they move over land or colder water. They are known by various names – hurricanes in the Caribbean, cyclones in the Indian Ocean, and typhoons in the northwest Pacific. The storms can cause great damage. Each year's storms are given individual names from an alphabetical list. The arrows on the map above show paths typically taken by hurricanes.

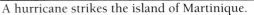

A hurricane strikes the island of Martinique.

Predicting hurricanes
In the countries worst hit by hurricanes, satellites are used to track the storms' paths. A storm warning can then be issued and people evacuated from the danger area. But it is difficult to track a hurricane exactly. So, aircraft are flown into the "eye" of the storm – the large, calm area in the center. They "seed" the clouds with silver iodine, salt, or silver crystals in an attempt to create another eye and divert the storm track. The picture above shows Hurricane Elena, photographed from the space shuttle *Discovery* in 1985.

Once a hurricane forms it generally moves westward, following the tropical trade winds.

Direction of hurricane

WATERSPOUTS
Waterspouts are whirling funnels of air which hang down from the base of cumulus or cumulonimbus clouds. When the twisting air touches the sea below, it sucks up a column of water and spray. Waterspouts are most common in warm, tropical seas. They can be 980 ft (300 m) wide and hundreds of feet (meters) high. A waterspout travels across the sea with its cloud. It rarely lasts for longer than 15 minutes. If the column of water is released suddenly, it can be devastating for ships and coastal areas.

Whirling air drops from cloud and touches down on sea surface.

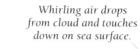

Water sucked up by spinning column of air.

This waterspout formed off the coast of southern California in December 1969. It was 2,950 ft (900 m) high. When it collapsed, it killed three people and destroyed many buildings along the beach, including the pier, shown in the foreground.

Most of the iceberg's huge size is below the water.

ICE AND FOG

Icebergs are found in the Arctic, North Atlantic, and Antarctic Oceans where they break, or "calve," off ice sheets and glaciers. Only a fraction of the berg shows above the water, as in the picture above, making it extremely hazardous to ships. Sea fog occurs when warm, moist air hits colder water. Fog reduces visibility and is doubly dangerous because it is so unpredictable. It can happen anytime, day or night, and lasts for a few hours or several days at a time.

TSUNAMIS
Tsunamis are triggered by underwater earthquakes or volcanoes. This causes the surrounding sea to bulge and then spread out in a series of ripplelike waves. As the waves travel through the open ocean, they can reach over 124 miles (200 km) in length, but are rarely more than 20 in (0.5 m) high. They move very fast though, at speeds over 435 mph (700 km/h). Tsunamis can pass by ships without being noticed. The real problem comes when they reach land. Then they slow down and rear up into huge waves, over 98 ft (30 m) high, which crash down, causing terrible destruction.

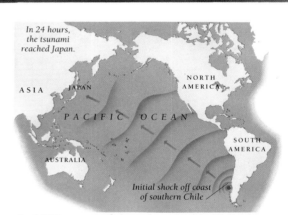

In 24 hours, the tsunami reached Japan.

Initial shock off coast of southern Chile

In 1960 a powerful earthquake hit Chile, in South America. The tsunami ripped across the Pacific, causing massive damage in Japan.

Tsunamis are set off by seismic activity under the water. They are not windblown waves.

They travel across the sea at high speed in a series of very long but very low ripples.

As they reach land, they rear up, sucking up water. Then they crash forward onto the shore.

CURRENTS

THE WATER IN THE OCEANS is never still. It moves in waves and tides, and in enormous belts of water called currents. There are two main types of ocean currents – surface and deep water. Surface currents are swept along by the wind. These great "rivers in the sea" may be more than 50 miles (80 km) wide and flow at speeds of 136 miles (220 km) a day. Some of these currents are huge. The West Wind Drift, which flows around Antarctica, carries about 2,000 times as much water as the Amazon River.

Surface currents may be as warm as 86°F (30°C) or as cold as 30°F (-2°C). They have a profound effect on the world's weather, helping to spread the Sun's heat around the globe. The winds also help distribute the Sun's heat. Without winds and currents, the poles would get colder and colder and the tropics hotter and hotter. The second main type of current is deep-water flow. In this case, the water moves because of differences in density (see below).

SKIMMING THE SURFACE

In the open ocean, wind-driven surface currents move in large, roughly circular patterns. These are called gyres. They circulate in a clockwise direction in the Northern Hemisphere, and in a counterclockwise direction in the Southern Hemisphere. There are two large gyres in the Northern Hemisphere, and three in the Southern Hemisphere.

DEEP-WATER FLOW

Deep-water currents are set in motion by differences in the density of seawater. The colder and saltier water is, the greater its density. Under the ice shelves at the poles, the water is very cold and weighted down with salt, which has drained in from the ice. The dense water sinks into the deep sea, as shown in the diagram on the right. Warmer, less dense water flows in to replace it closer to the surface. This type of ocean circulation is called thermohaline. "Thermo" means temperature and "haline" means saltiness. Dense water forms mainly in Antarctica and in the north Atlantic Ocean near Greenland (shown on the map above). From there, the water sinks and spreads outward toward the Equator. The water moves very slowly – just a few feet (meters) a day.

➡ Path of major deep-water currents
→ Deep-water spreading

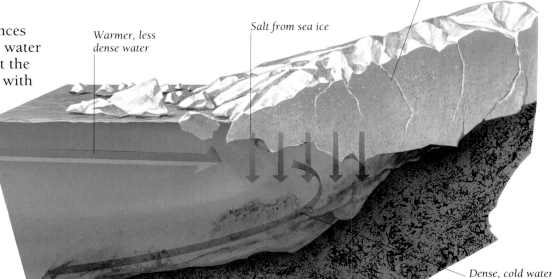

Warmer, less dense water

Salt from sea ice

Ice shelf

Dense, cold water spreads away from the poles.

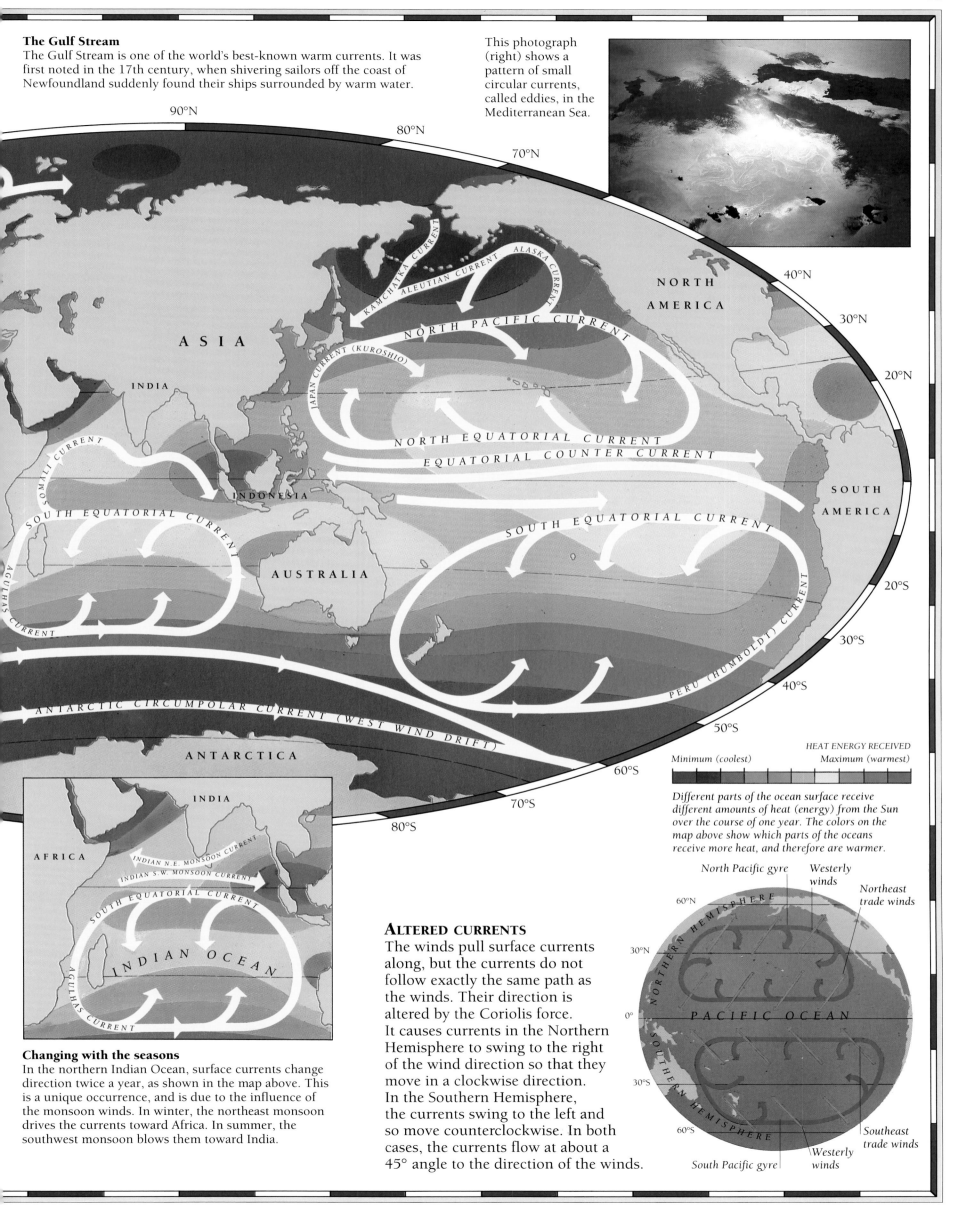

The Gulf Stream
The Gulf Stream is one of the world's best-known warm currents. It was first noted in the 17th century, when shivering sailors off the coast of Newfoundland suddenly found their ships surrounded by warm water.

This photograph (right) shows a pattern of small circular currents, called eddies, in the Mediterranean Sea.

90°N
80°N
70°N
40°N
30°N
20°N
20°S
30°S
40°S
50°S
60°S
70°S
80°S

KAMCHATKA CURRENT
ALASKA CURRENT
ALEUTIAN CURRENT
NORTH PACIFIC CURRENT
JAPAN CURRENT (KUROSHIO)
NORTH EQUATORIAL CURRENT
EQUATORIAL COUNTER CURRENT
SOUTH EQUATORIAL CURRENT
SOUTH EQUATORIAL CURRENT
SOMALI CURRENT
SOUTH EQUATORIAL CURRENT
AGULHAS CURRENT
PERU (HUMBOLDT) CURRENT
ANTARCTIC CIRCUMPOLAR CURRENT (WEST WIND DRIFT)

ASIA
INDIA
NORTH AMERICA
SOUTH AMERICA
INDONESIA
AUSTRALIA
ANTARCTICA

HEAT ENERGY RECEIVED
Minimum (coolest)   Maximum (warmest)

Different parts of the ocean surface receive different amounts of heat (energy) from the Sun over the course of one year. The colors on the map above show which parts of the oceans receive more heat, and therefore are warmer.

INDIA
AFRICA
INDIAN N.E. MONSOON CURRENT
INDIAN S.W. MONSOON CURRENT
SOUTH EQUATORIAL CURRENT
AGULHAS CURRENT
INDIAN OCEAN

Changing with the seasons
In the northern Indian Ocean, surface currents change direction twice a year, as shown in the map above. This is a unique occurrence, and is due to the influence of the monsoon winds. In winter, the northeast monsoon drives the currents toward Africa. In summer, the southwest monsoon blows them toward India.

ALTERED CURRENTS
The winds pull surface currents along, but the currents do not follow exactly the same path as the winds. Their direction is altered by the Coriolis force. It causes currents in the Northern Hemisphere to swing to the right of the wind direction so that they move in a clockwise direction. In the Southern Hemisphere, the currents swing to the left and so move counterclockwise. In both cases, the currents flow at about a 45° angle to the direction of the winds.

North Pacific gyre   Westerly winds
Northeast trade winds
60°N
30°N
0°
30°S
60°S
NORTHERN HEMISPHERE
SOUTHERN HEMISPHERE
PACIFIC OCEAN
South Pacific gyre
Westerly winds
Southeast trade winds

CHANGING SEA LEVELS

THE LEVEL OF THE SEA CHANGES daily because of incoming and outgoing tides, waves, floods, and storm surges. But the changes are not very great, nor do they last very long. Over millions of years, the average level of the sea rises and falls much more, and for much longer. These long-term changes have been caused by the various ice ages and the periods of warmer weather between them. As ice sheets covered the Earth, they locked up huge amounts of water, lowering sea levels around the world by as much as 330 ft (100 m). When the ice melted, sea levels rose again. Sea level has risen by about 4½ in (12 cm) in the last 100 years. Of course, a change in sea level is relative to the level of the land. So, there are two ways sea level can change: the rise and fall of the land, and the rise and fall of the sea itself.

This raised beach is in Morro Bay on the Pacific Ocean coastline of California.

PROOF OF SEA CHANGES

There is evidence that sea levels were once lower than today, but have risen. For example, freshwater sediment left by ponds and marshes has been found on continental shelves now covered by the sea. We can tell that sea levels have risen in the last 5,000 years, because the bones and teeth of land-living animals, such as mammoths and horses, have been found along coasts that are now under water. Geographical features such as those shown below also point to sea changes.

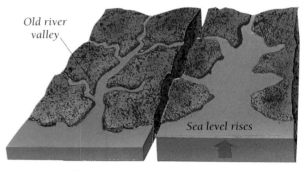

Old river valley

Sea level rises

Drowned valleys

If sea level rises, or the land sinks, the sea floods low-lying areas along the coast. Where the sea has flooded river valleys, it forms branching features called rias, or drowned valleys. The estuaries of southwest England are examples of these. They are evidence that sea levels were once lower than today.

Raised beaches

As sea level falls, or the land rises, old shorelines are sometimes left high and dry above sea level. These features are known as raised beaches. In some places, a staircase of raised beaches forms, one above the other. Raised beaches are found on several coastlines from the Arctic to the South Pacific.

RISE AND FALL OF THE LAND

Sea level may seem to rise or fall because land levels change. The illustration below shows how this happens. The land level can change as a result of movements in the Earth's crust. For example, when an oceanic plate is subducted, the continental plate rises. The land can also be lifted when ice caps melt. During the ice ages, enormously heavy sheets of ice, some up to 9,842 ft (3,000 m) thick, covered the land, pressing it down. When the ice melted, the land began to rise. This is called isostatic change. It takes time for the land to return to its previous level. In Sweden, where the ice was once thick, the land is still rising at a rate of about ⅘ in (2 cm) a year.

Old beach

Drop in sea level

New beach

Heavy ice presses on the Earth's surface, forcing it down.

When the ice melts, the water that is released causes the sea level to rise, but the land sometimes rises even faster.

The weight of the ice above pushes the crust downward and outward.

Melted blobs of oceanic crust rise up to join the continental crust, making the land higher.

At a subduction zone, the oceanic crust is driven down under the continental crust.

RISE AND FALL OF THE SEA

Sea level rises and falls when the volume of water in the oceans changes. These changes are called eustatic movements. They are often caused by seawater freezing or melting, in response to changes in the ocean temperature. A drop of 1½°F (1°C) in the temperature of the ocean can cause enough seawater to freeze to make the sea level drop by 6 ft 6 in (2 m). In the last 2,000 years, the Earth has been gradually growing warmer. Ice caps and glaciers have melted and the sea level has risen. The water in the oceans also expands as it gets warmer, and contracts when it gets colder.

THE WATER CYCLE

The Earth's water supply is constantly being recycled. The illustration on the right shows how the water cycle works. The Sun's heat evaporates millions of gallons (liters) of water from the Earth's surface – from the soil, green plants, oceans, lakes, and rivers. It rises into the air as water vapor, condenses to form clouds, and falls back to Earth as rain or snow. Some water falls directly into the oceans, rivers, and lakes; some soaks into the land and is taken up by plants or seeps into rivers. Then the whole water cycle begins again.

As air rises and cools, water vapor condenses into tiny droplets.

Water droplets join to form clouds, which release water as rain and snow.

Water evaporates from the surface of oceans, lakes, and rivers.

Water falling on the land returns to the seas and lakes in rivers, or seeps under the ground.

Carbon dioxide and other gases in the atmosphere keep the Earth warm by trapping some of the Sun's heat and preventing it from escaping back into space.

GLOBAL WARMING

For millions of years, carbon dioxide in the air has helped trap heat close to the Earth's surface, making it warm enough for life to survive. This is called the "greenhouse effect." When we burn fossil fuels (oil, coal, and gas), we add to the amount of carbon dioxide in the air. Other activities release different types of "greenhouse gases," which also increase this effect. Some scientists think that too much heat is being trapped and the Earth is getting too warm, too fast.

WORLDWIDE EFFECTS

If the Earth gets even a couple of degrees warmer, the effects could be devastating. Ice at the Poles could melt, raising sea level and flooding low-lying land along the coasts. Global warming could also disrupt weather patterns around the world, ruining harvests and increasing the risk and intensity of storms.

The layer of carbon dioxide acts like the glass walls of a greenhouse, trapping the heat inside. This is how the greenhouse effect gets its name.

CARBON DIOXIDE

A rise in the Earth's temperature could melt the ice caps over Greenland and Antarctica, with devastating results.

Bangladesh
One of the areas most at risk from global warming is Bangladesh, in southern Asia. Most of Bangladesh is situated in the fertile but flood-prone Ganges Delta. A rise in sea level of just 3 ft 3 in (1 m) would destroy 14 percent of the country's crop-growing area.

NORTH AMERICA · PACIFIC OCEAN · ARCTIC OCEAN · GREENLAND (PERMANENTLY FROZEN) · ATLANTIC OCEAN · EUROPE · THE NETHERLANDS · ASIA · BANGLADESH · AFRICA · Maldive Islands · INDIAN OCEAN

The Maldives are a group of tiny coral islands in the Indian Ocean. They are so low-lying that, if the sea were to rise by just 10 ft (3 m), these beautiful islands would be completely submerged.

Brahmaputra · Ganges · BANGLADESH · INDIA · GANGES DELTA · BAY OF BENGAL

This photograph shows the aftermath of a devastating flood that hit Bangladesh in 1991, killing many people and animals and ruining crops. About six percent of the country is permanently under water, and more than 60 percent of the total land area is flooded at some time of the year.

NORTH SEA · THE NETHERLANDS · The Eastern Scheldt Barrier

The Netherlands
The low-lying Netherlands has been at risk from flooding throughout its history. For many years, walls called dikes have been used to keep the sea at bay. But, as the Scandinavian landmass is rising, the Netherlands is sinking further. That, coupled with rising sea levels caused by global warming, could spell disaster.

The Eastern Scheldt Barrier is designed to keep the sea from flooding low-lying areas of the Netherlands. Without it, much land would be under water. But the barrier has had an effect on local marine life.

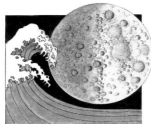

TIDES

TWICE A DAY, in most parts of the world, the sea rises and floods onto the shore. Twice a day it falls, or ebbs, away again. These daily changes in sea level are called the tides. They are caused mainly by the pull of the Moon and the Sun on the Earth. This pull makes the oceans wash back and forth across the Earth as though the water were in a giant bowl. Tides are also affected by the shape of the ocean basins, the shape of the nearby land, and by the Earth's rotation.

There are three types of tides. Which type occurs at a given location depends on many complex factors. Twice-daily, or semidiurnal, tides have two high and two low points each day. There is a six-hour interval. Daily, or diurnal, tides happen once a day, so there is only one high and one low tide each day. Mixed tides are a combination of the other two: there are two high and two low tides a day, but there can be a big difference in water height between the high tides in any one day.

Earth's rotation

Moon

Earth

Moon's gravitational pull on Earth's oceans

TIDAL FORCE

The Moon's pull on the Earth's oceans is over twice that of the Sun. The diagram (left) shows how the Moon pulls the water into a bulge on the side of the Earth that faces it. To balance this, the Earth's rotation causes the water on the opposite side to pile up in a bulge, too.

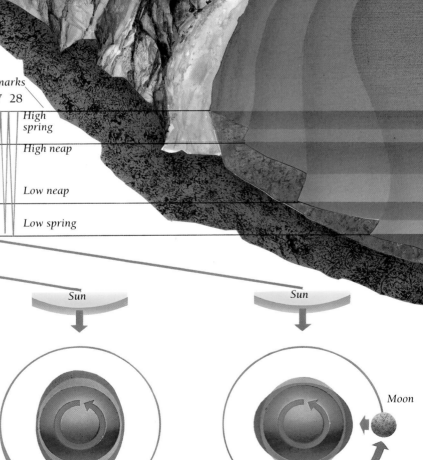

SPRING AND NEAP TIDES

The tidal cycles take place over one lunar day, or 24 hours and 50 minutes. A second cycle, of spring and neap tides, happens over 28 days. Spring tides have the greatest range between high and low points. Neap tides have the smallest range. This is shown in the diagram below and on the right. This tidal cycle depends on the relative positions of the Moon, Sun, and Earth. There are two spring and two neap tides a month, about a week apart.

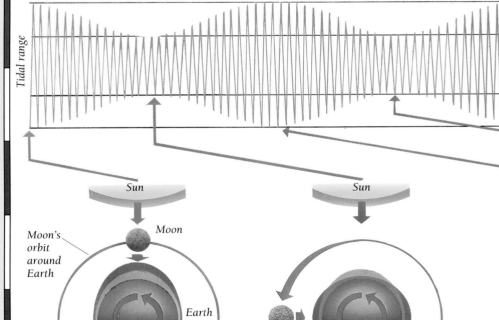

Days in month
1 2 3 4 5 6 7 8 9 10 11 12 13 14 15 16 17 18 19 20 21 22 23 24 25 26 27 28

Watermarks

High spring

High neap

Low neap

Low spring

Tidal range

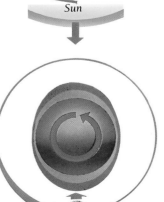

Sun

Moon's orbit around Earth

Moon

Earth

Sun

Moon

Sun

Moon

Sun

Moon

New Moon
At the time of the new Moon, the Moon and Sun pull in a straight line. The tidal bulges combine to form a spring tide.

First quarter
In the first quarter, the Moon and Sun oppose each other. The two bulges nearly cancel each other, causing a neap tide.

Full Moon
The second spring tide in the month happens at the time of the full Moon. The Moon, Sun, and Earth are in a line again.

Third quarter
The second neap tide happens in the Moon's third quarter. The Moon, Earth, and Sun once again form a right angle.

TIDAL RANGES

The tidal range is the difference between the water height at high tide and low tide. On the open ocean coasts, the tidal range is usually between 6–10 ft (2–3 m). Seas that are almost surrounded by land, such as the Mediterranean, have hardly any tidal range at all. In some bays and river mouths, the tidal range can be as great as 56 ft (17 m). Strong winds can make tides higher or lower than normal. These surges can cause floods when high or increase the risk of ships grounding when very low.

The two pictures above show the difference in an estuary (a river mouth into which the sea flows) scene at low and high tide. At low tide (left), the sea has receded and the mud flats and the creatures that live on them are exposed. At high tide (right), the sea has rushed in and covered the mud flats to a considerable depth. The creatures that live at or below the tide line are covered by water.

Going up?
Ships in tidal harbors rise and fall with the tide. At low tide, they can be left high and dry as the water recedes.

Exposed zone
The high-tide zone is the highest and most exposed. Wildlife here may only be splashed, not fully covered, by the water.

Wet and dry
The mid-tide zone is the largest on the shore. It is submerged when the tide is in and exposed to the air when the tide goes out.

Under water
Plants and animals at the low-tide mark are usually covered by water even when the tide is out. But the water's temperature and salinity may vary when the tide is in.

HIGH-TIDE ZONE

MID-TIDE ZONE

LOW-TIDE ZONE

LIFE ALONG THE SHORE

Shoreline creatures have to survive being alternately submerged and exposed. They live in distinct zones, depending on how good they are at coping with drying out. Some animals hide in their shells or burrow in the wet sand to avoid drying up when the tide is out. Seaweeds are covered with a mucuslike protective coating, which keeps them moist. They are anchored to the rocks by their rootlike holdfasts, to prevent them from being swept out to sea.

Channeled wrack

Spiral wrack

Bladder wrack

Knotted wrack

Toothed wrack

Sea thong

Kelp

Sugar kelp

Holdfast

Periwinkles

Mussels

Limpets

Dog whelk

Barnacles

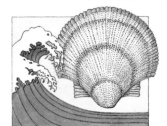

FISHING

FOR CENTURIES PEOPLE have caught fish from the sea for food. The first fishermen used spears, simple nets, and hooks – methods still used today. But fishing is also big business. About 74 million tons (75 million tonnes) of fish are caught each year, much of it by modern fleets using the latest equipment.

Only about 300 of the world's 20,000 species of fish are caught commercially. Two main kinds of fish are caught for food. These are called pelagic and demersal fish. Pelagic fish live near the surface of the sea, and demersal fish live on or near the seabed. Overfishing of some species is a serious problem. They are being taken from the sea too quickly for them to reproduce and keep their numbers up. Countries now set limits on the amount of fish caught. Apart from fish, the oceans' other food resources include shellfish, seaweed, sea cucumbers, and sea urchins.

COMMERCIAL FISHING

Commercial fishing fleets use the latest technology to locate fish and huge nets to catch them. Sonar is used to locate large schools. Pulses of sound are sent out from the boat and bounce back from the seabed below. If there is a school of fish nearby, the pulses take less time to return. The main types of nets used in commercial fishing are gill, or drift, nets, trawl nets, and purse seines. Apart from food fish, commercial fleets also catch other fish such as sand eels. This type is made into fish oil, and fish meal, which is used in animal foods.

These traditional fishermen from Kenya use net traps to catch fish.

ARTISANAL FISHING

Artisanal, or traditional, fishermen use a variety of equipment for catching fish and shellfish, including spears, handheld nets, rods and lines, fish traps, and pots. Traditional fishing boats range from dugout canoes to small motorized boats. Traditional methods require skill, and knowledge of the local tides and fish species. In many places, these skills are being lost as modern ships and technology replace them.

Up a pole
In Sri Lanka, fishermen sit on wooden stilts in the sea, fishing for sea bass and mullet with rods and lines.

Rock-wall traps
Traps made out of wood or stone strand schools of small fish as the tide goes out.

Cockle raking
At low tide, cockles and other shellfish can be collected by hand or by raking the sand.

Seaweed supply
Seaweed is harvested for food or fertilizer. It is also used as a source of vegetable gums, which are used to make ice cream and toothpaste.

Net traps
Some traps consist of a series of conical nets, with a cylinder at the end. They catch fish swimming with the current. They have large, net "wings" to guide the fish into the trap.

Cockle raking

Rock-wall trap

Net skimming

Pole fishing

Local fishing boat

Net trap

Brown seaweed

Lobster pot

Local craft
Small, local fishing boats can fish in waters that are too shallow for the larger fleets. They have small crews and their catches are usually sold close to where they are docked.

Net skimming
One type of net is skimmed over the shallow seabed to catch small fish and shrimps. The fisherman pushes the net in front of him, using two long poles.

Lobster pots
Wicker lobster pots are sunk to the seabed to catch bottom-dwelling lobsters, prawns, and crabs. Their positions are shown by floats on the surface of the sea.

Lobster (D)
20 in (50 cm)

Cockle (D)
Up to 2 in (5 cm)

At the end of a day's fishing, this boat's catch is transferred to shore for processing. Some larger trawlers process fish on board, cleaning and freezing their catch.

Purse seining
Purse-seine nets are used to catch whole schools of surface-living fish, such as tuna and sardines. The nets are so called because the ends are drawn together, as in a purse closing.

First the net is spread around the school of fish.

Then the two ends are pulled together, forming a large circle and the bottom of the net is closed, trapping the fish.

The net is drawn toward the boat and the fish are hauled out of it.

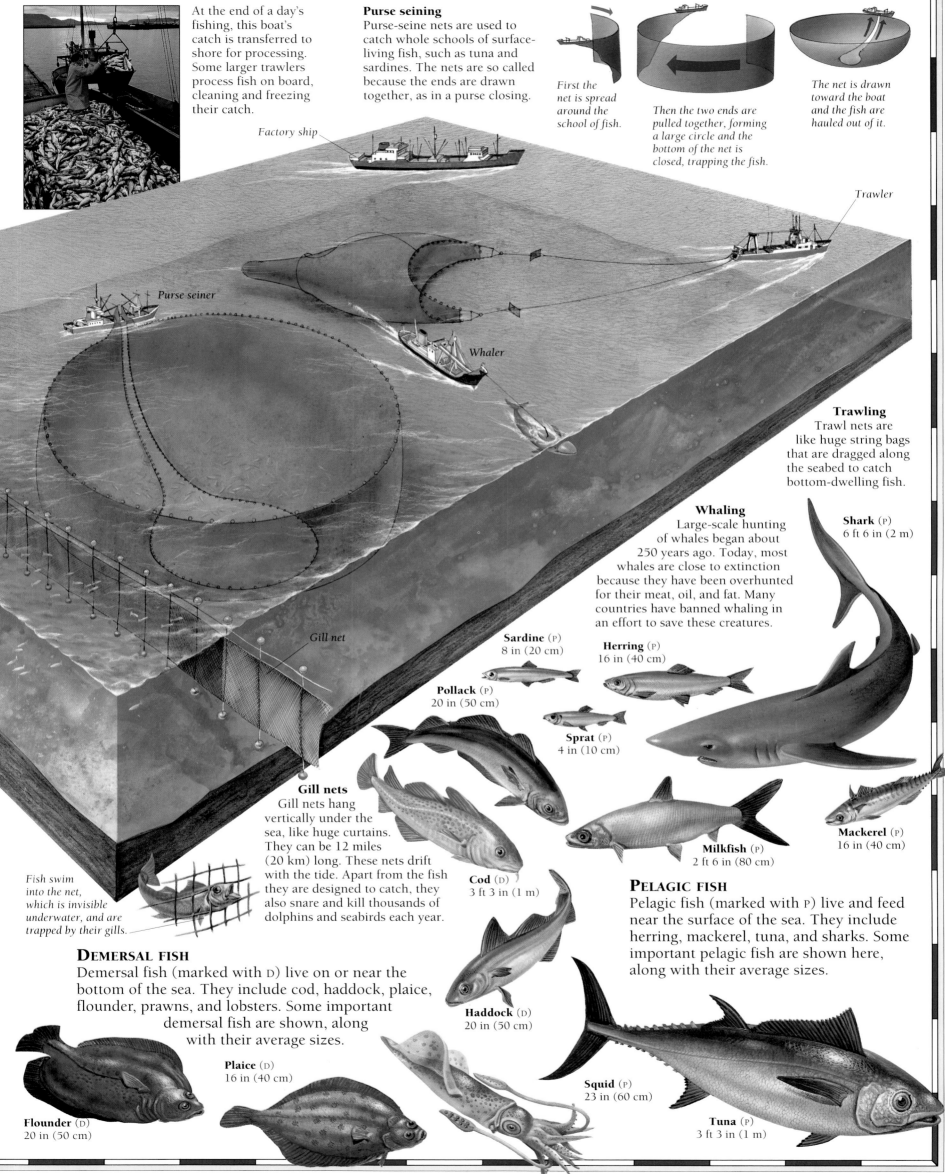

Factory ship

Purse seiner

Whaler

Trawler

Gill net

Trawling
Trawl nets are like huge string bags that are dragged along the seabed to catch bottom-dwelling fish.

Whaling
Large-scale hunting of whales began about 250 years ago. Today, most whales are close to extinction because they have been overhunted for their meat, oil, and fat. Many countries have banned whaling in an effort to save these creatures.

Shark (P)
6 ft 6 in (2 m)

Sardine (P)
8 in (20 cm)

Herring (P)
16 in (40 cm)

Pollack (P)
20 in (50 cm)

Sprat (P)
4 in (10 cm)

Mackerel (P)
16 in (40 cm)

Milkfish (P)
2 ft 6 in (80 cm)

Gill nets
Gill nets hang vertically under the sea, like huge curtains. They can be 12 miles (20 km) long. These nets drift with the tide. Apart from the fish they are designed to catch, they also snare and kill thousands of dolphins and seabirds each year.

Fish swim into the net, which is invisible underwater, and are trapped by their gills.

Cod (D)
3 ft 3 in (1 m)

PELAGIC FISH
Pelagic fish (marked with P) live and feed near the surface of the sea. They include herring, mackerel, tuna, and sharks. Some important pelagic fish are shown here, along with their average sizes.

DEMERSAL FISH
Demersal fish (marked with D) live on or near the bottom of the sea. They include cod, haddock, plaice, flounder, prawns, and lobsters. Some important demersal fish are shown, along with their average sizes.

Haddock (D)
20 in (50 cm)

Plaice (D)
16 in (40 cm)

Flounder (D)
20 in (50 cm)

Squid (P)
23 in (60 cm)

Tuna (P)
3 ft 3 in (1 m)

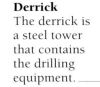

OIL AND GAS

ABOUT ONE-FIFTH of the world's total supply of oil and natural gas comes from under the sea. The first offshore oil well was sunk in 1896 off the coast of California. Today, exploring and drilling for oil and gas at sea is a huge industry, employing millions of people and using the very latest technology.

Geologists first have to study the structure of seabed rocks to see if they contain oil or gas. But the only way to make sure is to drill a test hole. If oil is struck, production can begin and a more permanent platform is built, like the one shown in the large illustration. People and supplies are brought on board. As the oil or gas is extracted, pipelines carry it to the refinery. When as much oil as possible has been extracted, the well is sealed up. This is known as well "capping."

HOW OIL FORMS

Oil formed millions of years ago from the remains of prehistoric sea creatures. When they died, their bodies sank and were covered in layers of mud and sand, which slowly turned into layers of rock. The pressure of these layers and the action of bacteria turned the creatures' remains into thick oil. Natural gas formed in a similar way. Oil tends to move upward through soft rocks until it reaches a layer of harder rock and is trapped.

Workers called "roughnecks" add sections to the drill string.

Derrick
The derrick is a steel tower that contains the drilling equipment.

Cranes
Cranes hoist supplies up to the platform.

Drill string
The drill string is made from lengths of steel pipe 33 ft (10 m) long. The drill bit is attached to the end.

Fireboat
In the case of fire, fireboats can pump out thousands of gallons (liters) of water a minute at the fire.

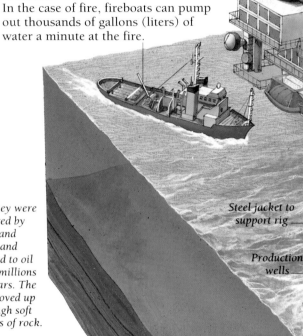

1. The dead bodies of countless prehistoric sea plants and animals sank down to the seabed (arrows).

2. They were covered by mud and sand and turned to oil over millions of years. The oil moved up through soft layers of rock.

3. Oil gets trapped by hard layers of rock called "caprock," or by movements of the Earth's crust.

Production platform

Seabed

Oil-bearing rock squeezed by weight of rock above.

Oil tapped by production wells

Steel jacket to support rig

Production wells

Sharp teeth

"Drilling mud"

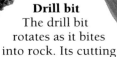

Drill bit
The drill bit rotates as it bites into rock. Its cutting teeth are made of steel or diamond. Drilling friction creates a lot of heat. Drilling fluid called "mud" is pumped down the drill string to cool the bit and to wash up the fragments of rock.

Production wells
To reach as much oil as possible, wells are drilled at different angles from one platform. Each wellhead is topped with a structure called a "Christmas tree" which is made up of valves and gauges.

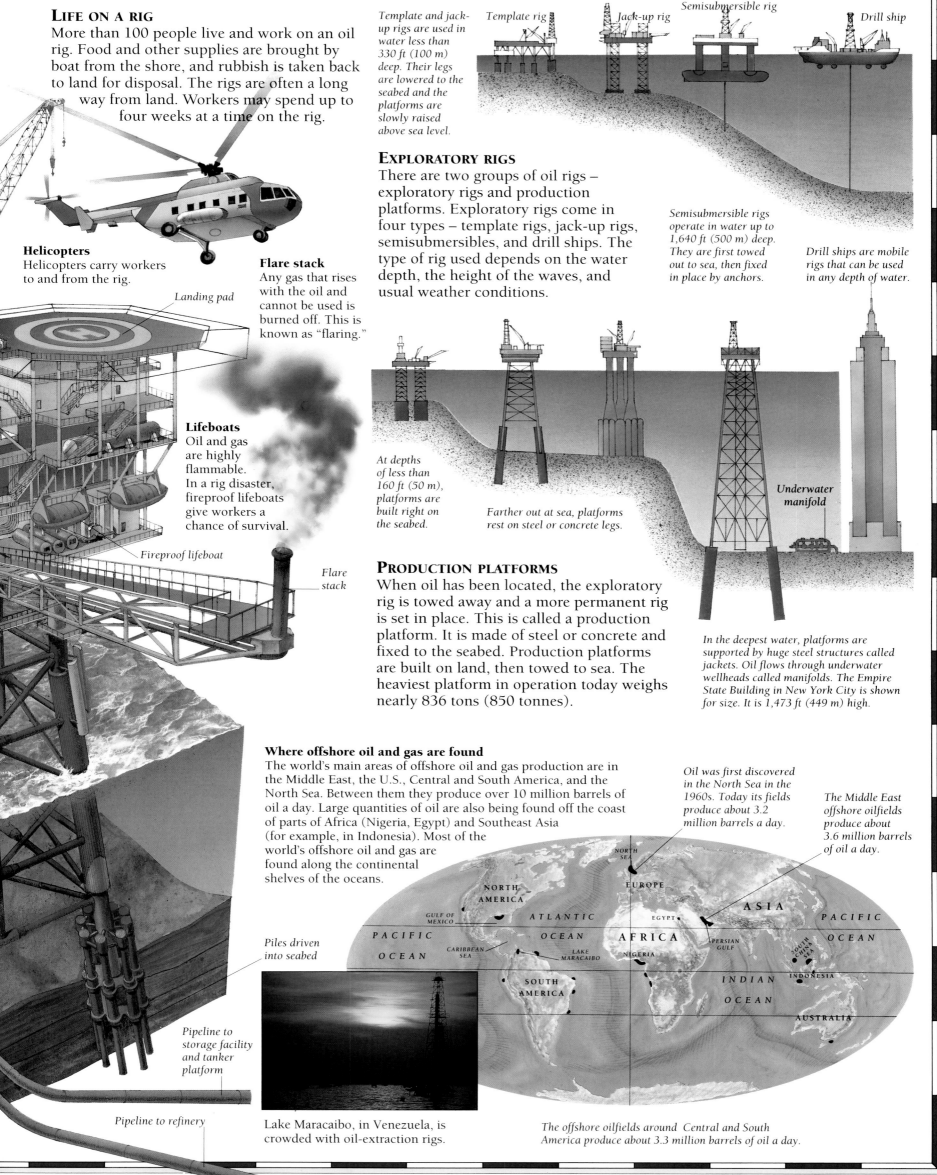

LIFE ON A RIG

More than 100 people live and work on an oil rig. Food and other supplies are brought by boat from the shore, and rubbish is taken back to land for disposal. The rigs are often a long way from land. Workers may spend up to four weeks at a time on the rig.

Helicopters
Helicopters carry workers to and from the rig.

Landing pad

Flare stack
Any gas that rises with the oil and cannot be used is burned off. This is known as "flaring."

Lifeboats
Oil and gas are highly flammable. In a rig disaster, fireproof lifeboats give workers a chance of survival.

Fireproof lifeboat

Flare stack

Piles driven into seabed

Pipeline to storage facility and tanker platform

Pipeline to refinery

Template rig *Jack-up rig* *Semisubmersible rig* *Drill ship*

Template and jack-up rigs are used in water less than 330 ft (100 m) deep. Their legs are lowered to the seabed and the platforms are slowly raised above sea level.

EXPLORATORY RIGS

There are two groups of oil rigs – exploratory rigs and production platforms. Exploratory rigs come in four types – template rigs, jack-up rigs, semisubmersibles, and drill ships. The type of rig used depends on the water depth, the height of the waves, and usual weather conditions.

Semisubmersible rigs operate in water up to 1,640 ft (500 m) deep. They are first towed out to sea, then fixed in place by anchors.

Drill ships are mobile rigs that can be used in any depth of water.

At depths of less than 160 ft (50 m), platforms are built right on the seabed.

Farther out at sea, platforms rest on steel or concrete legs.

Underwater manifold

PRODUCTION PLATFORMS

When oil has been located, the exploratory rig is towed away and a more permanent rig is set in place. This is called a production platform. It is made of steel or concrete and fixed to the seabed. Production platforms are built on land, then towed to sea. The heaviest platform in operation today weighs nearly 836 tons (850 tonnes).

In the deepest water, platforms are supported by huge steel structures called jackets. Oil flows through underwater wellheads called manifolds. The Empire State Building in New York City is shown for size. It is 1,473 ft (449 m) high.

Where offshore oil and gas are found

The world's main areas of offshore oil and gas production are in the Middle East, the U.S., Central and South America, and the North Sea. Between them they produce over 10 million barrels of oil a day. Large quantities of oil are also being found off the coast of parts of Africa (Nigeria, Egypt) and Southeast Asia (for example, in Indonesia). Most of the world's offshore oil and gas are found along the continental shelves of the oceans.

Oil was first discovered in the North Sea in the 1960s. Today its fields produce about 3.2 million barrels a day.

The Middle East offshore oilfields produce about 3.6 million barrels of oil a day.

NORTH SEA
NORTH AMERICA
EUROPE
ASIA
GULF OF MEXICO
ATLANTIC OCEAN
EGYPT
PACIFIC OCEAN
PACIFIC OCEAN
CARIBBEAN SEA
AFRICA
PERSIAN GULF
SOUTH CHINA SEA
LAKE MARACAIBO
NIGERIA
SOUTH AMERICA
INDIAN OCEAN
INDONESIA
AUSTRALIA

Lake Maracaibo, in Venezuela, is crowded with oil-extraction rigs.

The offshore oilfields around Central and South America produce about 3.3 million barrels of oil a day.

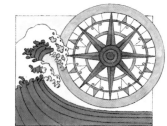

SHIPPING

FOR THOUSANDS OF YEARS, people have relied on ships for transport and trade. The first ocean explorers traveled in simple dugout canoes. Today's passenger-carrying ships include luxurious cruise liners, short-haul ferries, and speedy catamarans. As ships investigated and opened up the world, they also allowed distant countries to trade with each other. Most of the world's imports and exports are now carried by sea. Ships that carry goods and cargo are called merchant ships. They include container ships, bulk carriers, and the gigantic supertankers that transport oil (see below). Hundreds of kinds of ship are also involved in military duties and in the fishing industry.

The first ships and boats were rowed or paddled along. Sails were invented by the ancient Egyptians about 5,000 years ago. They remained the main driving force of ships until the mid-nineteenth century, when steam engines and propellers were developed. Most large ships today are powered by diesel engines.

SHIPPING ROUTES AND PORTS
The map below shows some of the world's main ports and shipping routes. Many of the ports grew up around the mouths of rivers. The world's busiest port is Rotterdam in the Netherlands. It is situated on the delta of the Rhine River. The set routes linking the major ports act like highways on land, and some parts are monitored to try to prevent collisions. The Suez and Panama canals are the most important shortcuts for ships.

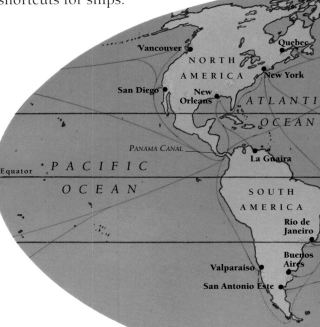

MODERN SHIPS
The ships shown below represent just a few of the many types of vessels using the sea today. Many are specially designed to carry cargo or passengers. Both can be carried long distances more cheaply by sea than by air. Some ships carry one type of cargo only; others carry a mixture. The world's fleet of merchant ships numbers more than 40,000 vessels. Other ships have specific functions, such as lifting extra-heavy objects, firefighting, or salvage work.

Passenger ferry
Nowadays most people prefer to go by airplane if they are traveling long distances. But passenger ferries are still in regular use on shorter trips. The largest ferry, in use in the Baltic Sea, can carry 2,500 passengers and 450 cars.

Royal Princess
The *Royal Princess* is one of the biggest cruise ships ever built. She sailed for the first time in 1984 from Southampton, U.K. to Los Angeles, U.S. The ship is like a floating hotel, with cabins for 1,200 passengers, a library, cinema, gymnasium, and four swimming pools.

Container ship
Container ships carry cargo in large metal boxes, or containers. The containers come in a range of standard sizes. They are designed to fit in the ship's hold or on deck and are loaded on by crane. The biggest container ships have room for 4,000 containers.

Bridge
The ship is navigated (steered) from here.

Passenger decks

Funnel

Funnel

Hull

Seagoing tug
Tugs are powerful boats, used for a variety of purposes. Some tow larger ships and guide them through difficult or dangerous waters. Others are used for repairing and servicing oil rigs.

Bridge

Passenger decks

Bridge

Funnel

Cargo containers

Bow (front)

Hull

Foils

Hydrofoil
Hydrofoils are boats with underwater "skis," called foils. As the boat gathers speed, the foils rise and lift the boat out of the water. The boat then skims across the surface of the water. Some hydrofoils can travel at speeds of more than 56 mph (90 km/h).

Twin hulls

Sea Cat
Launched in 1990, Sea Cat is the world's largest catamaran. (A catamaran is a boat with two hulls rather than a single hull.) It carries people across short stretches of water twice as fast as an ordinary passenger ferry.

Bow

Radar

Radar (radio detection and ranging) has been used in navigation since the 1940s. Radio waves are beamed out and bounce off objects such as ships. This enables the radar operator to see their position on a screen.

TRAFFIC SEPARATION

Some popular shipping routes become so congested that there is a high risk of ships colliding. The Strait of Dover in the English Channel, for example, is one of the busiest routes in the world. Fog and bad weather add to the problems. Traffic separation schemes, such as the one shown on the right, help reduce the number of accidents. A middle "lane" separates the northbound ships from the southbound ones. Aircraft, control ships, and radar are used to make sure that the rules are not broken.

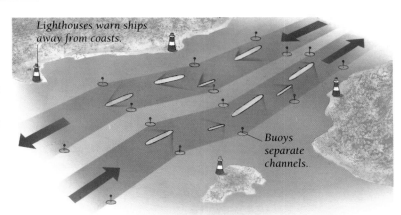

Lighthouses warn ships away from coasts.

Buoys separate channels.

SATELLITE NAVIGATION

The earliest sailors relied on the Sun and the stars to tell them their position and to help them plot a course. Modern navigators also use heavenly bodies, but in the shape of man-made satellites. A ship's on-board computer picks up radio signals from the satellite, which it uses to pinpoint the ship's position. The U.S. Navy uses a network of navigational satellites, called NAVSTAR.

Satellite

Radio signals

Ground station

Ground station

Bulk carrier

As their name suggests, bulk carriers transport very large amounts of a particular cargo. This might be grain, sugar, or coal. The cargo is loaded into enormous holds below deck.

Bridge

Cargo holds

Hull

RoRo supercarrier

"RoRo" stands for "Roll on, Roll off." A RoRo supercarrier is designed so that cargo, such as cars and other vehicles, can drive straight on and off the ship. It also carries containers.

Bridge

Containers

Deck cargo space

Heavy-lift ship

Heavy-lift ships carry extremely heavy cargo. This may be loaded by crane, or the ship's deck may be submerged underwater and the cargo floated onto it. Some heavy-lift ships carry cargo as huge as oil-drilling rigs.

Bridge

Heavy-lift cranes

Poop deck

Bridge

Forecastle deck

Three-island ship

In the early part of this century, many merchant ships were of a type called "three-island" freighters. The three "islands" were the forecastle deck, the bridge and the poop deck. From a distance at sea, these were the only parts of the ship you could see.

VLCC

VLCC is short for Very Large Crude Carrier. These are the gigantic supertankers that transport crude oil around the world. An ULCC (Ultra Large Crude Carrier) is bigger still. It can carry an amazing 492,000 tons (500,000 tonnes) of oil at a time.

Oil stored here

Multifunction support vessel

The multifunction support vessel is a weird-looking ship. It services oil rigs at sea, and provides emergency services in case of a disaster. It floats on huge powered pontoons (semisubmerged hulls). On the deck area above, there are crew quarters, a fully equipped hospital, a helicopter landing pad, and firefighting equipment.

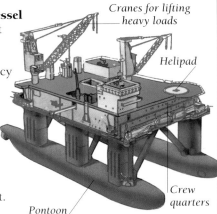

Cranes for lifting heavy loads

Helipad

Pontoon

Crew quarters

UNDERSEA ARCHAEOLOGY

UNDERSEA ARCHAEOLOGY involves the study of shipwrecks, sunken treasure, and even ruined cities which may have lain on the seabed for centuries. Before the invention of scuba gear in the 1940s, very little work could be done on deep-sea wrecks. Divers made a perilous descent in wooden diving bells. Despite this, some early salvage efforts were successful, retrieving mostly money and valuable objects such as silver, gold, and cannons.

Today, archaeologists have the latest diving technology and instruments to help them. By studying, mapping, and raising wrecks and artifacts, archaeologists have been able to discover valuable information about ships and shipboard life in the past. They have excavated coins, guns, clothes, shoes, and the remains of crew members themselves. Some of the most famous shipwrecks so far discovered include the *Titanic*, the *Wasa*, the Spanish treasure ships, and galleons that sailed with the Spanish Armada and which were wrecked off the west coast of Ireland.

This engraving from the 1600s shows an early salvage operation in progress.

MARINE ARCHAEOLOGISTS AT WORK

A marine archaeologist's job is much like that of an archaeologist on land. Once a site has been located, it must be surveyed and excavated before the artifacts can be raised to the surface and put on display. The large illustration shows some of the methods used by marine archaeologists. The work is painstaking – everything must be numbered, recorded, and studied. The marine archaeologist's task is made harder by the special problems of working underwater – the waves, currents, water pressure, low temperatures, and poor visibility.

Air in the bag is released gradually on the way up, to control the speed at which it rises to the surface.

Locating a wreck site

Thousands of wreck sites have been discovered all over the world, and there are many more waiting to be found. Some are found simply by chance. They are often in areas which are popular with sports divers. Others may be found after years of research and reading. Modern underwater instruments, such as sonars, can play an important part in locating sites.

Lifting objects with air bags

Heavy objects such as guns or fragile objects such as pots can be lifted to the surface by air-filled bags. These air bags can also be used to remove heavy loads of rocks or sediment from the site.

Drawing underwater

It is important to have a visual record of the site. Drawing is a good way of making such a record, although wax crayons or pencils and plastic "paper" have to be used.

Archaeologists excavate an ancient wreck in the Mediterranean Sea. The cargo consisted of wine and other goods packed in amphorae (jars).

Scaffolding grid

Site mapping

Before a site can be excavated, it has to be surveyed and mapped in order to provide an accurate record of its contents. The site is divided into small squares, using a scaffolding or tape grid. Then each square is surveyed.

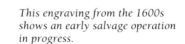

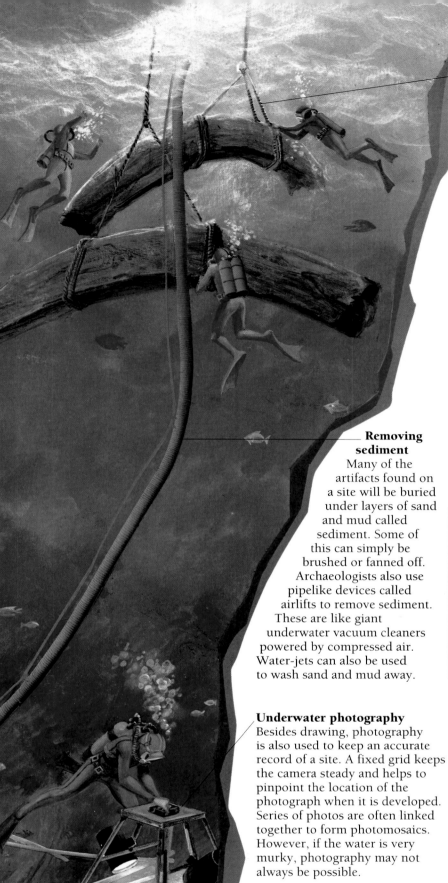

Raising the rafters
Large wooden timbers, such as these huge pieces from the stern of a wooden sailing ship, have to be winched to the surface so that they can be cleaned and preserved.

Preservation
Seawater preserves wood, leather, and other materials very well. But when they are brought to the surface, they need to be treated to stop them from drying out and crumbling. Various methods are used to preserve materials. Timbers are immersed in or sprayed with chemicals, such as polyethylene glycol (a type of wax). Iron may be roasted in a furnace with pure hydrogen to preserve it. Treatment can take years to complete.

UNDERWATER ARCHAEOLOGICAL SITES

There are two main types of archaeological sites to be found underwater. Wrecked ships and the artifacts they contain form one type. The other type are cities or harbors that have been drowned by changes in sea level or by natural disasters, such as tsunamis.

The *Batavia*
This archway was reconstructed from stones carried by the Dutch ship *Batavia*. It sank off the west coast of Australia in 1629. The wreck was found in 1961, but it was not excavated until 1972–76. Among other artifacts found were iron and bronze cannons, and silverware bound for India.

Removing sediment
Many of the artifacts found on a site will be buried under layers of sand and mud called sediment. Some of this can simply be brushed or fanned off. Archaeologists also use pipelike devices called airlifts to remove sediment. These are like giant underwater vacuum cleaners powered by compressed air. Water-jets can also be used to wash sand and mud away.

Roskilde Fjord
In 1959, divers found five different types of Viking ships in the waters of Roskilde Fjord, in Denmark. The ships had been deliberately filled with stones and sunk to block the fjord in about AD 1000. The wrecks were excavated by building a dam around them to keep the water away from the site.

The *Mary Rose*
This warship belonged to King Henry VIII of England and sank in Portsmouth in 1545. The wreckage was found in 1967 and raised to the surface in 1982. Thousands of artifacts were found on the ship.

Gold coins of Henry VIII's time

Underwater photography
Besides drawing, photography is also used to keep an accurate record of a site. A fixed grid keeps the camera steady and helps to pinpoint the location of the photograph when it is developed. Series of photos are often linked together to form photomosaics. However, if the water is very murky, photography may not always be possible.

Blocks (pulleys) preserved in seawater for 437 years

The Wasa *as built in 1628*

The *Wasa*
This was a Swedish warship that capsized and sank in Stockholm harbor on its first voyage in 1628. The *Wasa* was found by a marine archaeologist, Anders Franzen, in 1956. A huge rescue operation was launched to save the wreck, which was raised in one piece in 1961. It was gradually lifted off the seabed and into a dry dock, where it was sprayed with preservative.

The *Wasa* was raised on April 24, 1961. Here it finally breaks the surface, having been lifted by two floating cranes on either side. The *Wasa* and its artifacts are housed in a museum in Sweden.

Port Royal
In the seventeenth century, Port Royal was a wealthy pirate city near Kingston, Jamaica. In 1692, the city disappeared into the sea. It had been hit by an earthquake and tsunami. The city and 2,000 of its inhabitants were drowned. Most of the city only lay about 33 ft (10 m) below the surface, and some of its treasure was salvaged at once. But the city was not properly excavated until 1965–68. Three buildings were discovered still intact.

THE UNHEALTHY SEA

FOR MANY YEARS, the sea has been used as the biggest dumping ground on Earth. The oceans are huge, but they cannot go on absorbing waste forever. Today, marine pollution is a serious problem in many parts of the world. Huge amounts of sewage, industrial waste, oil, plastics, and radioactive waste are dumped into the sea every year. Pollutants can kill or damage marine animals and plants, and destroy fragile ecosystems such as coral reefs. They may also be dangerous to people. Ocean pollution cannot be stopped completely, but efforts are being made to clean up the sea. Several international agreements are now in force. One of these, the Regional Seas Programme, was set up in 1975 to clean up the Mediterranean Sea, one of the most polluted stretches of seawater in the world.

Industrial waste

Many industries are based near the coast or along rivers. They often discharge chemical waste into the water. This includes heavy metals such as lead, mercury, cadmium, copper, and tin, which comes from mining, smelting, paper production, and so on. Metals such as lead and mercury can become concentrated and kill fish and animals higher up the food chain.

Factory waste pipes often empty directly into the sea and can endanger beaches.

Some heavy industries near coastlines pour out airborne pollution. The chemicals then fall into the sea.

SOURCES OF POLLUTION

There are two main sources of ocean pollution. More than 40 percent comes from the land. It is brought to the sea by rivers. Most of the rest is dumped or pumped directly into the sea. Pollution is also carried by the air. It falls into the sea with the rain.

Pesticides are sprayed by both tractor and airplane.

Pesticides pollute rivers and streams, which then flow into the sea.

Agricultural chemicals

With the growing demand for farmers to produce more food, more chemicals are sprayed on fields to kill pests and give bigger harvests. About half of these pesticides and fertilizers are washed off the fields by the rain and into the rivers. They are then carried to the sea. Some fertilizers reduce the amount of oxygen in the water, so animals cannot breathe. Pesticides, such as DDT, build up inside animals, poisoning them and the animals that eat them (see opposite page). DDT also causes seabirds to lay thin-shelled eggs that do not hatch.

Assorted garbage, nylon fishing nets, floats, and bottles foul beaches and coastlines around the world.

Some chemicals are emptied directly into the sea.

Garbage

Each year millions of tons of plastic rubbish, glass bottles, tins and metal drums, wood, old nets, and ropes are dumped in the sea. This "garbage" kills many seabirds and mammals that get entangled in it. Materials such as plastic take many years to decay. They are called nonbiodegradable.

Pesticides such as DDT can contaminate offshore shellfish beds.

Mussels

POLLUTION BLACK SPOTS

In seas that are almost surrounded by land, pollution can become very serious indeed. Here, pollutants do not get diluted as they do in the open ocean. The problem is made worse if the seas are in areas of heavy industry or shipping, or if a lot of people live near them. The worst affected areas are the Mediterranean, the North Sea, the Baltic Sea, and the Red Sea.

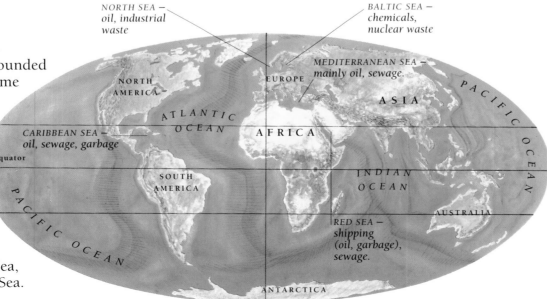

NORTH SEA — oil, industrial waste

BALTIC SEA — chemicals, nuclear waste

MEDITERRANEAN SEA — *mainly oil, sewage.*

NORTH AMERICA

EUROPE

ASIA

ATLANTIC OCEAN

AFRICA

PACIFIC OCEAN

CARIBBEAN SEA — *oil, sewage, garbage*

Equator

SOUTH AMERICA

INDIAN OCEAN

PACIFIC OCEAN

AUSTRALIA

RED SEA — shipping (oil, garbage), sewage.

ANTARCTICA

Oil spills

If an oil tanker crashes or runs aground, it can spill huge amounts of oil into the sea. It forms a slick that can be carried ashore by the wind and currents. Oil kills seabirds, whose feathers become clogged, and fish and mammals, who are poisoned by the oil they swallow. A spill has to be controlled quickly. Unfortunately, some of the detergents used to break the oil up are more dangerous to marine life than the oil itself.

Sewage dumping

In some places, untreated sewage is pumped straight into the sea. This can make the water unsafe for people to swim in because of the risk of infection. It can also rob the water of oxygen. Sewage contains nutrients that algae need. But too many nutrients can cause too rapid a growth. As they die, the algae use up extra oxygen from the water, and other creatures may suffocate. This process is called eutrophication (overfeeding).

Radioactive waste

Some parts of the deep sea have been used as dumping grounds for highly dangerous radioactive waste that has been encased in concrete. This can take thousands of years to break down and become safe. People are worried that it may leak into the water. In large quantities, it can kill fish and other creatures. In smaller amounts, it can cause cancers and abnormal growth.

A ruptured oil tanker spills huge amounts of oil per hour into the sea.

When the tanker *Amoco Cadiz* ran aground and burned off the coast of France in 1978, the oil pollution was the worst the world had seen up to that date.

If the oil catches fire, thick smoke billows into the sky, polluting the air as well.

Booms are placed around the oil to try to stop it from spreading.

Sewage being dumped at sea.

Incinerator ships

These burn toxic waste at sea. However, the burning itself gives off poisonous waste. They are now banned in many places.

Poisonous waste from the smoke falls into the sea.

Boat dumping radioactive waste barrels.

FATAL FOOD CHAIN

Animals cannot excrete the DDT in their bodies. Instead, it builds up in their tissues.

Some pollutants have devastating effects if they enter the food chain. They build up in animals' bodies, becoming more concentrated as they pass up the chain. Two of the worst offenders are the pesticide DDT and the metal mercury. Fish that have eaten DDT-contaminated food may contain 35 times as much DDT as the food they have eaten. The dose becomes even stronger in the next link of the chain, which is a larger fish or even a person. In 1952, a chemical factory in Japan leaked mercury into the sea. More than 100 people died and more than 2,000 were paralyzed by eating fish and shellfish poisoned by the mercury.

Squat lobster

Plaice eat small crustaceans and mollusks.

Plaice

Mackerel eat small crustaceans and fish. At each step of the food chain, the DDT poison builds up, so that the feeder at the next step up receives a larger dose.

Mackerel

Cod eat smaller fish. By this stage the poison has become highly concentrated.

Humans eating contaminated fish receive the biggest DDT dose of all.

Cod

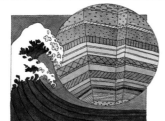

FUTURE USE OF THE OCEANS

WE ALREADY EXPLOIT MANY of the resources found in the world's oceans. These include both renewable resources that can be replaced, and nonrenewable resources that are used once, then lost. Fish, for example, have been a rich source of food for thousands of years. But only if stocks are properly managed and overfishing is prevented, will there be enough fish in the future. Nonrenewable ocean resources include minerals, oil, and natural gas. World oil and gas supplies are limited, but the oceans have vast, untapped energy resources. In the future, electricity derived from tidal or wave energy, or from the heat energy stored in seawater, may replace power from oil, gas, or coal. To safeguard the future use of the oceans, however, we must safeguard the future of the oceans themselves. Land-based pollution, such as sewage and chemicals, spilled oil, and waste dumped by ships are in danger of turning the oceans into a huge garbage dump. The future depends on keeping the oceans healthy and clean.

NONRENEWABLE RESOURCES

Nonrenewable resources cannot be replaced once they are used, at least not for millions of years. In the oceans, this means minerals such as oil and manganese. There are also metal-rich muds, found around ocean ridges, which contain zinc, silver, and copper; aggregates (sand and gravel); and deposits of tin, gold, and even diamonds. Oil is already exploited, and other minerals may become as important.

Fossil fuels

Approximately 20 percent of the world's oil supply comes from beneath the seabed. At present most fossil fuels – oil, coal, and natural gas – are taken from the relatively shallow waters near the shore. Today, stocks are running low and may have run out altogether in 50 years' time. To meet the continuing demand, fossil fuel reserves in deeper waters will no doubt be exploited.

Manganese nodules

Billions of tons (tonnes) of manganese nodules – small, potato-shaped lumps rich in valuable metals – are found on the seafloor. Manganese nodules were first discovered in the 1870s. But it was not until the 1950s that scientists became interested in mining them commercially. Several methods of gathering the nodules and bringing them to the surface have been tested, including a suction device similar to a huge undersea vacuum cleaner.

Salt is raked into piles at these sea salt pans near Goa, India (right).

Extracting salt from the sea

About 5.9 million tons (6 million tonnes) of salt are extracted from the sea every year. In hot countries, such as those in Asia and around the Mediterranean, seawater is channelled into large, shallow pans along the coast. The Sun's heat evaporates the water, leaving the salt behind. In some desert countries near the Persian Gulf, coastal desalination plants extract the salt from seawater to produce fresh drinking-water supplies.

Krill fishing

Someday you might eat the same meal as a whale – Antarctic krill. Scientists are studying ways of using krill as a food source for humans. Of the 4,900 million tons (5,000 million tonnes) of krill in the sea around Antarctica, up to 98.5 million tons (100 million tonnes) could be harvested each year. Some krill is already caught in nets, like the one shown on the left, and frozen or made into paste.

ENERGY RESOURCES

As supplies of fossil fuels run out, and as concern grows about the harm such fuels are doing to the environment, scientists are looking for alternative sources of energy. Energy from the Sun is stored in the Earth's atmosphere and oceans. This solar energy powers the winds, waves, and currents, all potentially clean and renewable sources of energy. About three-quarters of solar energy reaching the Earth is absorbed by the oceans. The heat energy of the water itself could also be used. A system called OTEC (Ocean Thermal Energy Conversion) uses the temperature difference between warm surface water and colder deep water to generate electricity. The map below shows the places where the OTEC system is already in operation, or where it could be used in the future.

La Rance tidal power station (above) in Brittany, France, lies across an estuary that empties into the Atlantic Ocean. The station opened in 1967.

Tidal energy

The tidal power station built across the mouth of the Rance River in France uses the energy of the tides to generate electricity. It consists of a dam with 24 tunnels running through it. Each contains a generator. As the tides rise and fall, the water rushes up and down the tunnels, turning the generators to produce electricity. Two other sites with great tidal energy potential are the Bay of Fundy, Canada, and the estuary of the Severn River, England.

BIOLOGICAL RESOURCES

The oceans' biological resources include natural fisheries and fish farming (or mariculture). Fish farming is big business in many parts of the world. Several species, such as tiger prawns and salmon, are now farmed intensively. Scientists are looking for new, unlikely food sources that could be exploited in the future, such as seaweed, krill, and deep-sea fishes.

Tiger prawn farming

In Hong Kong and southeast Asia, shellfish farming is a major industry. In these huge tiger prawn ponds in Taiwan (above), paddlewheels are used to increase the oxygen supply in the crowded ponds. Tiger prawns are also farmed as cash crops, for export abroad, in some South American countries such as Ecuador on the west coast. The prawns are kept in closely monitored ponds and fed on special algae to make sure they grow quickly and healthily.

Seaweed harvesting

Like krill, seaweed may become an important food source in the future. It is rich in vitamins and minerals, and grows abundantly in many areas, although it can be difficult to collect. The photo above shows kelp being harvested off the coast of California. In China and Japan, several types of seaweed are specially cultivated for food.

Oyster farming

Oysters and mussels are the most important "farmed" shellfish. They are grown in various ways – on huge rafts in artificial ponds, on poles, or on ropes hanging in the sea, such as those on the Spanish oyster boat on the right. This makes them simpler to harvest. The oysters are not given special food; they get their nourishment from the sea, just as they would in the wild. They are simply thinned out as they grow and protected from predators.

INDEX

ACKNOWLEDGMENTS

Dorling Kindersley would like to thank Martyn Foote, Christopher Gillingwater, Roger Bullen and DK Cartography, Anna Kunst, Lynn Bresler, and Peter Hunter, Dorian Spencer Davies and Fran Jones, Sarah Cowley, David Gillingwater, Louise Barratt, James Mills-Hicks for cartographic advice, John Cope, and Jane Parker. Susanna van Rose would like to acknowledge the help and advice of the following people and organisations: British Antarctic Survey; Simon Conway-Morris at Cambridge University; Rob Kemp at Royal Holloway, University of London; Martin Litherland at the British Geological Survey; Ian Mercer at the Gemmological Association; Ron Roberts; Robin Sanderson.

3-D representations of the seafloor supplied by the Institute of Oceanographic Sciences Deacon Laboratory from data provided by the British Oceanographic Data Centre, NERC, on behalf of the OOC/IHO General Bathymetric Chart of the Oceans (GEBCO). Permission to use Map of World Ocean Floor by Bruce C. Heezen and Marie Tharp, 1977 (© Marie Tharp 1977) as reference kindly granted by Marie Tharp, 1 Washington Ave, South Nyack, NY 10960.

Additional illustrations Richard Ward, Jon Rogers, Andrea Corbella, Fiona Bell Currie, Kuo Kang Chen, and Andrew Robinson.

Picture research Sarah Moule, Joanna Thomas, Clive Webster

Picture Credits
t=top, b=bottom, l=left, r=right, c=center, a=above

Ardea Ltd., London/A. Warren: 117bc
Dr Ian Boomer: 39tr
The Bridgeman Art Library/Royal Geographical Society, London: 7tc
Bruce Coleman Ltd.: 97cr; /G. Cubitt: 124clb; /I. Everson: 124br; /J. Foott: 125bl; /J. Stein Grove: 87tr; /Dr Charles Henneghien: 53cr;/B. Wood: 92bl; /G. Ziester: 52cr;/C. Zuber: 114ca
John Cleare/Mountain Camera: 6bl, 28cl, 34c, 34bc
Steven J. Cooling: 35bl
© Photothèque Electricité de France: 125tr
Ecoscene/Farmar: 45tr
Mary Evans Picture Library: 12bl, 16tr, 23tr, 72tr, 76cra
Robert Harding Picture Library/Bildagentur Schuster/Scholz: 103c;/A. Tovy: 93tr
A. Woolfitt/Readers Digest: 121cr; 26cl
The Image Bank/L. Fried: 115tl; /D. King: 105br; /J. Schmitt: 95tr
Institute of Oceanographic Sciences/B. Bett: 78c, 79bl
Dr Rob Kemp, Royal Holloway, University of London: 54bc
Frank Lane Picture Agency: 85cr; /H. Hoflinger: 107tr; /D.P. Wilson: 113tc, 113tr; /D. P. Wilson/E. & A. Hosking: 74tr; NHPA/B. Hawkes: 70bl; /S. Krasemann: 101cla; /D. Woodfall: 122cl; /USDA Forest Service: 7cr, 7br
Patricia Macdonald: 49br
The Natural History Museum, London: 10bl, 57bc
Natural History Photographic Agency/A.N.T.: 43tl
Netherlands Board of Tourism: 111br
Peter Newark's Western Americana: 55tr
Oxford Scientific Films Ltd./M. Gibbs: 97cla; /H. Hall: 75tr; /Ake Lindau/Okapia: 50cl
Planet Earth Pictures/R. Hessler: 83bl, 88r, 90b, 98bl; /Joyce Photographics: 102c
J. Lythgoe: 76tc, 83bc, 125br; /D. Perrine: 66t; /C. Petron: 120bl; /P. Scoones: 97clb; /F. Schulke: 73cb; /N. Wu: 81tl; Rex Features Ltd./Sipa Press: 123tl; /Sipa Press/L.Chamussy: 111crb
Tim Ridley: 123br
Ann Ronan at Image Select: 41tl, 64tr, 120tr
By permission of The Royal College of Surgeons of England/Courtesy of Mr. G.P. Darwin: 83br
Science Photo Library/Julian Baum: 7tr/Martin Bond: 54cl/Jean-Loup Charmet: 8bl/Tony Craddock: 32tr/Earth Satellite Corporation: 19tr, 25tr and cover/François Gohier: 10br/NASA: 25cl, 39cr, 43cr/Pekka Parviainen: 9cr/Alfred Pasieka: 64cr/Peter Ryan/Scripps: 41bl/Soames Summerhays: 21tl; John S. Shelton: 24c
Science Photo Library/Julian Baum: 7tr/Martin Bond: 54cl/Jean-Loup Charmet: 8bl/Tony Craddock: 32tr/Earth Satellite Corporation: 19tr, 25tr and cover;/ S. Fraser: 70br, 101ca, 122t; /François Gohier: 10br/NASA: 25cl, 39cr, 43cr; 107tl, 109tr;/ D. Parker: 99br; /Pekka Parviainen: 9cr/Alfred Pasieka: 64cr/Peter Ryan/Scripps: 41bl/Soames Summerhays: 21tl; John S. Shelton: 24c
South American Pictures/T. Morrison: 79cr; Sygma/Giraud: 106bc
Tony Stone Images: 51cr/Oliver Benn: 62cbr/Chris Haigh: 60cbr/Delphine Star: 48tr
Telegraph Colour Library/Colorific/Black Star/K. Sakamoto: 85t; Tropix/J. Wickins: 125cr
Courtesy of the Vasa Museum, Stockholm: 121bc
Viewfinder: 116cra
Vikingeskibshallen i Roskilde: 121c
Tony Waltham Geophotos: 6cr, 17tr, 29tr, 30cl, 110tc
Woods Hole Oceanographic Institution: 77cr.
Zefa 49bl

Every effort has been made to trace the copyright holders and we apologize for any unintentional omissions. We would be pleased to insert the appropriate acknowledgment in any subsequent edition of this publication.